Usability
Engineering

Xristine Faulkner

palgrave

Published by
PALGRAVE
Houndmills, Basingstoke, Hampshire RG21 6XS and
175 Fifth Avenue, New York, N. Y. 10010
Companies and representatives throughout the world

PALGRAVE is the new global academic imprint of
St. Martin's Press LLC Scholarly and Reference Division and
Palgrave Publishers Ltd (formerly Macmillan Press Ltd).

ISBN 0–333–77321–7

This book is printed on paper suitable for recycling and
made from fully managed and sustained forest sources.

A catalogue record for this book is available
from the British Library.

11   10   9   8   7   6   5
09   08   07   06   05   04   03

Printed in Great Britain by
Ashford Colour Press, Gosport, Hants

Dedication
For Rosie and Clarrie – who enjoy getting their teeth into a good book…

Contents

Preface   ix

Chapter 1 An introduction to usability engineering   **1**

    Chapter overview   1
1.1   An outline of usability engineering   1
1.2   The need for usability   2
1.3   What usability and usability engineering mean   6
1.4   Usability and user friendliness   8
1.5   Usability engineering   10
1.6   Usability, usability engineering and usability evaluation   12
1.7   What happens without usability engineering?   13
1.8   The usability engineering lifecycle   15
1.9   A map of the book   16
    Chapter summary   16
    Self test list   17
    Exercises   17
    References   18
    Further reading   19

Chapter 2 Usability – know the user!   **21**

    Chapter overview   21
2.1   Getting to know the user   21
2.2   End-user classes   23
2.3   Levels of expertise   25
2.4   Categorising users   30
2.5   Methods for gathering information about users   30
2.6   Putting it into practice   34
2.7   Observation   39
2.8   Activity sampling and activity logging   41
2.9   The interview   42
2.10 Knowing the user – a checklist   47
    Chapter summary   47
    Self test list   48
    Exercises   48
    References   54
    Further reading   55

Chapter 3 Usability – know the task!   57

    Chapter overview   57
3.1   Background   57
3.2   Norman's Action Cycle Model   58
3.3   The Gulf of Execution and the Gulf of Evaluation   60
3.4   The user's task   61
3.5   Task analysis   63
3.6   A small task…   66
3.7   The ethnographical approach   75
3.8   Adopting the right attitude for design…   78
    Chapter summary   81
    Self test list   82
    Exercises   82
    References   83
    Further reading   84

Chapter 4 Making usable products   85

    Chapter overview   85
4.1   The importance of design   85
4.2   Problems with specification   90
4.3   What does the customer want?   92
4.4   The initial stages   92
4.5   The feasibility study   93
4.6   Requirements   95
4.7   Strategies for representing design   99
4.8   Involving the user – some problems   108
    Chapter summary   109
    Self test list   110
    Exercises   110
    References   111
    Further reading   112

Chapter 5 Usability metrics   113

    Chapter overview   113
5.1   So how do I know it's usable   113
5.2   Usability attributes   116
5.3   More on attributes   125
5.4   The aims of usability engineering   127
5.5   Defining objectives in usability engineering   128
5.6   Usability engineering as a process   128

5.7	Extensions to the usability specification	129
5.8	Checklist for developing a usability specification	130
5.9	How to obtain the usability metrics	130
	Chapter summary	133
	Self test list	134
	Eexercises	134
	References	135
	Further reading	136

Chapter 6 Usability evaluation **137**

	Chapter overview	137
6.1	Evaluating systems	137
6.2	Formative and summative evaluation	138
6.3	Analytical and empirical evaluation	139
6.4	How to carry out evaluations	140
6.5	Experiments	145
6.6	Talk aloud, thinking out loud	156
6.7	Cooperative evaluation	157
6.8	Wizard of Oz	166
6.9	Laboratory studies	167
6.10	Field studies and field trials	168
6.11	Functionality/feature checklists	168
6.12	Scenarios	169
6.13	Valuation method	169
6.14	Incident diaries	170
6.15	Logging use	171
6.16	The purpose of evaluation	171
	Chapter summary	172
	Self test list	173
	Exercises	174
	References	174
	Further reading	175

Chapter 7 Design heuristics and expert evaluations **177**

	Chapter overview	177
7.1	Expert evaluations	177
7.2	Usability heuristics	188
7.3	The seven stages of action and design	192
7.4	Heuristics – advantages and disadvantages	193
7.5	Expert appraisals – advantages and disadvantages	195

Chapter summary		195
Self test list		196
Exercises		197
References		197
Further reading		197

Chapter 8 The spanners and what next… **199**

	Chapter overview	199
8.1	On spanners, science and engineering	199
8.2	When should evaluation take place?	202
8.3	On definitions	203
8.4	Who sets the goals?	204
8.5	A rose by any other name…	204
8.6	Whither usability engineering?	207
8.7	What next?	210
	Chapter summary	212
	Exercises	212
	References	212

Chapter 9 A case study– the Tuttles **215**

	Chapter overview	215
9.1	Background to the Tuttles	215
9.2	The specifications	217
9.3	The usability specification	217
9.4	Evaluation material	219
9.5	Instructions for observers	219
9.6	Summary of evaluation running order	220
9.7	Subject allocation sheet	221
9.8	Observation forms	221
9.9	Usability observation form	225
9.10	The task list	226
9.11	Questionnaire on the Tuttle systems	227
	References	229

References	231
Glossary	237
Index	241

Preface

In his opening to *The Parliament of Fowls*, Geoffrey Chaucer says:

> The lyf so short, the craft so long to lerne
> Th'assay so hard, so sharp the conquerynge
> The dredful joye, alway that slit so yerne:[1]

Actually, Chaucer was talking about love but he had never tried writing about the 'craft' of usability engineering or, I can safely say – having attempted both – he would have realised that love is a doddle!

This book has been a 'dredful joye'. But I've enjoyed writing it immensely and I hope that it will be fun to read. I learned a lot about usability engineering during the writing. I read a lot, admired a lot, wished I had time to read a lot more and bored people with my obsession. There are some fantastic minds working in the field, and some fantastic personalities too – people who are dedicated and driven by a real desire to improve things but have the humility and humour you need when you work with people. Where possible I've offered pointers to the papers, books and articles I've found useful, intelligent, humane, amusing or have challenged my own beliefs. I hope that once you have finished with *Usability Engineering* you will go on to read them. They have things to say that I am unable to cover in this text. I have added a list of suggested reading material after each chapter and I have made comments about them. I make no secret that there are people in the field it is difficult not to admire!

The idea for this book emerged over several months but probably the impetus for it was created by *The Human Computer Interaction Educators Workshop* held at the University of Glasgow in March 1998 where I finally accepted that there was a gap between the way that software engineers and HCI practitioners viewed software. This book attempts to show how the marriage between software engineering and HCI might take place through usability engineering and is my attempt at rationalising what has occurred so far. I will be the first to admit that I have been very selective in what I present and I understand only too well that the process I describe is not widely adopted in the field. I believe it should be. That Glasgow workshop changed my outlook. First, I finally realised how miserable I would be if I didn't have contact with a computer studies department. For me, HCI is a central part of a computer studies or computer science degree and I enjoy

---

1. The life so short, the craft so long to learn
   The endeavour so hard, so keen the conquering
   The terrible joy that always cuts so deep

making contributions from a user-centred perspective to other people's courses – as well as figuring rather (too?) hugely in my own! But I also accepted that, for me, an interface has to be engineered and that I want HCI to be a fundamental part of that process of engineering a system. I believe that can best be done through the process of usability engineering. I also accepted that this book had to be written and thus threw my ordered life into the introspection that writing brings. I gave myself up to the tantrums and selfishness of the writer and boring people with the latest chapter I was working on. Thanks are due to many people at that original Glasgow workshop. I hope they won't feel too much like Victor Frankenstein when they see the effect of those arguments and discussions.

Neil Finn has a line in one of his songs, *Souvenir*: 'Count yourself lucky that you don't write the software.' In the past, HCI has been lucky; it has largely ignored the writing of the software and has left that up to software engineers. However, I believe many of the problems we are experiencing with computer systems is because of the lack of integration between software engineering and HCI. For me, usability engineering is an attempt to bring software engineering and HCI together. This book is meant as a short introduction to usability engineering. It offers a view that usability engineering is not simply evaluation but is a mixture of software engineering and HCI. It attempts to show how this might be carried out. However, it is a snapshot in time, and space is limited, so I have had to be very selective. It is not meant as an introduction to HCI and so does not cover some areas that would form a natural part of an HCI textbook.

Each chapter begins with an overview and concludes with a summary and a self-test list of words for which definitions can be found in the text and at the back of the book. In each chapter I have included the vignettes I adopted for *Essence of HCI* but this time I have also added a second category of boxes – 'A spanner in the works…'. This is a viewpoint that contradicts or challenges some aspect of the ideas I have discussed in the text. By this process I hope to encourage argument and discussion and to make the text as lively and realistic as possible. It is important to return to the original sources for these arguments, otherwise where the views contradict my own it would be unfair of me to say that I have given the spanner-wielder every opportunity to persuade. It is impossible for me to be unbiased and I don't pretend to be; no-one would believe me if I did! Read them and decide for yourself.

The case study at the end of the text is based on work done by students taking the final-year option in *Usability Engineering and Evaluative Methods* at the School of Computing, South Bank University. This is a unit taught by Fintan Culwin and myself. In order to put this material together I have adapted material over several years of the Tuttles project. However, I feel I would like to say a special thank you to the first year of that course – that is the students in the 1995–6 cohort and those in the 1997–8 cohort. In particular, to Terry Roberts whose efforts last year during the Tuttles project largely produced the case study you see reproduced here; also to Glenn Elliott who helped to make that first year such a success.

I should like to say a huge thank you to Fintan Culwin who is the best colleague anyone could wish for and I'm never sure what I've done to deserve such a friend! As a child I always envied the heroes and heroines in folk tales who had a special person to make things turn out right. In so far as it has been humanly possible Fintan has fulfilled that role for me. He read chapters, suggested improvements, supported and cajoled me through the writing, kept me on schedule, offered advice and didn't turn tetchy if I ignored it. How he finds time to be such a dynamic teacher, prolific writer and excellent colleague and friend to so many of us at the School of Computing puzzles me. There are those of us who believe he has a clone... By the way, his one and only fault is that he doesn't accept the need for Grand Marnier in a margarita!

Additional material, references, stories, help or encouragement were provided by Harry Agiush (SBU), Allan Blair (SBU), William Boyd, Peter Chalk (SBU), Edward Callen, Fintan Culwin (SBU), Dan Diaper (Bournemouth), Steve Draper (Glasgow), Glenn Elliott, John English (Brighton), Dan Farinha, Tony Flower (SBU), Andy Gowers, John Hall, John Hughes (Lancaster), George Papatzanis, Matt Parker, Keith Patrick (SBU), Nigel Phillips (SBU), Suziah Sulaiman, Verna Verwayne, Neil Vinall and Mick Wakefield. The first year of the Brewsers project provided some of the documentation dotted throughout the text but Sharron Cumberbatch and Cleo Piera brought order into chaos! Maria Korsakova and Robert Dunford have to be mentioned for their evaluation documents.

Thanks are due to all those people (and dogs) who have been cajoled into having their photographs taken. All photos are from my collection and the one of me was taken by John Hall and the commercial office was taken by William Boyd. My parents have provided all sorts of practical support ranging from collecting newspaper articles to dog-sitting. They have been there with love, understanding and a reliability I can take for granted. Dan Farinha offered a timely analogy of the electron in super position and Ian Marshall removed a serious distraction by giving me the clue I needed to complete Myst. At Macmillan, Jackie Harbor has, as always, been there with support and encouragement and best of all conviction. Graham Douglas was in charge of production and I'd like to say thank you for his efficiency, professionalism and sense of humour. And last but not least, I must thank my enthusiastic human factors students who have brought me stories, jokes, articles and coffee and without whom I wouldn't have a job!

Finally, I should like to crave the reader's indulgence and mention Rosie and Clarrie who have been the most uncritical, constant and tolerant companions. I don't know how difficult it is to live with me, but I suspect it's horrid. I stay up all night writing, think the book is the centre of the universe and play Shostakovich's Fifth Symphony when I'm exasperated. They have never snapped at me when I'm being difficult or whined to do something else when I'm writing. The book has never been a bone of contention between us and whatever their private thoughts they have given me the lead in return for letting sleeping dogs lie! They will never know my gratitude but it makes me feel better for saying this. As Andrew Marvell has rightly noted a Nymph's best friend may well be her Faun; they are no fawns but then I'm no nymph either. However, I suspect that Marvell would agree that the sentiments are the same… So, for all those many, many, many times I've made a dog's dinner of living with you – this one is for you, girls…

xristine@sbu.ac.uk

An introduction to usability engineering

CHAPTER OVERVIEW

This chapter:

▶ examines the concepts of usability and usability engineering (looks at their definitions);

▶ provides a brief look at the history of usability;

▶ examines the need for a usability engineering approach to the production of computerised systems;

▶ suggests what might go wrong if the principles of usability are ignored;

▶ looks at a lifecycle model for the process of usability engineering.

1.1 An outline of usability engineering

One of the biggest problems that the designers of a human computer system face when developing a system is making sure that the finished product is what the user really wants and needs. It is far from easy to ensure that a product is suitable for the purpose for which it was designed given the complicated specifications many computer systems are endeavouring to fulfil.

In order to be able to produce a suitable system for the end-user, the software development team needs to know what the user really wants and needs. If what the user wants and needs is known, then the best system can be produced for that particular task and that particular user working in that particular environment. In the field of ergonomics this is often reduced to Know the user! Know the task! In the *Essence of Human Computer Interaction* (Faulkner, 1998) I argued that in our own discipline, the field of Human Computer Interaction (HCI), we perhaps needed to add Know the environment! to make sure that we did include it. In this book on usability engineering I shall include the user's environment in the discussion on the user – see Chapter 2.

However, although the aim of those involved in the production of computerised systems has been to develop systems that are useful and effective, actually doing that has not proved as easy as formulating the intention. Usability engineering can be seen as a direct response to the failures of developers to produce truly effective and usable systems.

Usability engineering endeavours to solve the problem of ensuring that a system is fit for the purpose for which it was designed. It does this by a process of discovering what will make an acceptable system for the user and then matching the finished product against those previously agreed criteria for acceptability.

Usability is not exclusive to HCI. It can be found in industry – used by companies to improve the way in which their information technology (IT) services operate (Trenner and Bawa, 1998) or to produce better products to sell (Jordan, 1996). It has to be said that some of the techniques available to HCI practitioners have been around in ergonomics for some time. In that sense it is far from new. Usability engineering attempts to address the practical rather than the heavily theoretical. It is my intention in this book to try to provide a practical guide for all those who wish to pursue a usability engineering approach to the development of computerised systems.

1.2   The need for usability

How much equipment that is difficult and cumbersome to operate does the average householder have in the home? Why do some products seem easy and effective to use and others leave the user baffled? If all products could be designed to appear to be natural and efficient to the user that would be excellent. For a start it would save time since problems over poor usability are time-consuming. For example, Allwood conducted a field study in the 1980s which showed that difficulties with computer systems could waste between five and ten per cent of working time (Allwood, 1984). Nielsen has suggested that a group of experienced users wasted 'at least 10 minutes every day because of usability problems' (Nielsen, 1993). In saving time companies would save money because workers would accomplish more. Jordan *et al* in the introduction to their excellent book on usability evaluation say that usability is establishing itself as:

> …an important issue with respect to the marketing and sales of products, thus it can have significant commercial implications.
>
> Jordan, 1996

Furthermore, Patrick Jordan, in his more recent book, suggests that design issues, and he includes usability issues in this, might be one of the few places where manufacturers have the opportunity to gain any real commercial advantage over their competitors. He suggests that this is because manufacturing processes have themselves become so standardised that there are only small benefits to be made from them. However, in comparison, very little regard has been given to the concept of usability so there is much more opportunity to make significant gains in that area (Jordan, 1998).

However, there are different reasons for systems being unacceptable or failing to deliver what users expect of them. Andy Smith suggests that:

> Overall it would seem that roughly only 30 per cent of IT systems are fully successful and that some 70 per cent either fail or only produce some marginal gain to the organization.
>
> Smith; 1997, p9

Landauer, in his book *The Trouble with Computers*, goes as far as saying that computers have not brought about the gains in productivity that we might have expected them to bring or indeed think they have brought. He has impressive evidence to back this assertion and blames the fact that there haven't been huge gains in productivity on the problem that systems are still far from easy to use. He suggests that the way forward is to ensure that systems are usable by adopting UCD as a means of producing systems for people and by UCD he means:

> …user-centred design, user-centred development, and user-centred deployment. They don't need separate acronyms because at the base they're all the same: techniques for getting empirical evidence on how systems help and hinder people in their work.
>
> Landauer; 1995, p8

Maguire believes the problem is that although:

> …there is a substantial body of human factors and ergonomics knowledge about how such design processes can be organised and used effectively, much of this information is not yet widely applied.
>
> Maguire; 1997, p6

Natural and efficient products can make the user's task seem a lot more pleasant. This would remove the frustration that is often caused by trying to do something with a system that is far from easy to understand or easy to use. Though, happily, there is evidence that users are no longer quite so willing to tolerate products that are difficult to use (Jordan, 1996). The concept of usability was born out of this desire and need to make things easier and more efficient for the user. Certainly, the proliferation of terms like 'user friendly' would suggest that manufacturers believe simplicity of use is now a selling point (Jordan, 1996). Indeed, whole advertising campaigns have been centred on this idea of simplicity. In the UK, the first advertisements for Apple's *iMac*, for example, emphasised how easy and simple it was to set the system up. The user simply plugs the system in and switches it on and the computer is up and running. Microsoft have used babies in their television advertisements, in the UK at least, to imply that its systems were very easy to use indeed. Many advertisements for computers and software imply that the systems are so easy and obvious to use that a manual is not required. One group of students I taught, however, believed that designing some systems was impossible without a huge manual to explain usage. Figure 1.1 shows their humorous attempt to show me that a command line Automatic Teller Machine (ATM) would not be possible without an accompanying tome!

Figure 1.1 Command line system with help

Therefore, it has to be said that computer systems still do not live up to the expectations those of us in the field of HCI might have for them and the user's relationships with them is still far from satisfactory. Whatever some of the adverts might claim for their products the reality is that computer systems are still far from easy to use. The major problem with them appears to be that the way in which tasks might be accomplished is not always obvious. *The Sunday Times*, for example, had this to say about a survey carried out on computer users:

Three out of four computer users cannot get their machines to do what they want and a minority hit them in sheer frustration…

The Sunday Times, 22 February 1998

The result from a survey like that is disappointing reading for anyone working in the field of HCI. It implies that 75 per cent of users are struggling with machines that cannot easily be manipulated and which do not appear to support the tasks that users wish to perform with them. However, it is not simply a matter of creating systems that are easy to use. The systems must also be able to do things that users want them to do. Getting a computer to do what a user wants it to do means knowing what the user wants to do in the first place as well as enabling the task to be carried out as easily and in as obvious a fashion as possible.

How do you know if a product does what the user wants it to do? How do you know that the product is sufficient for the user's task? The concept of usability engineering emerged out of the desire to develop a procedure whereby it could be demonstrated that a particular product was usable and fulfilled the criteria which a particular user performing a specific task, in a given environment might require of it.

How do you know if the user is satisfied with the product? How do you know if what you have produced fulfils user expectation? In law this would coincide with the concept of fitness for purpose. Many so-called defective products are simply products that do not meet the customer's expectation. An interface which is difficult to use may cause the product to be defective to the extent that the customer is entitled to reject it. In such a case, it could be argued, that under the Sale of Goods Act the software was not of a satisfactory quality. Usability evaluation methods and heuristics can be used to produce evidence that the product is of a satisfactory quality and does live up to the user's expectations.

These expectations are utterly justifiable and need to be quantified. Root and Draper in a study of questionnaires as an evaluation tool suggested that:

…software technology should be, and probably is, moving towards greater concern for the user in the design of the interface; the logical endpoint of this process is the adoption of an objective evaluation of the user interface to a program as standard "good practice", in much the same way that well-commented, well-structured code is currently a mark of well-designed software.

Root and Draper, 1983

Notice that the endpoint is seen as the adoption of 'objective measures'. The implication being that somehow the very subjective responses of users to the software they use can be measured in an objective way. I have already argued elsewhere (Faulkner, 1998) that in its early stages new technologies are unable to consider the user and it is a measure of a technology's maturity that user considerations come into play. Usability engineering is perhaps the logical development in this search for objective measures for the user interface. Usability metrics can therefore be viewed as a direct response to this desire to create something that is objective and measurable out of something that appears to be highly subjective.

1.3 What usability and usability engineering mean

The words 'usability' and 'usability engineering' have been in use for some time now. Usability evaluation methods are used in industry to measure the usability of products so usability is not a concept that is found associated with computers alone. It has a long history. Consequently, an examination of its past might explain how some of the ideas and attitudes we are dealing with today have been handed to us as part of the heritage of usability.

1.3.1 The history of usability

Brian Shackel raised the concept of ergonomics for the computer as early as 1959 but the idea of usability and usability engineering was slow to emerge from these tentative origins. Shackel suggests that the first definition of usability was probably attempted by R B Miller in his paper of 1971 (cited by Shackel, 1990). This definition was based on 'ease of use'. A detailed formal definition was put forward by Shackel (Shackel, 1981), modified by Bennett (Bennett, 1984) and then integrated as Shackel's formal definition (Shackel, 1986; 1990). This produced a definition based on effectiveness, learnability, flexibility and attitude.

In his definition of effectiveness Shackel (1986) implied ideas of speed and performance. For him 'effectiveness' referred to a required percentage of the specified users and related to a required proportion of the specified target range of the users. In order to be effective a system had to allow the task to be performed within specified time limits, and for a particular range of users which would be specified in advance.

Shackel's concept of learnability specified a time frame during which the specified users should acquire a level of familiarity and proficiency with the system. Learnability was based upon a specified amount of training they would require. Furthermore, Shackel's interpretation of learnability acknowledged that it should relate to the relearning time of intermittent users of the system too (Shackel, 1986).

For Shackel, flexibility was seen as allowing a specified degree of adaptation and variation in the way in which tasks might be done or the environments in which the system might act (Shackel, 1986).

Interestingly, Shackel defined attitude as 'within acceptable levels of human cost in terms of tiredness, discomfort, frustration and personal effort'. Furthermore, it was expected that satisfaction should not only continue during further encounters with the system but it should actually be enhanced by the use of the system (Shackel, 1986).

It has to be remembered that Shackel had a close association with ergonomics and his definitions show the influence of this discipline not only in his choice of the concepts themselves but in the way in which those concepts are handled and defined.

However, Shackel's original definitions have gone through a process of change. The terms 'usability' and 'usability engineering' no longer mean what was first outlined. Since the terms have been around for some time and have consequently undergone this series of transformations it might be as well to look at what we really mean when we use the words 'usability' and 'usability engineering' since like a sticky sweet left in a pocket, they have gathered rather a lot of fluff!

1.3.2   More recent definitions

The International Organization for Standardization (ISO) defines usability as:

> ...the effectiveness, efficiency and satisfaction with which specified users can achieve specified goals in particular environments...
>
> ISO DIS 9241-11

By 'effectiveness' what is meant is that the user is able to carry out the intended task. There is no concept of time in this 'effectiveness'. There is no concept of ease of use either. The task simply has to be accomplished for the system to be considered effective. In other words, if there are two systems and the user can accomplish the task with the first system and not with the second, then the first system is effective and the second is not. This is in sharp contrast to Shackel's concept of effectiveness as being a measurement of time as well as performance.

By 'efficiency' a sense of time is implied. If the task can be accomplished in five minutes using one system but in ten minutes using the other, then the faster performance time of the first system implies a more efficient system. Shackel had no separate concept of efficiency in his definition. Efficiency was part of his concept of effectiveness.

The ISO makes no mention of learnability here. Though it could be argued that an efficient system would not have a prolonged learning time frame.

Finally, the ISO refers to user satisfaction with the system. User satisfaction is complex and it can be related to all kinds of aspects of the system. There are ways of measuring what is a very subjective concept. This will be dealt with in a later chapter. But for the time being user satisfaction can be defined as being how acceptable the system is to the users, how comfortable they feel with the operation of the system or whether they prefer one system over another. This would coincide partially with Shackel's idea of attitude though Shackel couched this concept in the much more humane terms provided by his close association with the field of ergonomics.

A spanner in the works...

Draper, in a succinct and challenging paper on task, argues persuasively that the ISO is not just 'pessimistic' but might not be 'pessimistic enough'. He suggests that HCI practitioners should be pessimistic about the definition because:

'...it implies there may be no generalisation across users or machines or tasks.'

Draper, 1993

In later chapters we will return to Draper's contention that there is a need for pessimism amongst the HCI community and examine ways in which usability engineering can rise to the challenge of generalisation. Quite clearly, if effective Human Computer Systems (HCS) are to be built, it would be economically impossible, at the moment, to produce individual systems based on every user's highly distinct needs in terms of both expertise and task. Ultimately, there needs to be some method of generalising across users, platforms and perhaps even across tasks.

1.4   Usability and user friendliness

In some ways, usability builds on the older idea of user friendliness. This was a term that was popularly used to describe whether or not a system was easy for the user to operate. Nielsen suggests that the term 'user friendly' is:

> ...unnecessarily anthropomorphic [and] implies users' needs can be described along a single dimension...
>
> Nielsen, 1993

Nielsen's objection to the anthropomorphic nature of the term is an interesting one since computers appear to be all too frequently addressed by their users as if they are sentient beings. This tendency has already been noted by those working with children but I have observed it in adults too and even in software engineers who are often described as being rational and prosaic! However, Nielsen is not alone in his objections to user friendly as a means of describing the ideal system. Norman and Draper banned it from *User Centred System Design* as early as 1986, evidently moved to exasperation by the inability of anyone to explain precisely what advantages a user friendly system might offer. But it still lingers on, as it did then, in marketing literature. Rereading the glossary definition of 'user friendly' provided by Norman, Draper and Bannon reminded me how awful interfaces used to be then and that, in reality, 'user friendly' quite often meant condescending and over familiar in a sickening and sometimes downright rude fashion. However, a major problem with 'user friendliness' seems to be that it was vague and amorphous and did not explain what was really required of a system. But I mourn its loss now though because vague and amorphous it may have been it has found its way into the Oxford Dictionary with a definition I can appreciate and obviously not the one that Norman *et al* had in mind nor the one that was prevalent then:

> user-friendly adj. esp *Computing* (of a machine or system) designed to be easy to use.
>
> *Concise Oxford Dictionary*, 1996

And although HCI people might be disgusted by the term, strangely enough non-HCI specialists seem to know what to expect from a user-friendly system. Perhaps they all looked it up in the dictionary too. It seems to have caught the imagination of the general public and has entered the vocabulary so that all sorts of things are now described as 'user friendly'. More recently other 'friendliness' has entered the vocabulary so that 'environmentally friendly' and 'freezer friendly' are now used in everyday speech.

Barrie Sherman, as early as 1985, defines 'user friendly' thus:

> User friendly means adapting parts of the system to the operator rather than the operator having to adjust and probably not managing to do so efficiently; that is why it is such a desirable quality to build in, a quality moreover which generally only needs to provide patience, commonsense, and a sense of humanity.
>
> Sherman, 1985

Sherman's definition is probably a lot more concrete than many HCI practitioners would have been able to offer when asked to define the term. He quite clearly knows what he expects of a system even if it doesn't manage to live up to those expectations. However, despite the public's preoccupation with the term, user friendliness is unacceptable in that it does not really say that the system needs to be effective and efficient for the task that is being performed. A system with a good interface but which did not support the task adequately could still be said to comply with ideas of user friendliness even though it was totally worthless so far as getting the job done was concerned. Usability, on the other hand, carries with it the idea that the product will be useful for the task it has been designed to cope with.

Most people in the field of usability engineering would agree whole heartedly with the first part of Sherman's statement though; this is what systems really ought to be like. However, despite applying much patience, humanity and common sense, HCI practitioners have not always achieved the 'user friendly' solution that Sherman implies ought to be attainable if the effort was made. There appears to be something else that is required to make systems really effective and pleasant for end-users. However humane HCI practitioners have endeavoured to be they have still failed to produce usable systems. It is as a direct response to the failures in past systems that usability and usability engineering have emerged as a more controlled attempt to solve the problem of unusable systems.

1.5   Usability engineering

From the idea of producing usable computer systems there also emerged the concept of usability engineering which would be a process by which the usability of a product could be attested and perhaps guaranteed. Bennett's work had provided the idea of a usability specification with planned levels of performance which the development process would endeavour to achieve (Bennett, 1984). These ideas were developed and honed by Good *et al* (1986) and Whiteside *et al* (1988). We will examine the work of Whiteside, Bennett and Holtzblatt in Chapter 5 when we look at usability metrics.

Tyldesley (1990) describes usability engineering as:

> …a process whereby the usability of a product is specified quantitatively, and in advance. Then as the product itself, or early 'baselevels' or prototypes of the product are built, it is demonstrated that they do indeed reach the planned levels of usability.
>
> Tyldesley, 1990

Notice that Tyldesley says this is a quantitative evaluation of usability. By this Tyldesley means that actual performance measures will be made of the system. He also stipulates that these will be set before the system is developed. In other words, before the product is built its levels of usability will already have been agreed. There is nothing so very strange about this and we do agree levels of acceptability for very ordinary items before their delivery. For example, at a restaurant you might order your steak well done or rare. A steak outside the specified range would be unacceptable.

In later chapters of this book we will examine just how systems can be specified and agreed with the user in advance of the production of the actual system. This is in contrast to more traditional methods of developing a computerised system whereby the system would not have its performance levels specified prior to delivery. Very often, developers had no idea if a system would be acceptable to the user and appropriate for the task, until that system was *in situ*. Obviously, modifying a system that has already been developed but has been found to be unsuitable is more expensive than designing-out problems before the system has been developed. Therefore, usability engineering can be said to be a more economically viable method of developing software since the developer is certain that if the usability levels agreed with the user are reached, then the system will be acceptable to the user. There are sound economic reasons for following a usability engineering approach.

The idea that emerged from the efforts of the various workers in the field is best summed up by Hix and Hartson (1993) who say what needs to be said rather succinctly:

> The bottom line is that *if you can't measure it, you probably can't manage it*. [Their italics, not mine].
>
> Hix and Hartson, 1993

The idea of an engineering approach to the problems of producing usable software was taken up enthusiastically by some people in the field. In the UK the Department of Trade and Industry (DTI) set up the Usability Now! programme with the aim:

> …to promote the importance of usability in IT systems and suggest how it can be achieved.
>
> DTI, 1990

The DTI initiative produced, amongst other things, a delightful, introductory text (DTI, 1990), a regular glossy newsletter, a directory of practitioners and some case studies. It was an impressive programme that attempted to impart useful tips for designing systems and evaluating them from a user-centred perspective. In the UK, at least, this helped to put usability on the map. As a natural progression, discussions about usability led to discussions about what should be taught to computer science and computer studies students in order to give them a firm understanding of the user. In America this led to a model syllabus proposed by the Association of Computing Machinery (ACM, 1992) while in the UK, the British Computer Society was responsible for the new HCI syllabus (BCS, 1995). This inevitably led to discussions about whether or not it was possible to produce usability engineers, that is those software engineers who understood the user's difficulties, through the new Human Computer Interface (HCI) syllabus and if so how this could be done (Culwin and Faulkner, 1997).

The theme of both the ACM's syllabus and that of the BCS was one of integration. For both organisations there seemed to be a need for HCI to become a fundamental component of the computer science/computer studies curriculum. HCI was no longer seen as a luxury; it was no longer part of the decoration – the cherry on top of the cake – but had become part of the recipe. The image I have used elsewhere is that no longer could we stick cherries on top of the cakes in order to make the product look nice but we had to bake cherry cake! For me, usability engineering is the answer to how we might go about baking cherry cakes.

From the metric-oriented beginnings and a somewhat academic start, the ideas of usability and usability engineering have gathered wider connotations. This book attempts to examine the major concepts of usability and to provide a framework for those readers who wish to use the principles of usability engineering in systems development.

Interestingly enough, while usability, usability engineering, usability evaluation and usability engineers have been elbowing their way into the world of HCI, User Centred Design (UCD) has jostled for position too. In 1986 it launched itself at us via the Norman and Draper text mentioned above but in the guise of User Centred System Design. Undoubtedly, in 1986, Norman and Draper and the contributors to that collection knew what they meant by User Centred Design. However, ten years later, in 1996 Karat is not so sure that he knows just what it is and asks whether or not UCD can be precisely defined. He then goes on to say that what best defines it for him is papers by Gould (1988) and Whiteside *et al* (1988). He points out that neither paper uses UCD as a label to describe their activities (Karat, 1996). What both papers are about is involving the user and both acknowledge the importance of usability engineering. The way in which UCD can be accomplished is through the application of usability engineering.

1.6 Usability, usability engineering and usability evaluation

Usability engineering in this book is interpreted as an approach to the development of software and systems which involves user participation from the outset and guarantees the efficacy of the product through the use of a usability specification and metrics. The process also includes adherence to the design–evaluate–redesign cycle (Downton, 1991). In this book usability, usability engineering and usability evaluation are used to describe the various components that will make up a User Centred Design approach. Usability refers to the measure of success of the product – whether it be software, computer systems or a product. Usability engineering is the entire process of producing usable products and a usability engineer is the person who facilitates that. Usability evaluation is the process by which systems and products are evaluated using any of the methods available to the usability engineer or usability evaluator. The terms usability, usability engineering and usability evaluation are not interchangeable in this book; they mean quite distinct activities. Although the former and the latter go towards making up the process of usability engineering, they do not comprise usability engineering alone. It also needs the addition of software engineering.

As we have seen, other writers and experts in the field do not interpret these terms in exactly the same way. Whiteside, Bennett and Holtzblatt (1988) for example use 'usability engineering' to refer to the process of applying usability metrics. For Nielsen (1993) usability engineering is more of a process of evaluation and redesign. When I refer to usability engineering I imply the whole process of development from requirements gathering to installation. A usability engineer is someone who is closely concerned with the development of software and is not someone who simply carries out evaluation. These views are expressed elsewhere in papers by Fintan Culwin and myself, for example (Culwin and Faulkner, 1997; Faulkner and Culwin, 1999).

Usability engineering is therefore an entire process which adheres to the precepts of UCD and pays close attention to the needs of the user. More than that it attempts to demonstrate that the finished product is actually what the customer wants and needs and has been engineered following a rigorous and principled method of software engineering.

1.7   What happens without usability engineering?

Whatever our problems in defining our terms, one thing appears to be constant and that is that design should centre on the user. The reasons for this will become clearer during the course of this book. But the major drawback with not consulting the end-user or not considering the needs of end-users, is that systems do not do what users want them to do. Sometimes the problem is even more fundamental than that and the failure to consult the end-user can have devastating effects on the user's ability to even use the product at all. For example *The Higher* ran this report in 1991:

A company got in a group of technical engineers to design a laser engraving machine. Unfortunately they forgot to consider the operator. Design consultants found that for someone to use the machine they had to have at least three arms, all of which were three feet long, and that person had to be under three feet tall.

The Higher, 22 November 1991

In this example it is physically impossible for the machinery to be operated by people but most of the time human beings will adapt to difficult, uncomfortable and awkward systems if they have to or cease to use them if they don't have to. The implications of this in terms of frustration and the reduction of productive work are too serious to overlook.

I recently received a letter from my father. It is shown in Figure 1.2. I include it here because it states in the user's own words the kind of problems that are all too often experienced with systems. Although the letter amused me greatly, it also made me sad that users should have to struggle with systems that are far from easy to use. Like many users, my father captures the frustration of trying to use a system that is far from transparent.

Figure 1.2 A novice user operating a word processing package

Chris

I am trying out a new word processing package on my new computer. Y'know the one that Trevor gave me. It works OK, says he. But when I type names and addresses i.e. parts of lines, it sort of word-wraps them along a couple of lines. I'll give you an example at the end of this. Well Mum said scribble Christine a note. She always says Christine when she's giving orders. So I found this splurge in the Mail yesterday, which I thought might interest you (enclosed). It's a follow-on to what we were discussing when we were with you. It's taking me hours to write this I feel like a stone-mason chiselling it in stone! I don't know how you ever wrote that book. If I ever become an author… I wouldn't say my chances were all that great. I would write only short stories…. Very short stories! Anyway, I'll finish off by typing our address then you can see what I mean. So here goes:

> Mr & Mrs Blah Blah Blah
> 111 Blah Blah Blah
> Blah
> Blahshire
> BLA H4
> Cheerio for now… Oh Mum sends her love.
> XXXXXXXXXXXXXXXXXXXXXXXXXXXXX

W-E-L-L it seems to be alright this time. Trouble is I can't remember what I did differently. Shucks.

What happens when usability is not considered might not be simply that a product is not usable and therefore is not purchased and a manufacturer fails to make a profit. The implications of failing to adopt a usability approach are far more wide-reaching. For example, in the United Kingdom, the failure of the London Ambulance Service's (LAS) Computer Aided Despatch (CAD) system can be seen as a prime example of the lack of a usability engineering approach.

The LAS CAD system failed on 4 November 1992. There had been a number of problems prior to the failure but shortly after 2 am the system slowed down and then locked up completely. The staff made attempts to reboot the system by switching off and restarting the machines as they had been previously instructed to do. However, this did not solve the problem on this occasion. Calls already in the system could not be printed out and obviously could not be answered. The staff had to account for all calls they had received and being unable to continue to use the CAD system, reverted to a manual, paper-based system. After the failure of the CAD system it was suggested that deaths may have occurred because of this incident but inquests later showed this to be untrue.

The report on that failure concluded thus:

> Ultimately, the LAS is judged by the quality of service which it provides to the public. The single most effective way of restoring public confidence would be for an actual and visible improvement in performance to take place and be seen to have taken place.
>
> LAS, 1993

There can be no more poignant request for the adoption of usability engineering as a disciplined approached to producing guarantees for usable software and computer systems than that.

1.8 The usability engineering lifecycle

Usability engineering is a process. It seeks to ensure that usable software is produced and that user requirements are met. The system is guaranteed to be what the user wants and needs. In order to understand the relationship between future chapters of this book it is useful to look at the usability engineering lifecycle model. This is shown in Table 1.1.

Table 1.1 The usability engineering lifecycle model

Task	Information produced
Know the user	User characteristics
	User background
Know the task	User's current task
	Task analysis
User requirements capture	User requirements
Setting usability goals	Usability specification
Design process	Design
Apply guidelines, heuristics	Feedback for design
Prototyping	Prototype for user testing
Evaluation with users	Feedback for redesign
Redesign and evaluate with users	Finished product
Evaluate with users and report	Feedback on product for future systems

1.9   A map of the book

The following chapters will examine the processes and methods involved in following a usability engineering approach to the development of systems. Table 1.2 shows the points at which each of the milestones will be reached in the text. Although there are some divergences, generally speaking, the book follows the process through in order. However, in the case of evaluation methods there is some movement backwards and forwards through the text. Some of the methods for gathering information about what is required can be used to evaluate the system and some of the methods used for evaluation are useful in honing requirements and specification. For example, Cooperative Evaluation discussed in Chapter 6 can be used as an evaluation tool but is excellent for examining the requirements and improving the specification. Occasionally, some of the methods and processes will appear in more than one place; for example, the Wizard of Oz method of evaluation is discussed in Chapters 5 and 6. Where this happens I have attempted to alert the reader and to explain why this is necessary.

Table 1.2
A map of this book

Milestone	Chapter in the book
Knowledge of the user	Chapter 2
Knowledge of the task	Chapter 3
User requirements capture	Chapter 4
Usability goals	Chapter 5
Design process	Chapters 4, 5
Apply guidelines, heuristics	Chapter 7
Prototyping	Chapter 6
Evaluation with users, apply metrics	Chapters 6, 2, 5
Redesign and evaluate with users	Chapters 6, 7, 2
Evaluate with users, apply metrics and report	Chapters 6, 7, 2, 5

CHAPTER SUMMARY

▶ It is difficult to ensure that a finished system is exactly what the end-user wants and needs.

▶ Usability engineering tries to solve this problem by a process of discovering what will make an acceptable system for the user and matching the finished product against previously agreed criteria.

▶ Manufacturers are aware of the commercial implications of adopting a usability approach.

▶ Natural and efficient products can make the user's task seem a lot more pleasant. This would remove the frustration often caused by trying to do something with a system that is hard to understand.

▶ Today end-users are less likely to tolerate difficult-to-use systems.

▶ Software which does not conform to the Sale of Goods Act could render the developer liable.

▶ It could be that concentration on the end-user is a sign of the growing maturity of new technology and software development.

▶ Shackel suggested a four-point definition of usability which was later developed.

▶ The ISO defines usability in terms of effectiveness, efficiency and user satisfaction.

▶ The failure to consult the end-user can have devastating effects on the product.

SELF TEST LIST

- attitude
- effectiveness
- efficiency
- learnability
- quantitative evaluation
- usability
- usability engineer
- usability engineering
- usability evaluation
- usability metrics
- User Centred Design
- user friendliness
- user satisfaction

EXERCISES

1   Make a list of household products that you enjoy using and ones you dislike using. Why do you respond to these products in this particular way?

2   Examine advertisements for products. How many talk about 'user friendly' or 'ergonomically designed'? What do they mean by these terms?

3   How would you define usability? What makes a product usable?

4   Make a list of any equipment you own that has required an effort on your part to learn how to use it. Think of what problems you have had and why particular aspects of the equipment may have caused you difficulties.

5   Ask a friend to try to operate a piece of equipment you own, for example, use the grill to make toast, or switch on the oven, play a CD. Try to work out together how easy/difficult the task was and why.

REFERENCES

Allwood C (1984) 'Analysis of the field survey' in Allwood C M and Lieff E (eds) *Better Terminal Use*, pp. 72–7, University of Goteberg: Syslab-G.

ACM SIGCHI (1992) *Curricula for Human-Computer Interaction*. ACM Press.

BCS HIC Group (1995) BCS Model Syllabus 'Challenging Computing Curricula'. *Interfaces,* no. 28.

Bennett J (1984) 'Managing to meet usability requirements' in Bennett J L *et al* (eds) *Visual Display Terminals: Usability Issues and Health Concerns*. Prentice Hall, Englewood Cliffs, New Jersey.

The Concise Oxford Dictionary (1986) 9th edition. BCA, London.

Culwin F and Faulkner C (1997) 'Integration of Usability Considerations within the CS/SE Curriculum'. Proceedings of 3rd CTI Dublin Conference.

Downton A (1991) *Engineering the Human Computer Interface*. McGraw Hill, Maidenhead.

Draper S W (1993) 'The notion of Task in HCI' in Ashland S, Henderson A, Holland E and White T (eds) *Adjunct Proceedings of INTERCHI '93*.

DTI (1990) *A Guide to Usability, Usability Now!* Open University.

Faulkner C (1998) *Essence of Human Computer Interaction*. Prentice Hall, Hemel Hempstead.

Faulkner C and Culwin F (1999) 'Integration or Disintegration' in the proceedings of the SIGCSE conference, New Orleans.

Gould J (1988) 'How to design usable systems' in Helander M (ed.) *Handbook of Human–Computer Interaction*. Elsevier, North Holland.

Hix D and Hartson R (1993) *Developing User Interfaces*. John Wiley, New York.

Jordan P (1998) *An Introduction to Usability*. Taylor and Francis, London.

Jordan P, Thomas B, Weerdmeester A, and McClelland I (1996) *Usability Evaluation in Industry*. Taylor and Francis, London.

Karat J (1996) 'User Centred Design: Quality or Quakery?' in *Interactions*, vol. 11.4, ACM.

LAS (1993) *Report of the Inquiry into the London Ambulance Service*. London: LAS.

Landauer, Thomas (1993) *The Trouble with Computers*. MIT Press, Cambridge, Massachusetts.

Maguire M (1997) *RESPECT User Requirements Framework Handbook*, Deliverable D5.1. RESPECT Consortium.

Nielsen J (1993) *Usability Engineering*. AP Professional, Cambridge, Massachusetts.

Norman D and Draper S (1986) *User Centred System Design*. LEA, Hillsdale, New Jersey.

Root R W and Draper S W (1983) 'Questionnaires as a Software Evaluation Tool' in the proceedings of CHI '83, Boston (pp. 83–87).

Sherman, Barry (1985) *The New Revolution*. John Wiley, London.

Shackel B (1981) 'The concept of usability' in Bennett J L *et al* (eds) (1984) *Visual Display Terminals: Usability Issues and Health Concerns.* Prentice Hall, Englewood Cliffs, New Jersey.

Shackel B (1986) 'Ergonomics in Design for Usability' in Harrison M D and Monk A F (eds) *People and Computers: Designing for Usability.* Proceedings of the Second Conference of the BCS HCI Specialist Group, September 1986.

Shackel B (1990) 'Human Factors and Usability' in Preece and Keller (eds) *Human Computer Interaction.* Prentice Hall, Hemel Hempstead.

Smith, Andy (1997) *Human Computer Factors: A Study of Users and Information Systems.* McGraw Hill, London.

Trenner, Lesley and Bawa, Joanna (1998) *The Politics of Usability.* Springer-Verlag, London.

Tyldesley D (1990) 'Employing Usability Engineering in the Development of Office Products' in Preece and Keller (eds) *Human Computer Interaction.* Prentice Hall, Hemel Hempstead.

Whiteside J, Bennett J and Holtzblatt K (1988) 'Usability Engineering: our Experience and Evolution' in Helander M (ed.) *Handbook of Human–Computer Interaction.* Elsevier, North Holland.

FURTHER READING

Landauer, Thomas (1993) *The Trouble with Computers.* MIT Press, Cambridge, Massachusetts.

This is closely argued and impressive if somewhat disturbing. It needs peace and quiet to follow parts of the argument – I gave up reading it on the train. But it certainly rewards the time and effort put into it. I've made it sound like hard work which it isn't in its entirety but you do need to make sure you follow the first part of the argument.

LAS (1993) *Report of the Inquiry into the London Ambulance Service.* London: LAS.

This is an excellent report for anyone interested in what happens when usability engineering and socio-technical design are ignored. The report is thorough, perceptive and understanding; a must for anyone interested in HCI.

Norman D and Draper S (1986) *User Centred System Design.* LEA, Hillsdale, New Jersey.

I can't in all honesty recommend the entire volume because of its age – though for me it's still a nostalgia trip. I do suggest reading the introduction, looking at the glossary and reading the Lewis and Norman paper on 'Designing for Error' which sums up the ideas of UCD. Incidentally, if you can't lay your hands on a copy then Lewis and Norman are still reproduced (try Baecker *et al* 'Readings in HCI: Towards the Year 2000'), probably because it is such a good paper, abounding with that rare commodity – common sense. It is an entertaining read as well as an informative one.

Shackel B (1990) 'Human Factors and Usability' in Preece and Keller (eds) *Human Computer Interaction*. Prentice Hall, Hemel Hempstead.

This provides a good historical perspective for usability engineering. It is a short paper and easy to read.

Usability – know the user!

This chapter:

▶ looks at the user in terms of individual characteristics and as part of a workplace;

▶ looks at ways in which systems can be designed for non-workplace scenarios;

▶ offers suggestions for getting to know users;

▶ suggests methods of categorising users according to task and expertise;

▶ examines and suggests methods for eliciting knowledge about the user and the task;

▶ suggests points in the usability lifecycle model at which the various methods can be used.

2.1 Getting to know the user

Shackel (1986) provides a picture of what developing systems for people ought to be like:

> The ergonomic approach at this human–machine level is to examine the tasks and the operational sequences which the human will have to carry out and then to work outwards, thus coming to consider the human's interaction firstly with the machine, next with the immediate workspace, and finally with the general environment in which the human and the machine are to work.
>
> Shackel, 1986

This chapter and the next will attempt to pursue this approach starting with the user, moving out to the task and then on to the environment.

The basic tenet for usability engineering is the same as used by ergonomics and Human Computer Interaction (HCI): Know the user! Know the task! So important are the differences between users and what they do that Nielsen suggests that this might account for the major part of usability considerations (Nielsen, 1993).

When we say 'know the user' we mean that there should be a firm understanding of who the users of a product are, what level of expertise they have, what they are likely to assume about systems and the environment in which they are operating. Gould in his paper 'How to Design Usable Systems' urges early and continual focus on the users of the projected system. He adds that designers are often reluctant to define the users and even when they have done so seem reluctant to take their definition seriously (Gould, 1995). This means that systems are frequently built that are not at all suitable for the groups of users that the product was originally targeted at. Gould cites the example of a toolkit system for non-programmers which is too complicated for the target user group to use. From this example it would seem that it is important to remember who the users are since designers seem prone to forget. However, it is possible for the contrary circumstance to occur where a system is developed that offers a level of support that will never be required. I recently listened to a student who had just gained a First and who had produced an excellent final-year project. He explained somewhat ironically how the first version of his programme had a very easy to use Graphical User Interface (GUI). He had spent some time developing this only to realise that it would never be needed since the program was carrying out a research algorithm and would only be used by him! Even more seriously, it slowed down the action of the program. He said the final version had one button that said 'Go'! I have wondered long and hard if usability engineering could have prevented this over enthusiastic student from making this error and I have finally decided it would since usability engineering concentrates on knowing who the users are and what they are trying to do. It isn't about providing the easiest, it is about providing the most appropriate.

The first job to be done, then, is to discover who the users of the proposed system will be. If it is expected that the group will eventually be more heterogeneous than it appears at present then this will have to be taken into consideration. It is pointless attempting to define an average user of the system, since it is unlikely that anyone will fit into the 'average' definition. It is equally futile aiming the system at the lowest common denominator since this could render it unsatisfactory for the bulk of the users.

The nature of the intended users is not simply the body of workers that are presently employed. It has more implications than that. For example, a system that is being built for a group of novice users who form a stable workforce and once trained are not likely to leave within a short space of time will not have the same intentions as a system aimed at a workforce which is fluid. This is especially relevant where this fluidity will involve a constant influx of novice users. Clearly, in the case of the second system training must be minimal and it may be necessary to trade off a simple to learn system for other features. In the case of the stable workforce, it is not so critical to trade off training against other aspects of system performance.

The users of the projected system will have different relationships with that system according to their roles inside the organisation. They will also have different levels of expertise. It is therefore necessary to examine users both in terms of their organisational role or end-user class and their broad computing ability.

It also has to be remembered that computer systems are used outside the workplace. Getting to know the user might involve more than visiting a workplace if the system is to be designed for the general public. Such systems probably pose one of the biggest challenges to HCI – mostly because they need to be usable at once. In some cases, it could be that the user perceives an advantage of learning the system and will therefore put in the effort to learn. The ATM (Automatic Teller Machine) possibly falls into this category. However, many systems designed for use by the general public will have to be usable at once or no effort will be expended to use them.

An aside...

It is important though that users are approached. Never use yourself as sufficient testing of the usability of the product. Scott Kim learned this when he was demonstrating Metafont (a programming language used for typeface design). When the system was shown to expert typeface designers they wanted to work directly on the screen with the design rather than type in programs to produce the images. Scott Kim, on the other hand – 'the resident programmer/artist' – 'liked Metafont's mix of artistic and technical considerations' (Kim, 1995).

2.2 End-user classes

The user class can be defined as a subset of the total population of end-users. The members of an end-user class should be similar both in terms of their use of the system to perform tasks and in terms of their personal characteristics or classification. Users grouped in an end-user class should have very similar patterns of system behaviour and therefore their usability requirements ought to be similar too. It could be that a user who performs more than one functional role within an organisation will be grouped in more than one appropriate end-user class.

There are four user classes that need to be identified:

▶ **Direct users** Direct users use the system themselves in order to carry out their duties. For example, a data entry clerk uses a computer system in order to enter data, a secretary might use a word processor in order to produce letters.

- **Indirect users** These are users who ask other people to use the system on their behalf. For example, a would-be passenger might ask a travel agent to consult an airline's booking system for available flights to Dublin. A customer wishing to order a book might ask the shop assistant to consult the on-line catalogue.

- **Remote users** Remote users do not directly use the system themselves but nevertheless depend upon it for output. For example, the customers of a bank will depend upon the bank's system for information regarding the state of their accounts.

- **Support users** A support user is part of the administration and technical team which supports the work of other people. The task of the support user is to ensure the smooth running of the system. Support users might be helpline staff, system administrators, technicians and so on.

In addition these end-users will also have a relationship with the system which is based on whether or not using the system is part of the jobs they do. We can therefore identify two extra categories of mandatory and discretionary users which may overlap with the categories above:

- **Mandatory users** Mandatory users have to use the system as part of their jobs. They have no choice in the matter. If the system is awkward to use this will make the jobs of mandatory users more difficult and arduous.

- **Discretionary users** Discretionary users do not have to use the computer system as part of their jobs. They can choose whether or not to accomplish their tasks with a computer system. Obviously, the easier a system is to use and the less time-consuming it is to learn, then the more likely a discretionary user is to use the computer system for the particular task in hand. If the task takes longer with a computer system, the discretionary user may choose to use some other method. However, some discretionary users, particularly those who have control over their jobs, may well find learning to use a system an interesting distraction.

A spanner in the works…

Liam Bannon (Bannon, 1995) tells an ironic story of how he was given the specification for a new system. He quite rightly asked to meet with the end-users but was told that he was not allowed 'for political, organizational reasons, to meet with even a single user…' He, therefore, had to proceed as best he could.

Grudin makes similar observations (Grudin 1991). In an ideal world usability engineers do attempt to know the user but this may not always be possible in which case it will be necessary to rely on what information is available.

2.3 Levels of expertise

Besides placing users into classes according to the nature of the task that they carry out when using the computer system, it is also necessary to examine their level of expertise and background. This will be instrumental in deciding just what type of system to implement for the target group and it will also dictate the type of help facilities and training that will be needed for the support of the system.

Normally, when users are classified according to levels of expertise they are placed into the following broad categories: novice, intermediate and expert. However, quite clearly there are ways of breaking down those broad categories and adding others according to the profile of the particular organisation for which the system is being designed. For example, a discretionary user might also be intermittent in their use of computers so a broad categorisation of intermittent and discretionary users could be added. Categorising is useful in that it presupposes the possibility of generalising across user types and thus makes the task of design and development a lot easier than it would be if no such generalisations were allowed.

> **A spanner in the works...**
> However, it is not quite so straightforward as it might seem. There needs to be some care in assigning these broad categories. There needs also to be considerable care in the assumptions that might be made from such broad categorisation of users.
> In a study of a group of users of a UNIX system, Draper (1985) concluded that the common-sense assumptions made about the nature of expertise were in reality not very accurate. He went so far as to suggest that there were no experts. Obviously, such a statement would depend on the definition of expert in the first place. However, some useful material can probably be derived. His study suggests that most users specialise, that is they learn a body of commands that they need to carry out their particular tasks. This means, in practice, that some so-called 'novices' may know commands that the 'experts' do not know, since these experts do not have the need to know them. It also puts into question the accepted wisdom of categorisation.
> If Draper's argument is correct then providing systems that cater for expert users at one end and novice users at the other is not really the answer to the problem at all since everyone is in some sense both an expert and a novice.

Draper's study was of UNIX command line shell. However, it should be possible to extrapolate from it to other software. Take for example the case of the word processing package. The way in which it is used will depend upon the type of users, what they are doing and their expectations or the purpose of the task. Someone who is using the package to produce camera ready copy for publishing will need to be able to use many more of the facilities available – such as complex formatting, table of contents and footnotes. Whereas someone who uses the same system to produce personal letters quite clearly may not have the need to learn all those extra facilities.

Obviously, usability engineering would need to take this into consideration if it is to provide an optimum solution.

2.3.1 Novice users

The novice user of a system will have little or no experience of computers. There may be some hesitation on the part of novices to learn how to use them. It is important that usability engineers do not assume that everyone is as enthusiastic about computers as they are!

Novices need frequent feedback from the system to reassure them that they are progressing towards their goals and that all is well. They find it easier to be presented with choices rather than having to consider actions for themselves. They like the system to progress at their speed, they like to read the screens and see what is going on. They want to be reassured that they cannot break the system or that they won't do anything to hurt it. Strangely, breaking the system seems to be a problem that is uppermost in many users' minds. So much so that jokes abound about just this aspect of a system's performance. One such joke, in the form of definitions, is shown as Figure 2.1 below.

Figure 2.1 Breaking the system: definitions of users

> **novice user** – someone who is afraid that if they touch the keyboard they will break the system.
> **intermediate user** – someone who has broken the computer and doesn't know how to fix it.
> **expert user** – someone who breaks other people's computers.

Systems need to be robust above all else. Usability engineers need to reassure users that if something does go wrong, it is not the fault of the user.

Novices need to be guided through processes and supported. They need good, easy to find and easy to understand help systems. They need to be in easy reach of human help. People prefer to get help from each other rather than from the system. Usability engineers need to accept that and design into the way in which work is carried out, the provision of human help. Gould argues that users should always be in sight of another user so that they can ask for help. Asking for help should be encouraged so that there is never any sense of shame or embarrassment implied in not knowing, or in needing assistance (Gould, 1995). Those of us who can remember a time before the Web, when newsgroups and e-mail lists were not quite so busy as they are now will know how easy it was to get help via those sources and how generous some very busy and dare I say famous people were with their time. People like helping people as well as being helped by people. The Answer Garden – a system that creates and then grows a tree structure that contains answers to commonly posed questions – could be used in this way with the usability engineer receiving questions not answered by the Answer Garden. Obviously, any repeated questions can be inserted into the system which can then be monitored in order to see which problems re-occur.

In any humane computer system actions should be easily undone without side effects, since this encourages users to explore without being afraid of 'breaking the system'. For novice users this is very important indeed. The sense that the system can be safely experimented with will increase the confidence of the novice user and encourage use of the system. Functionality should be limited to the tasks in hand and the system should always volunteer activities for the novice user to choose from rather than expecting novices to suggest functionality to the system. It is much easier to select from a given set of choices rather than guess what those choices might be. Imagine a restaurant without a menu where the diners are expected to guess what might be served and will not be able to place an order until they have guessed correctly. It would be a nightmare.

An aside…

Strangely enough, I saw this happen in Atlanta, Georgia in the spring of 1998 while I was attending a conference there. A group of colleagues and I went to a very smart restaurant in Atlanta. Some of us ordered cocktails without any problems then one of the party asked for a beer. Instead of producing a list of possible choices, the waiter asked which beer the guest would like, adding there were thirty to choose from. There followed a guessing game!

Large systems can be intimidating for novice users. Furthermore, it is not always necessary to show novice users all parts of a system at once; sometimes it is possible to have more advanced parts of the system hidden until the user has gained confidence and experience. The more advanced features of the system can be gradually revealed as and when the user needs the extra functionality. Some of the very flexible and quick development tools have versions of this so that systems can be set as browse only or edit with the tools for editing available at various levels.

A spanner in the works…
Carroll and Rosson found that:

'…many users were not discovering and using functions that could have made their jobs easier… Instead of becoming generalized experts themselves, users learn a basic set of knowledge…'

Carroll and Rosson, 1989

2.3.2 Intermittent users

Intermittent users provide a real challenge for usability engineers. These are people who may use the system only occasionally, or use it for periods of time and then go several months without using it again. They are very likely to display both expert and novice characteristics; though as we have seen Draper argues that this would be true of all users (Draper, 1985). They need good on-line help and good supporting manuals. They are liable to remember broad aspects of the system but not its details so it is important that such users are supported in their search for help and that functionality is consistent across the application.

2.3.3 Expert users

The accepted wisdom is that expert users know everything there is to know about the system. The truth is that expert users will need to use help systems. Draper argues that expert users are indeed the major users of help systems. He suggests that this might be because they consult help systems on other people's behalves, or perhaps novice users find help systems too daunting and so avoid using them (Draper, 1985). This would in comparison make expert-user use of manuals look proportionally higher. Experts will also carry out tasks that are new to them. Like the other categories of users they may on these occasions need to consult help systems. Generally speaking they will not need the feedback and support that a novice user might need. This is mostly to do with the fact that they will be more confident in their interactions with the system and they will also have clearer ideas about how they can achieve any feedback that they believe they need. For example, users of the Macintosh operating system who wish to delete a file will point, click and drag the said file to the wastebasket. The wastebasket will bulge convincingly as the file is placed inside. Users accustomed to this system will know that the file is inside the wastebasket where it will remain there until they select 'empty waste bin' from the main menu or drag the file out again! The dustbin will then return to its normal shape showing that the file has been deleted. If we examined that same process on VAX/VMS we would note that the user would have to build in their own feedback. The sequence of commands for deleting a file under VAX/VMS would be:

```
$ dir
$ delete file.txt;1
$ dir
```

The first dir command lists all the files in that directory. This enables the user to verify that the file that is to be deleted actually exists in this particular directory. The second command deletes the offending file. The third dir command again lists all files in the directory and enables the user to confirm that the file has indeed been deleted. For an expert user this process is easily available but a novice user might well be puzzled as to how confirmation of actions is achieved. Figure 2.2 shows the actual interactions with the system.

Figure 2.2 Deleting a file
using VAX/VMS

```
$ dir
myfile.txt;1
thisfile.txt;3
important.txt;1
book.txt;2
file.txt;1
$ del file.txt;1
$ dir
myfile.txt;1
thisfile.txt;3
important.txt;1
book.txt;2
```

Expert users need to be provided with accelerators through the system. In a GUI this might be in the form of shortcut keys and defaults. In a command line system, commands can be grouped and the commands themselves abbreviated or redefined as necessary.

People who use computers frequently may well use a variety of platforms and a variety of applications. At present, standardisation is far from complete and a wide range of commands are in existence to more or less accomplish the same activities. For example, take terminating a session with a system, all of the following commands might be used by different applications and platforms:

```
exit, system, logout, finish, bye, quit, close
```

It is therefore useful for expert users to be able to redefine commands, or to add synonyms for commands in order to achieve the desired result whatever system they are using. For example, Figure 2.3 shows a section from a login.com file on a command line system I use. The system has allowed me to redefine commands and give them whatever names I want to.

Figure 2.3 Command line
login.com file for redefining
commands

```
$ chatty :== set broadcast = phone
$ quiet :== set broadcast = (nophone)
$ quiet
$ up :== set def [-]
$ home :== set def [xristine]
$ mail :== mail/edit
$ who :== show users
$ room :== show quota
$ del :== delete/confirm
$ zap :== delete *.*;*/conf
```

2.4 Categorising users

Care needs to be taken when assigning users to categories. If we measure an individual's feet we can classify them according to shoe size and say that Bridie takes size 37 shoes. But that may not always be the case. If Bridie puts on weight her shoe size may go up. The shape of the shoe might also dictate whether she decides to buy a size 36 or 38. The same thing applies to end-users. When we classify users we need to do so in context and be very clear what those categorisations mean. My own students are encouraged to describe someone who has never touched a computer before as a naïve user. Novices will normally have some, albeit very limited, experience at the keyboard, either through games or some contact with a computer system – such as a library cataloguing system. Experts should be proficient in the use of computer systems. However, we regularly classify users as expert users but novices in a *particular environment*. Our only assumption about experts is that they will be less scared of breaking the system!

An aside...

It must be stressed that these categories must mean something to the design team. They are not absolutes; they are tools to get the job done and all tools should be malleable and bend to the circumstances they need to be used in. Never apply rules rigidly to the development of Human Computer Systems. Users are people; they do not conform to rules. If you have ever tried identifying birds, butterflies or flowers from a field guide you know how difficult that can be. People are much the same. Fitting them into a field guide is tricky.

2.5 Methods for gathering information about users

There are several ways in which information can be gained from the intended users. These methods will elicit information about the user group or the user task and can be used for gathering information about both. Task analysis (dealt with in the next chapter) is geared to eliciting information about task.

Sometimes it is difficult to separate user characteristics from the task and the usability engineer should bear this in mind when carrying out activities to elicit information about task and user group characteristics.

The subsequent sections will examine the following methods for gathering information about users:

- informal and formal discussion;
- observation;
- putting an expert on the design team;
- questionnaire;
- interview.

If the system is to being built for an organisation it is important to prepare the ground before visiting the workplace. The design team should know as much about the organisation as possible before it visits. The intention of the visit is to gather information about the end-users, their tasks, the environment and the socio-technical makeup of the organisation but this will all be easier if the background and history of the organisation have been studied first. It is important to respect the culture of the organisation. For example, Ben Shneiderman talks about one manager who called to warn the visiting team that graduate students should not wear jeans since end-users were not permitted to do so! (Shneiderman, 1998).

2.5.1 Informal and formal discussion with users

Gould recommends talking with users. He believes that discussions with users can bring to light all sorts of information about the system and the way in which it needs to operate (Gould, 1995). Users are not expert designers but they do have opinions about whether or not a particular design will work in their environment. They can often give insights into the current system that designers fail to see. It is possible to learn a lot about what users want simply by *listening* to what they have to say.

There is another advantage to talking with users in that they are made to feel part of the process of designing and building a system. This can have significant benefits when the system is finally introduced. For example, supposing the user group is not committed to the idea of a new system then involving them in the process of building it will enable them to see that the system is being built for them and that designers are considering their needs. Secondly, involving them in the decision making about the development of the system means that end-users will feel responsible for it. If they make suggestions about the system's performance and design they will feel that they have a vested interest in it and will be more likely to help make the system work. The experience of the London Ambulance Service (LAS) over its Computer Aided Despatch (CAD) System shows what happens when the designers of systems fail to consult effectively with the end-users (LAS, 1993). The report on the failure of the LAS CAD system says that:

> … there was incomplete "ownership" of the system by the majority of its users… the staff expected the system to fail rather than willing it to succeed.
>
> LAS, 1993

There is the added advantage that users who are involved with the system during its development will know what it consists of and will need less training when the system is finally brought on-line. However, this is a double-edged sword. Designers must be careful not to train end-users in a system while it is being developed and then convince themselves that the system is easy to learn because certain end-users have grasped it in what appears to be next to no time. Also, users are not expert designers and sometimes may know that something is difficult to use but have no suggestions to make. One of my students once asked a user who had difficulty with a particular icon what she would like in place of the icon he had provided. The user answered quite rightly that she didn't build programs so she didn't know what there was to suggest! Users can help point out problems but they may not be able to provide answers.

However, focusing on end-users by interviewing them and talking to them means that it is difficult to ignore them. The system is being built for those particular users. The users are not there for the system. By talking to the end-users of the system they will inevitably be uppermost in the mind of the designer and they are more likely to obtain the system they need and deserve because the designer will know what the user group is really like.

2.5.2 Understanding the user's workplace

It is important for the system's designer to have a clear idea of the tasks the users do and the environment in which they carry out these tasks. In ergonomics the environment in which the task takes place is one of the paramount considerations but HCI practitioners may need to remind themselves of the fact that user and task exist within an environment. For example, it would be pointless designing a voice input system which was to be used in a very noisy environment. It would be equally unacceptable to design a voice-input system for a very quiet or even silent environment (for example a library). Not only would such a system interfere with other people performing tasks but talking into a system in a silent environment would probably prove very embarrassing for many users, at least at first, though perhaps the familiarity with mobile phones might reduce this problem.

If system developers visit customer locations and talk to the users, see what they are doing and experience what they experience; mistakes in the development of the system are less likely. For example, designers of a system for secretaries were told by the users that they did not want audible alerts when something went wrong. The end-users did not wish the rest of the room to know that mistakes had been made. Information like this is invaluable in designing systems and it is not likely to emerge without close contact with the end-user group.

Notice I use the term 'end-user group'. It might be interesting to talk to the managers of end-user groups but those people can never provide the insights into the job that the actual end-users of a system can. All too often those responsible for the management of end-users know how a task is supposed to be done, how it used to be done or how they wish it was done but quite often the end-users themselves perform those tasks in quite a different way. By talking to end-users in their own environment usability engineers will not make the mistake of getting an idealised version of what happens. Seeing users in their own environment and getting them accustomed to your being there means you are more likely to hear the truth and are less likely to be subjected to a special show, put on for your benefit.

Figures 2.4, 2.5 and 2.6 show workplaces.

Figure 2.4 A commercial office

Figure 2.5 An academic's office

Figure 2.6 A study

2.6 Putting it into practice

So far we have looked at the importance of talking to users and gaining insights into their behaviour and the organisation they are part of. We now need to look at some of the methods open to the usability engineer for the collection of information about the user. These methods will be useful for several different stages in the usability engineering lifecycle.

Table 2.1 Lifecycle with techniques available at each stage

Task	Information produced	Method
Know the user	User characteristics	Interview, questionnaire, observation
	User background	As above
Know the task	User's current task	As above
	Task analysis	
User requirements capture	User requirements	
Setting usability goals	Usability specification	
Design process	Design	
Apply guidelines, heuristics	Feedback for design	Interview, questionnaire
Prototyping	Prototype for user testing	
Evaluation with users	Feedback for redesign	Interview, questionnaire
Redesign and evaluate with users	Finished product	
Evaluate with users and report	Feedback for future systems	Interview, questionnaire

The methods that follow can be used to gain broad information about the user, the task and the environment. This would be useful in the early stages when it is necessary to look at user requirements. Secondly, the same techniques can be used during task analysis and the design of the system. Thirdly, the techniques can be used during development as part of a prototyping and evaluating exercise. Finally, they can be used as part of the usability evaluation process.

Each stage should produce its own documentation. This will be dealt with as each of the stages is examined. We will also add other techniques as the book progresses.

2.6.1 Expert on the design team

One of the ways in which information can be gathered about end-users is to involve one or more of the users in the project by putting them on the design team. That way, there is always a representative from the user group to voice the hopes and fears of the group. Sometimes the end-users can give valuable insights into the design of the system and may, sometimes, provide alternative solutions. However, there are drawbacks in involving one particular user all through the project in that it is possible that the particular user becomes accustomed to the way in which the design team operates and is no longer representative of the group as a whole. Some projects overcome this difficulty by changing the representative from the end-user group so that this does not happen. This also allows more users to be involved in the development process but it can seriously skew evaluation results later on.

2.6.2 Questionnaires

One of the ways in which the usability engineer can gather information about current work practices or opinions on the system is by the use of the questionnaire. Questionnaires are good sources of subjective responses (a measure of user attitude) but they are less reliable when it comes to collecting objective data. They can produce vast amounts of data that is useful for the usability engineer though analysing it can be tedious. However, they are time-consuming to produce and need to be properly tested before they can be given out to the target audience.

Producing a good questionnaire is very, very time-consuming!

Questionnaires can be either interviewer administered where an interviewer asks the questions and fills in the answers as the subject responds or self-administered where the subject reads and fills in the answers without any assistance.

Interviewer administered questionnaires are time-consuming to administer. If more than one person is to interview subjects then they have to be trained to deal with the questionnaire in the same way, or the results cannot easily be compared. There has to be agreement about what each question really means, how the responses are to be interpreted and how much assistance the subject is to be given. The advantage of interviewer administered questionnaires is that there is a control of the returns of the questionnaire.

Self-administered questionnaires require fewer person-hours to deliver but there are several problems that can occur. For a start, there is poor control over the return of the questionnaire and because of this there is a likelihood of bias in that the group that responds might have a particular axe to grind. The questions have to be very clear, since there is no opportunity to explain to the subject what is meant.

Questions can be open or closed. Open questions are good for gaining information on a broad basis because they allow the respondents to answer in any way they choose. For example, an open question might be:

> What aspects of the system did you like most?

The closed question limits the subject's response to a given range of possible answers. For example, a closed question based on the example above would be:

> Which aspects of the system did you like most?
> a) the colours   b) the sound   c) the ease of navigation

The problem with open questions is that they can produce too much data that cannot be easily analysed because it is so diverse. Whereas it is much easier to classify the responses to closed questions and therefore to analyse the data. However, closed questions can distort findings simply because they suggest things to people that might not otherwise occur to them.

2.6.3   Problems encountered in designing questionnaires

The wording of suitable questions for a questionnaire is not simple and there are many places where problems can occur. The questionnaire must be prototyped and tested before it is distributed to users. It is all to easy to find out, once the questionnaire is returned, that subjects have interpreted a question in a way that the design team has not anticipated. Or that additional material is needed in order to be able to interpret the data. Obviously, if a questionnaire can be identified with the particular subject who completed it, then the team does have the opportunity to ask for additional material. But quite often this is not possible because it is desirable to have the anonymous responses in order to guarantee confidentiality and to ensure that responses are more likely to be honest.

It is also important not to bias the reply by using emotionally significant terms, or by implying some fault in the subject, or by suggesting a reply in the question. Questions that begin 'You have... haven't you?' fall into this category and are difficult for the subject to answer honestly.

Embarrassment of the subject and perhaps biasing of the results can also arise where the subjects feel that their particular answers imply some inadequacy on their part. For example, a long list of applications which subjects are asked to tick if they know how to use them may make a user who has none, or very few, to tick feel inferior. Some subjects may well tick applications they do not know or use simply because they think it looks better if they do.

Precision in framing questions can also be a problem. Questions that give answers like 'seldom', 'frequently', 'often' are impossible to answer accurately. It will be unclear to the subject just what these terms mean as they are far too subjective. It is important to ensure that questions which require frequency as a reply have those frequencies stated or allow the subject to offer them.

2.6.4 Questionnaire types

Multi-choice questions and checklists

The simplest form of questionnaire might ask the user for a yes/no response – see Figure 2.7. Some questionnaires add a 'don't know/don't have an opinion' category.

Figure 2.7 Simple yes/no questionnaire

Have you ever used Draw n' Draft?	Yes ☐	No ☐

Checklists are also useful. These might gather information about what systems a user has used or what aspects of a system they have used – see Figure 2.8. They do not require a subject to remember which aspects of the system have been used – which could be a problem for subjects filling in the questionnaire out of context. However, there is the problem that subjects may be tempted to 'beef up' their replies by ticking more than is strictly true.

Figure 2.8 A checklist

Which of the following have you used? Tick all that apply.

Word processor ☐
Spreadsheet ☐
Database ☐
Drawing package ☐
Presentation software ☐
Translation package ☐

Scalar questionnaires

A scalar questionnaire asks the subject to register an opinion based on a predefined scale. These scales have numerical values attached to them or a linguistic scale – see Figure 2.9.

Figure 2.9 A multi-point rating scale

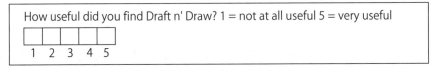

Some questionnaire designers deliberately miss out a middle category from questions like this in order to force the respondent into an opinion either way. A middle category can be very much like adding a 'don't know/don't have an opinion' category to a question and when this is present some 10 to 40 per cent of respondents will shift their answer to that section (Plous, 1993). Some respondents seem to prefer not to give a definite answer! Questions without middle categories are good for collecting general opinions and they avoid the disadvantage of allowing people to sit on the fence. The disadvantage of using no middle category is that it does force people to decide between opinions they may not really have strong feelings about and it may cause them to register artificial opinions.

A Likert scale is a scalar questionnaire where the strength of opinion is gathered – see Figure 2.10.

Figure 2.10 A Likert scale

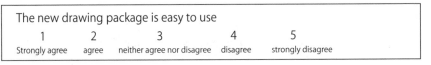

A semantic differential scale uses antonyms (opposites) to represent two opposing views. The scales between these views are then given – usually with a neutral view in the middle. An example is shown in Figure 2.11.

Figure 2.11 A semantic differential scale

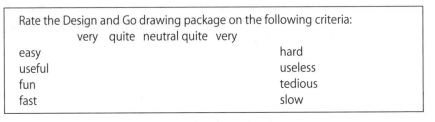

A ranked order questionnaire asks the respondents to rank their opinions but these are specified by the question itself. Figure 2.12 gives an example of a ranked order question. Again, it can be difficult for subjects to choose between categories that seem equally important or do not have any quantifiable differences for that particular subject. It is also possible that artificial responses will be registered.

Figure 2.12 A ranked order questionnaire

> Place the following in order according to how frequently you use them with the most frequently used first and the least frequently used last.
>
> Spell checker   Thesaurus
> Grammar checker   Template

Incidentally, there are packages available to help with the analysis of questionnaires. If the intention is to use such a package then it would be wise to experiment first with the design of the questions. Sometimes it is necessary to use a different question structure simply to enable the analysis to be done automatically. Students at South Bank have used such packages in the creation of questionnaires. They have also designed and built questionnaires in the more traditional way and used spreadsheets and databases in order to carry out the analysis. Our experience seems to be that it really does depend on what type of questionnaire you want to design. The packages do allow for the collection of answers to open questions but, obviously, these would have to be analysed manually. Sometimes there is no alternative but to ask an open question.

At the time of writing I have just emerged from listening to presentations from students who have carried out a series of investigations, frequently using questionnaires. Time and time again they have exclaimed that the questionnaire they thought perfect was problematic when it was given to subjects. However, the major problem encountered was that their questionnaires were too long and subjects were unhappy to give up the necessary time to fill them in. If the questionnaire is to be used as part of an interview and administered in work time with the blessing of management, there may not be a problem. If the questionnaire is to be used in the street on the general public, keep it very short indeed. Dorothy L. Sayer's heroine Harriet Vane remarks in *Gaudy Night* that 'English people won't fill up questionnaires… As a nation we are not questionnaire-conscious.' (Sayers, 1970). I suspect that this characteristic is not a reserve of the English and no-one much likes filling them in so make them short and attractive.

2.7 Observation

It is useful and interesting to watch workers or members of the public perform a task. Particularly if they can be persuaded to ignore the observer and carry on as usual. It can also be useful if they can be persuaded to talk through the task as they carry it out. However, it is important not to disturb the way in which someone typically works on a task nor must any extraneous conditions or tools be imposed. Talking through a task quite clearly does that, although some people – myself included – quite happily talk to themselves when doing things and have no problem talking through a task with someone there! It is important to ensure that any user who agrees to be observed is happy about that and that users are performing the task they normally perform and in the way in which they normally perform it. If the evaluation team has the confidence of the users they are less likely to be treated to a show!

It is important to remember that people being watched can act in a different way because of the presence of the observer. This is not always conscious and there may well be no intention on the part of the subject to deceive. This is called the Hawthorne effect. The Hawthorne effect is named after a study carried out at the Hawthorne electrical assembly works in Chicago in the 1920s. The aim of the study was to examine the effect of lighting upon work. However, as the study progressed it became obvious that it was being affected by extraneous factors. At one point productivity increased steadily as lighting levels were reduced to the point where workers complained that they could no longer see! It is important to remember then that observing users means that you may inevitably alter the way in which they work. Draper (1993) argues that experimentation suffers from the same problem and that because of the influence of the experimenter very little can realistically be derived from experiments! (Draper, 1993).

A spanner in the works...

Ben Shneiderman points out that:

'The goal of an observation is to obtain the necessary data to influence interface redesign. Unfortunately, it is easy to misinterpret observations, to disrupt normal practice, and to overlook important information.'

Shneiderman; 1998 p108

Gould suggests using video recordings of users (Gould, 1995). I have to admit to being somewhat cynical about this process. It is all too easy to be subjected to a show when the video recorder comes into play. Gould does emphasise that these recordings should be brief and suggests two minutes (Gould, 1995). Any longer really is a complete waste of time in more ways than one. But short recordings would be useful if you can ensure that you are not being given a special show. These recordings must not be done secretly so obtaining the trust of the end-users is important if a realistic picture is to emerge. This really does depend on the team's ability to develop a good, honest relationship with the end-users. I have noticed that some of my students working with end-users are able to gain a lot more out of them than others. It probably amounts to learning how to interact with end-users, learning to respect them and listening to them. Gaining the trust of end-users is an important aspect of this.

An aside...

I do not wish to imply that it is impossible to persuade users to act naturally on the camera – it is, but can require patience. I spent one summer as a photographer for an archaeological site. Much of the work consisted of creating a photographic record of the collected data but I was also asked to obtain a record of everyday life on the site in order to obtain publicity material. At first, every time I appeared with a camera I was subjected to huge smiles with trowels raised in an artificial pose but, after a while, the archaeologists grew accustomed to having me around and ignored me.

Incidentally, Don Norman is very scathing about the use of video material. He believes that usability laboratories are full of unseen video tape (Norman, 1992). He is very likely right. A video recording of a user working at a system might take 30 minutes to shoot. It takes time to set up the equipment in the first place. To watch it requires a further 30 minutes. That means that one hour, plus set up time, has gone into a half an hour observation. Much of the second viewing will be of things that are unimportant. If video recordings are to be made it is very important to ensure that a note is made at the time of anything that is interesting so that when you return to look at the video you can jump to the relevant points in the tape and thus save time. Furthermore, these recording must be brief if they are to be successful. Figure 2.13 shows a document developed by the 1998–9 Brewsers Project students at the School of Computing, South Bank University. The students designed this document for observation of our evaluation subjects. An extra column for the point reached on the video would be needed if it were to be used for video observations/interviews.

Figure 2.13 A document for logging activity

Interface		Subject No:		
Observer's name		Evaluator's name		
Start time		Finished time		

Time	Task	Subjects actions	Help given /Evaluators action	Comments

2.8 Activity sampling and activity logging

Another method of gathering information about user activity is by logging. This can be done by either a member of the design team or the performer of the task or by the system itself. When done by the task performer it can interfere with the way in which a task is performed so the usability engineer needs to remember that. Logging carried out by the system is far less intrusive. However, when logging is carried out in this way it is important that the end-user knows this will happen. Knowing that logging is taking place may well affect performance, especially at first, but the likelihood is that over a period of time, the end-user may well forget that logging is taking place and perhaps a less biased picture may emerge.

It has to be said that a huge quantity of data can be generated by system logging – which can be very tedious and time-consuming to deal with (unless it is automated).

It is important to remember that the *Display Screen Equipment Regulations Workstation Requirements Schedule* states that under no circumstances must quantitative or qualitative checking – either the quality or the quantity of work – be carried out on end-users without their prior knowledge (Directive 90/270/EEC).

Even without the presence of the requirement, it would be unethical of a usability engineer to subject users to anything without their prior knowledge or consent.

2.9　The interview

The social sciences have developed several kinds of interviews which can be used and adapted by usability engineers wishing to obtain information from users. Interviews can range from structured to unstructured and all stages in between. The social sciences have also developed ethnographical interviews which have been ported across to HCI with varying degrees of success.

In the unstructured interview the interviewer asks the users a series of open-ended questions. The idea is that the user will steer the interview in the direction of issues which they perceive as being important. This type of interviewing technique is probably most appropriate when the usability engineer has little idea about what the user's concerns actually are, or in the early stages when the usability engineers are trying to capture general information about the users, their tasks and their environments. It is a good method for building user confidence in that it allows them to direct the interview and gives them the sense that they are actually airing their concerns. It is important in the development of systems that users believe that usability engineers are really interested in what they have to say.

It is vital that the interviewer has some questions to ask the subject in case the interview is halting. Sometimes users are happy to talk about their experiences and need little prompting but this is not always the case. If the interviewee is shy or reluctant to discuss the issues with the interviewer then it will necessary to find a method of encouraging talk. It is just as well to have a few questions planned in case there is a problem. The questions can be as open-ended as the interviewer deems fit since this might encourage the interviewee to talk. Usually, with shy interviewees some short questions which are general and easy to answer are a good way of breaking the ice.

On the other end of the scale, structured interviews expect the users to select a response from a given set of responses. For these interviews a set of questions will have been planned in advance and the interviewees will be expected to indicate their answers from a list of suggested answers. These interviews make no attempt to gather individual opinions but attempt to find a gross response. This method is quite often used in public opinion surveys. These highly structured interviews are effectively interviewer-administered questionnaires.

Obviously it is possible to design an interview which comes somewhere between these two extremes. There are semi-structured interviews in which the interviewer will have a series of questions that can be used to draw out the interviewee if necessary. But the structure is more fluid than the structured interview in that the interviewees are allowed to express whatever opinions they hold; there is no need to match their opinions with a predefined list. These interviews are frequently the most useful in that the interviewer can ensure that the necessary ground has been covered adequately but at the same time it is possible to gather individual responses from the worker and to gain some indication of their ideas and personal responses.

Prompted interviews are flexible interviews but with a built-in means to prevent the interviewee from drying up. In the case of prompted interviews the interviewer might encourage the interviewee to say more or to expand upon important issues by adding supplementary questions such as 'What do you mean when you say… ?', or 'Can you explain that in a little more detail?' and so on.

Where users are nervous or hesitant an unstructured interview is probably a waste of time. I once had the task of having to interview someone who was very upset about something – not a computer, I hasten to add. She needed to tell me what the problem was but every time she tried to explain, she started to cry. I suggested I asked questions and she answered them. In fact, in this case, it worked well. She had to concentrate on my questions and we could tiptoe carefully around the bits that were painful. However, no usability engineer should be in the situation where they are interviewing someone who is weeping. It ought not happen. If an interviewee becomes upset, for whatever reason, then the interview must stop. But the technique of short questions is probably useful for the shyest and most self-effacing of workers. After a while, most people will relax and the interviewer can allow the interview to develop into an unstructured one.

Structured interviews are easier to manage. The interviewer goes into the interview with a set a questions, and when the last question is reached that is the end of the interview. But structured interviews only work with the right set of questions. It is important therefore to test the questions carefully beforehand just as would be done with a questionnaire.

Unstructured interviews are hard work for the interviewer. There needs to be some method of recording the interview. If a tape recorder is used then it has to be used discretely but the interviewee must know that the interview is being recorded. Secret recordings are unethical and unacceptable. Recording an interview may put an added burden on the subject though in fact most people do seem to settle down and relax eventually as long as the recording equipment is discrete. The problem is that if the tape recorder is relied upon as a means of recording the interview a decision has to be made about what will be done with the finished recording. Don Norman has already commented about this at some length in his witty and erudite essay 'I Go to a Sixth Grade Play' (Norman, 1992). He suggests that where typed transcriptions are made from tape recordings it may take as much as ten hours for each hour of tape recording.

If the intention is to rely entirely upon the tape recording of the interview and the transcription made afterwards then it is probably wise to use two tape recorders, just in case there is a problem. This is the method adopted by those working in the field of Knowledge Elicitation for Knowledge Based Systems. However, two tape recorders will be twice as daunting and twice as problematic as one. It is important, for example, to make sure the tapes do not run out at the same time. If two tape recorders are being operated then it is vital to have a second person present along with the interviewer in order to run the equipment. This makes the interview all the more problematic for a nervous subject. Equipment needs to be tested too. One of my project students carried out a cooperative evaluation with his mother who had only just started using a computer. Interviewing relatives is notoriously difficult as the familiarity can get in the way but this interview was very well done and both parties put aside personal considerations. However, half way through the recording the project student suddenly remarked that they hadn't tested the equipment to make sure it was recording correctly to which his mother replied: 'Don't worry, it'll be all right.' The subject here was confident about being recorded and was an excellent subject in other ways too; she was being handled well and she was relaxed and her response is a testimony to that. However, subjects should not normally be subjected to oversights like that even if they are your mum! In testing equipment never let the subject hear part of the recording before the interview is complete. Some people find the sound of their own voice somewhat surprising and off-putting and may become too shy to proceed.

It is probably better to make sure that sensible notes are made at the time, or at least a record made that there is a need to return to a particular point on the tape. That way time will be saved and you will not need to listen to the whole thing again. It might be entertaining to listen to one hour of tape after the first interview (and I suggest that you do that to find out how well you conducted the interview) but it is difficult to be quite so enthusiastic about listening to ten interviews of one hour each.

An aside...

One subject a project student and I were working with recently was asked by me if he minded being recorded. We were carrying out a talk aloud evaluation (see Chapter 6). He said that he didn't mind at all. At the end of the session, the project student asked if the tape recorder had been a problem for the subject. The subject replied that it had made him talk more and be more descriptive because he wanted to make sure that what he said would still make sense to us afterwards! We are still trying to figure out whether this is good or bad.

Nielsen *et al* (1986) used a semi-structured interview technique on integrated software packages. The aim of their questionnaires was primarily to look at tasks and the reasons that tasks were structured in a particular way. Figure 2.14 shows this process diagrammatically and is adapted from Nielsen. The questions are shown in Table 2.2 with their intentions. These questions will be used in the next chapter as a means of eliciting information about a small task.

Figure 2.14 Semi-structured questions

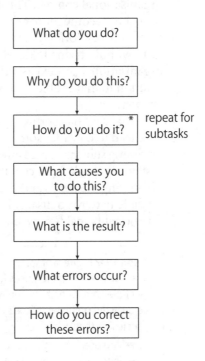

Table 2.2 Questions to elicit task detail

Questions	Purpose
1 What do you do?	Obtains the user's goal
2 Why do you do it?	Obtains method
3 How do you do it?	Obtains the subtask. Used recursively for each subtask
4 What are the preconditions for doing this?	To find out what outside influences there are
5 What are the results of doing this?	To examine the product and see what the purpose is
6 What errors occur?	Error capture
7 How do you correct them?	Error correction

Some interviews use cards for the interviewee to pick options from or to arrange in an order of priority. This technique has been used to good effect by knowledge elicitation teams (Killin, 1989). However, it does imply that the interviewer has the cards prepared in advance and that implies the expertise to prepare them. If the domain is unfamiliar this is no easy task. Market research has employed the technique of matching cards to opinion. This is more easily done.

Ethnographical interviews have been ported across from the social sciences. There are really an attempt to deal with the growing complexities of understanding the users and their tasks in a widening social and organisational context. The demand for a solution to this problem has probably become more critical with the growth of Computer Supported Cooperative Work (CSCW). It is difficult enough to support users and tasks without trying to develop systems which fit into a social and organisational context as well. The ethnographical approach may be the solution to that problem. It will be examined in more detail in the next chapter.

Perhaps we have grown a little complacent about the use of interviews and need to consider some alternative views. Interviews are useful for obtaining subjective measures. They can be used to identify problems in the system, to check the acceptability of concepts. They are also useful for identifying the needs and preferences of users and as an indication of possible patterns of usage. However, prediction of possible use of functionality inside a system needs to be treated with caution.

A spanner in the works...

In a study of user preferences Root and Draper (1983) suggested that there was in fact little correlation between what users said they would prefer and what they actually did prefer when the system was implemented. They came to the conclusion that:

'…asking users the value of some proposed change without giving them experience of it is an essentially useless guide to their satisfaction with it in practice.'

Furthermore, it is unfortunately the case that people away from the work environment and sometimes the task itself seem to have little ability to remember in detail. Holtzblatt and Jones (1995) have noted that workers seem to talk about their jobs in the abstract. Frequently, they fail to describe the actual task as they do it but they may describe the process in a vague and abstract way. They frequently generalise which as we shall see later, can be a problem. It is apparent that if interviews are to be used in order to produce material for requirements capture or task analysis then it must be an interview done in the context of the task itself. It is better to get the worker to demonstrate the task and talk through it. Holtzblatt and Jones go so far as to say that:

'…process descriptions are idealized models of what should be or could be a way of working, but they rarely describe the actual flow of people trying to accomplish a task.'

Holtzblatt and Jones, 1995

2.10 Knowing the user – a checklist

The process of getting to know the user should enable the usability engineer to build up a suitable picture of the user group. A checklist for user characterisation is shown in Table 2.3 – to which items can be added or deleted as necessary. For example, it may not be necessary or expedient to gather information about age or educational background.

Table 2.3 User characteristics

User information:
- age range
- educational background
- skills
- user classification

Use of the system:
- discretionary or mandatory user

Job details:
- end-user class
- brief job description
- main tasks
- responsibilities
- control of work load

CHAPTER SUMMARY

▶ The basic tenet for usability engineering is Know the user! Know the task!

▶ Designers need to discover who the users of the system will be and find out about their workplace and methods of work.

▶ The users of the projected system will have different relationships with the projected system according to their roles inside the organisation. They will also have different levels of expertise.

▶ There are four user classes: direct users, indirect users, remote users and support users. End-user classes should be similar in their use of the system to perform tasks and in their personal characteristics or classification.

▶ Users can also be classified according to their level of expertise and experience with the computer system.

▶ There are objections to the accepted wisdom that there is a clear scale between novice and expert users.

▶ Informal discussions are a good way of finding out broad information about the end-user's preferences and background.

▶ Users who are involved with the system during its development will know what it consists of and will need less training.

▶ Questionnaires are good sources of user attitude but they can be time-consuming to prepare, administer and analyse.

▶ Observation is a good way of finding out how tasks are done and seeing what the problems are. It is important that the observer does not interfere with work flow.

▶ Activity logging and activity sampling, particularly when carried out by the system itself, are good ways of getting an idea of how end-users operate with a system.

▶ The social sciences have developed several kinds of interviews which can be used and adapted by usability engineers wishing to obtain information from users. These range from structured to unstructured interviews.

▶ Structured interviews are easier to manage than unstructured ones but unstructured interviews can often provide a wealth of information that the interviewer may not have anticipated. They are harder work for the interviewer though.

SELF TEST LIST

● accelerators	● indirect users
● answer garden	● Likert scale
● checklists	● mandatory users
● direct users	● multi-choice questions
● discretionary users	● novice
● end-user class	● remote users
● expert users	● scalar questionnaires
● Hawthorne effect	● structured interviews
● intermediate user	● support users
● intermittent users	● unstructured interviews

EXERCISES

1 Ask a friend to describe doing a task that you don't know how to do.

2 Observe the friend doing the task just described to you. Note any differences in the description and your observation.

3 Take notice of people interacting with systems around you. For example, how do they manage to work vending machines, ticket machines, open windows and so on.

4 Examine the questionnaire below and suggest ways in which it could be improved. It was designed by second-year students to gather information about spell checking activity for e-mail and snail mail messages. They made one very serious error and several minor ones that they discovered only when they started to analyse the results.

E-Mail vs. Snail Mail Questionnaire
For all questions, unless stated, please tick only **one** box, or circle **one** opinion.

1. What is your gender?　　　　Male ☐　Female ☐

2. What is your age group?　　18–25 ☐　26–35 ☐
　　　　　　　　　　　　　　36–45 ☐　46–64 ☐
　　　　　　　　　　　　　　65+ ☐

3. What is your academic background?　Arts ☐　Science ☐
　　　　　　　　　　　　　Comp. ☐　Business ☐
　　　　　　　　　　　　　Science

4. Do you use e-mail?　　Yes ☐ (*go to q.5*)
　　　　　　　　　　　　No ☐ (*go to q.13*)

5. Which e-mail software do you use?　VAX/Unix MAIL ☐
　(*Please tick all that apply*)　　VAX/Unix PINE ☐
　　　　　　　　　　　　　　Windows-based ☐
　　　　　　　　　　　　　　(*e.g., Pegasus/Outlook*)
　　　　　　　　　　　　　　Web-based ☐
　　　　　　　　　　　　　　(*e.g., Hotmail/Yahoo*)
　　　　　　　　　　　　　　Other: _____

6. Are you aware of the spell check facilities available within your e-mail software?　Yes ☐　No ☐

7. Do you spell check your e-mail messages?　Yes ☐ (*go to q.8*)
　　　　　　　　　　　　　　　　　No ☐ (*go to q.9*)

8. How often do you spell check your e-mail messages?

Every message ☐
Most messages ☐
Occasionally ☐

9. Please rate the usefulness of the e-mail system:

1 —————— 2 —————— 3 —————— 4 —————— 5
Not useful   *Very useful*

10. How do you agree with the following statement:

'I write long e-mail messages.'

1 —————— 2 —————— 3 —————— 4 —————— 5
Strongly disagree   *Strongly agree*

11. Do you think that other people spell check their e-mail messages?

Yes ☐
No ☐

12. How do you agree with the following statement:

'Most e-mail messages contain spelling errors.'

1 —————— 2 —————— 3 —————— 4 —————— 5
Strongly disagree   *Strongly agree*

13. Do you use word-processing software?

Yes ☐ *(go to q.14)*
No ☐ *(thank you for completing this)*

14. Which word-processing software do you use? *(Please tick all that apply)*

Microsoft Word ☐
Lotus Word Pro ☐
WordPerfect ☐
Other: ——————————

15. Are you aware of the spell check facilities available within your word-processing software?

Yes ☐
No ☐

16. Do you spell check your word-processed documents?

Yes ☐ *(go to q.17)*
No ☐ *(go to q.18)*

17. How often do you spell check them?

Every document ☐

Most documents ☐

Occasionally ☐

18. Please rate the usefulness of word-processing software:

1 _____ 2 _____ 3 _____ 4 _____ 5

Not useful   *Very useful*

19. How do you agree with the following statement:

'I write long word-processed documents.'

1 _____ 2 _____ 3 _____ 4 _____ 5

Strongly disagree   *Strongly agree*

20. Do you think that other people spell check their word-processed documents?

Yes ☐

No ☐

** Thank you for completing this questionnaire**

5 An exercise we have carried out at the School of Computing, South Bank University, is quite interesting and might be worth reproducing out of interest. After one of my project students had carried out a series of evaluation exercises, we noticed that subjects were changing their ratings of parts of an interface they had seen previously. We decided to find out how far we could influence their decisions by how we presented the scalar questionnaires and built a series of questionnaires to do just this. We asked subjects to rate their response to a series of prototypes, using a scalar questionnaire. We then waited a fortnight and asked them to rate the same system and noted any differences in their ratings. We then assigned values to the scales and asked them to rate the systems again. Then we went back to scalar values and asked the subjects to say what they thought the values meant and to again rate the systems. The material the student used is attached.

Figure 2.15 Interface to the prototype: opening screen

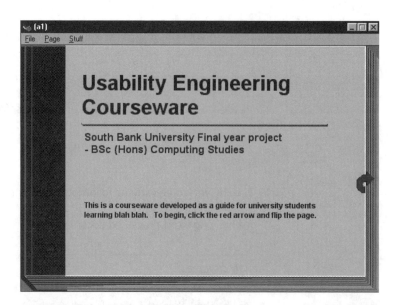

Figure 2.16 Interface to the prototype: index screen

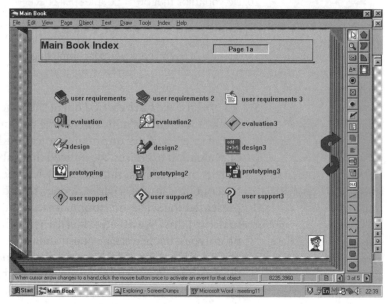

Evaluating 'b2.tbk'
QUESTIONNAIRE

Date: _____/_____/_____ S_No: _____ Name: _____

---

b2.tbk (page 1). Rate initial page on scale of 1–4 (1 is lowest value & 4 is highest value)

```
 ┌──────────┬──────────┬──────────┐
 □          □          □          □
 1          2          3          4
```

b2.tbk (page 2). Rate second page on scale of 1–4 (1 is lowest value & 4 is highest value)

```
 ┌──────────┬──────────┬──────────┐
 □          □          □          □
 1          2          3          4
```

Evaluating 'b2.tbk'
QUESTIONNAIRE

Date: _____/_____/_____ S_No: _____ Name: _____

---

b2.tbk (page 1). Rate initial page on scale of 1–4.

(1 is the worst the interface could be – i.e., 0%
2 is a third as good as the interface could be – i.e., 33%
3 is two-thirds as good as the interface could be – i.e., 66%
4 is the best the interface could be – i.e., 100%)

```
 ┌──────────┬──────────┬──────────┐
 □          □          □          □
 1          2          3          4
```

b2.tbk (page 2). Rate second page on scale of 1–4.

(1 is the worst the interface could be – i.e., 0%
2 is a third as good as the interface could be – i.e., 33%
3 is two-thirds as good as the interface could be – i.e., 66%
4 is the best the interface could be – i.e., 100%)

```
 ┌──────────┬──────────┬──────────┐
 □          □          □          □
 1          2          3          4
```

Evaluating 'b2.tbk'
QUESTIONNAIRE

Date: _____/_____/_____ S_No: _____ Name: _____

---

b2.tbk (page 1). Rate initial page on scale of 1–4.

(1 is not acceptable
2 is acceptable
3 is good
4 can't be improved)

not acceptable	acceptable	good	can't be improved
□	□	□	□
1	2	3	4

b2.tbk (page 2). Rate second page on scale of 1–4.

(1 is not acceptable
2 is acceptable
3 is good
4 can't be improved)

not acceptable	acceptable	good	can't be improved
□	□	□	□
1	2	3	4

REFERENCES

Bannon L (1995) 'From Human Factors to Human Actors: The Role of Psychology and Human Computer Interaction Studies in System Design' in Baecker, Grudin, Buxton and Greenberg (eds) *Readings in HCI: Towards the Year 2000.* Morgan Kaufmann, San Francisco.

Draper S (1985) 'The Nature of Expertise in UNIX' in Shackel B (ed.) *Human-Computer Interaction.* INTERACT '84 , pp. 465–71. North-Holland, Amsterdam.

Carroll J M and Rosson M B (1989) 'Paradox of the Active User' in Carroll J M (ed.) *Interfacing Thought.* MIT Press, Cambridge, Massachusetts.

Gould J (1995) 'How to Design Usable Systems' in Baecker, Grudin, Buxton and Greenberg (eds)*Readings in HCI: Towards the Year 2000.* Morgan Kaufmann, San Francisco.

Grudin J (1991) 'Interactive Systems: Bridging the Gaps Between Developers and Users' in Baecker, Grudin, Buxton and Greenberg (eds) *Readings in HCI: Towards the Year 2000.* Morgan Kaufmann, San Francisco.

Holtzblatt K and Jones S (1995) 'Conducting and Analyzing a Contextual Interview' in Baecker, Grudin, Buxton and Greenberg (eds) *Readings in HCI: Towards the Year 2000*. Morgan Kaufmann, San Francisco.

Killin J (1989) 'Interview Techniques'. The Knowledge Based Systems Centre, South Bank Polytechnic. Internal paper.

Kim, Scott (1995) 'Interdisciplinary Cooperation' in Baecker, Grudin, Buxton and Greenberg (eds) *Readings in HCI: Towards the Year 2000*. Morgan Kaufmann, San Francisco.

LAS (1993) *Report of the Inquiry into the London Ambulance Service*. London: LAS.

Nielsen J, Mack R, Bergendorff K and Grishchkowsky N (1986) 'Integrated Software Usage in Professional Work Environment: Evidence from Questionnaires and Interviews', conference proceedings of CHI '86, pp. 162–7.

Nielsen J (1993) *Usability Engineering*. A P Professional, Cambridge, Massachusetts.

Norman D (1992) *Turn Signals are the Facial Expressions of Automobiles*. Addison Wesley, Reading, Massachusetts.

Plous, Scott (1993) *The Psychology of Judgement and Decision Making*. McGraw Hill, New York.

Root R W and Draper S (1983) 'Questionnaires as a Software Evaluation Tool' in Janda A (ed.) *Human Factors in Computing Systems*, conference proceedings of CHI '83, pp. 78–82. ACM Press, New York.

Sayers D (1970) *Gaudy Night*. Hodder and Stoughton, London.

Shackel B (1986) 'Ergonomics in Design for Usability' in Harrison M D and Monk A F (eds) *People and Computers: Designing for Usability*. Proceedings of the Second Conference of the BCS HCI Specialist Group, September 1986.

Shneiderman B (1998) *Designing the User Interface*, 3rd edition. Addison Wesley, Reading, Massachusetts.

FURTHER READING

Gould J (1995) 'How to Design Usable Systems' in Baecker, Grudin, Buxton and Greenberg (eds)*Readings in HCI: Towards the Year 2000*. Morgan Kaufmann, San Francisco.

This is a highly readable, frequently entertaining and thorough description of how designers need to work with users.

Holtzblatt K and Jones S (1995) 'Conducting and Analyzing a Contextual Interview' in Baecker, Grudin, Buxton and Greenberg (eds) *Readings in HCI: Towards the Year 2000*. Morgan Kaufmann, San Francisco.

This is worth reading for a detailed account of how to conduct interviews. Holtzblatt and Jones even suggest schedules.

Kvale, Steinar (1996) *Interviews*. Sage Publications, Thousand Oaks, California.

This is a text written for sociologists, psychologists and the like but the best work done on interviews has been done in the social sciences so this is a good text to look at. It is very thorough and has plenty of tips and examples. It also takes the reader through the entire process from designing a study to writing it up. In order to see interviewing techniques at work I suggest Hugh Benyon's book. Although now a little dated, Benyon obtained the most amazing amount of detail from the people he interviewed and worked with.

Benyon, Hugh (1973) *Working for Ford*. Penguin Books, London.

Benyon worked for Ford and was involved in the day-to-day lives of people working there. His account is at once humorous and poignant. It is a fascinating study of a workplace and should give ideas about how factories function and the sort of problems usability engineers might face when trying to change the way that things get done.

Usability – know the task!

This chapter:

▶ looks at the user's task;

▶ examines Norman's Action Cycle Model;

▶ looks at the Gulf of Execution and the Gulf of Evaluation;

▶ introduces *task analysis*;

▶ explains, with a worked example, the interview techniques examined in the previous chapter and contrasts this method with that of ethnography.

3.1 Background

The purpose of this chapter is to provide a means of identifying the user's task and analysing the components which make up that task. In order to make software products usable we need to know what the task is that the user will be performing with them. Therefore, we need to examine what it is that users do. Two approaches are to be adopted here. The first method of examining task will be one of the traditional methods of task analysis. The second method is more controversial and newer in the context of HCI, and that is the approaches provided by ethnography.

This book will adhere to the definitions of goal and action used by Norman and the reader may assume these definitions throughout the rest of the text. If an alternative definition is implied then that will be given. As Preece *et al* (Preece, 1994) have rightly commented, different authors are being what I would describe as very promiscuous in their definition of the terms 'goal', 'task' and 'action' and they can mean any number of things to different people. Sometimes they mean different things to the same author! Unlike Lewis Carroll's Alice I am afraid that we cannot assume that writers on task say what they mean and mean what they say! Instead, like Carroll's Humpty Dumpty they seem to believe that words mean what they say they mean! A few years ago the same problem existed with the terms conceptual models and mental models but this seems to have stabilised. We can only hope that the same will be true for goal, task and action or at least writers find some alternative words if they wish to imply something else instead of sticking extra layers on as if they are making papier-mâché hats for Christmas.

I do not wish to be unduly critical; in a new field defining terms can be problematic and writers are limited in what they can use because as T. S. Eliot quite rightly says:

> I've gotta use words when I talk to you.
>
> Sweeney Agonistes

I just wish they would use words discreetly and discretely.

3.2   Norman's Action Cycle Model

In order to do something the user must start with a concept of something that needs to be done. We can see this as a goal that needs to be achieved. In order to achieve a goal the user has to do something, or manipulate something in the world. The user then will look at what has been done or manipulated and decide whether the goal has been achieved.

Norman suggests an Action Cycle Model which he describes as being 'an approximate model' (Norman, 1988). He believes that the stages are not discrete and that people may not necessarily pass through all of the stages in order. However, it is a useful model because it accounts for action and it has the added advantage of accounting for error through the Gulfs of Evaluation and Execution.

We will examine the Gulf of Execution and the Gulf of Evaluation later in the chapter.

The Action Cycle is formed of seven stages: one stage for goals, then three for execution and three for evaluation.

Norman defines these as follows:

- ▸ forming the goal;
- ▸ forming the intention;
- ▸ specifying an action;
- ▸ executing the action;
- ▸ perceiving the state of the world;
- ▸ interpreting the state of the world;
- ▸ evaluating the outcome.

Figure 3.1 shows this diagrammatically.

Figure 3.1 Norman's
Action Cycle

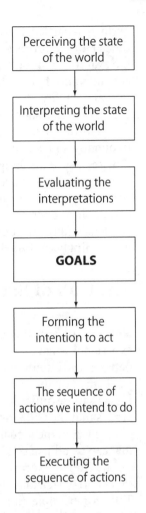

Norman says that the goal is translated into an intention to perform some action. This intention has to be translated into a series of internal commands or an action sequence which, when performed, will hopefully lead to the achievement of the goal. However, the action sequence is a mental event; it has not yet been performed. The action sequence must then be executed. Once this has occurred, the action can then be evaluated. This begins with perceiving the state of the world which is then interpreted according to what the expectations of the actor were. The state of the world is then compared with the intentions of the actor.

Using Norman's definitions we can say that the goal is the state that the human wishes to achieve. The task is the activity required in order to bring about the state the human wishes to achieve (the goal). An action is the physical interaction with the system in order to carry out the user's goal.

Norman points out that for many everyday tasks it is likely that goals and intentions are not well specified. They occur in an opportunistic fashion and are not planned. Norman defines opportunistic actions as those that take place because a situation arises where it would be advantageous to perform a particular task. There is no extensive planning beforehand but the person performs the task if and when the opportunity arises. He gives the example of not planning to go to the library but going about the day's activities and then finding oneself near the library and deciding that the relevant activity of going to the library should occur.

Norman also states something that is well worth considering now: *people do not always behave in a logical fashion*! It is an argument I have quite frequently and is a subject I will return to later in the book. It would be unwise of systems designers to expect people to behave logically and I always give the example of Mr Spock on *Star Trek*. Spock is characterised as strictly logical and seeing how he struggles with the way in which his human companions operate is amusing because it is so alien to us. Human beings are delightfully unpredictable, intuitive, inspirational and sometimes maddeningly irrational. We need to remember that when we design.

3.3   The Gulf of Execution and the Gulf of Evaluation

Norman suggests that a large number of the difficulties that people experience when they perform everyday tasks are due to a poor relationship between the intention of the actors and the physical actions that can be performed on the object they are working with, and the state of that object. He calls these difficulties the *Gulfs of Execution* and *Gulfs of Evaluation*. He argues that the Gulfs reflect the distance between how the user believes the system is and the actual physical state of the system and the components that can be adjusted (Norman, 1988).

The Gulf of Execution shows the difference between what the user wants to do and what can actually be done using the controls that are available. Take, for example, filling-up a bath tub and suppose that someone wanted to fill the bath as quickly as possible. In order to do that it would be necessary to turn both taps full-on so that the water flowed as fast as possible. However, it is unlikely that the bath tub would fill with water of the required temperature. In order to achieve a bath of the desired temperature, it will not be possible to run both taps at full capacity. Therefore, the task cannot be carried out in the way in which this particular operator wishes it could be done and a compromise has to be made: either the bath tub is filled quickly with water that is not of the desired temperature or it is filled more slowly with water of the desired temperature.

The Gulf of Evaluation shows the mismatch between the real state of the system and the intentions and expectations of the user. The Gulf of Evaluation reflects the amount of effort that the user needs to bring to the system in order to work out what the physical state of the system actually is, and to work out whether or not their intentions and desires have actually been met by the system.

An example of the Gulf of Evaluation is to be found in the cause of the crash of an A-320 aircraft into a mountain near Strasbourg. Crash investigators believed that a 3.3 degree flight-path was necessary for landing; however, a 3300-feet/minute descent mode was instead fed into the computer. The cockpit screen displayed '33' thus indicating a descent mode in hundreds of feet/minute but the pilot mistook the display for 3.3 and therefore did not realise that the plane was descending far too fast. Obviously, if the display had shown the angle of descent and the altitude as separate displays, the one as two digits (3.3) and the other as four digits (3300) the mistake would have been less likely. The pilot had to work quite hard to decipher the true state of the equipment (Petroski, 1996).

An aside...

A good example of the bridging of the Gulf of Evaluation is to be found in the controls of the Boeing 777. The pilot's commands are interpreted and sent to the engine and control structures. However, the onboard computer is programmed to move the stick controls and throttles to reflect the plane's condition as it was affected by airspeed (Petroski, 1996).

3.4   The user's task

In the first chapter of this book we looked at a definition of usability provided by the ISO. It would be as well to look at that again now:

> ...the effectiveness, efficiency and satisfaction with which specified users can achieve specified goals in particular environments...
>
> ISO DIS 9241-11

The ISO states that we are looking at 'specified goals'. The interpretation of the goal in the ISO definition can be taken as the same as that provided by Norman and we can consider the system as being able to satisfy the user's goals by providing suitable tasks that can be done in order to accomplish the goal. The question is how do designers know what the user's goal really is?

An aside...

Let's look at the apocryphal story of the gang of workmen who were sent to dig up the road. The gang dug a hole several metres deep. When the hole was complete a supervisor came along, stared into the hole for a moment or two and then instructed the workers to refill it. The gang moved along the road, dug another hole and the process continued. After several holes, the gang leader approached the supervisor and said that the workers were unhappy. They were being asked to dig holes and fill them in again and they thought this a waste of time. The supervisor explained that the plans of the town's drains had been lost so they were trying to locate them. The workers went back happily to their task.

Figure 3.2 Digging
the road up

What is the purpose of the story? It is an important one quite aside from the fact that workers should always be told the purpose of their work! What is the goal of the workers – is it to dig a hole or to find the drains? Quite clearly it is to find the drains. In this process the method of doing that is by digging holes. Suppose a computer system had to be built to replace the workers digging holes. The mechanics are irrelevant; let's pretend we can build the system. The goal of the system is to find the drains. If the computer can do that without digging holes then that is a better solution unless, of course, having holes in the road was somehow desirable.

When usability engineers look at what the user does they must be certain that they are looking at the user's goals more intently than they are looking at the user's task. If designers look at the goal they know what users want to achieve. If they look at the user's tasks they see what the users are doing. The computer solution might not need to perform the same actions as the system it is replacing. However, the goal will very likely have to be the same.

With all this in mind we can look at task analysis.

3.5 Task analysis

The process of task analysis should produce a clear understanding of what the system must do. The next stage is to convert that understanding of the task into an appropriate human computer system. However, in this book there is insufficient time to give detailed consideration to the problems of software engineering a product. I have tended to make assumptions that the usability engineer will be accomplished in software engineering but I accept that this is not always the case.

The method of task analysis examined in this book is Hierarchical Task Analysis (HTA). The reason this method is used is that the structure looks like that used for Jackson Structured Programming (JSP) and many software developers will already be familiar with JSP. HTA has the advantage that, like JSP, it can be represented diagrammatically, or in the form of outlines – similar to the document outlines found in some word processing packages.

3.5.1 The task model

A task is a human activity that will achieve a goal. It is equivalent to Norman's concept of action. If HCI had an ideal methodology then the user's task isn't really what the replacement computer system should be concerned with. It really ought to look at goals and then try to work out the processes involved in reaching those goals from the point of view of a computer system. Unfortunately, that is not entirely feasible so the user's task is analysed and quite often replicated in the computer system.

> **A spanner in the works...**
> Draper believes that this renders task analysis dubious since all it does is to reproduce bad work practices (Draper, 1993). Ergonomists have, for some time, used task analysis as a means of capturing worker activity and they invariably make notes of the bad parts of the system so that those practices are not introduced into the new system. They also make note of good practices so that those aspects can be carried over into the new system. There is no real reason that task analysis should continue to enforce bad work practices but the usability engineer has to be quite certain that those bad aspects of the system have been identified. It is also necessary to remember that just because they have been noted it does not mean to say that they can be designed out!

A task consists of a task goal and it is modelled as a hierarchy of subtasks. The decomposition simply continues as far as is necessary. That will depend on what the aim of the system is. For example, if the system is to produce a letter but it is already known that a tool exists for doing that then there is no need to decompose past the level of producing a letter. However, if the aim of the system is to produce a word processing package then the task will have to be decomposed down to keystroke level.

When the user's tasks are understood the result is appropriate design. Figure 3.3 shows a pen provided at HCI '98 which is an annual conference held in the United Kingdom for those interested in HCI matters. The providers of the pen thought carefully about what delegates to the conference might want to do – they would want to take notes perhaps, or highlight the papers they wanted to hear, or perhaps parts of papers they found interesting, contentious or annoyed them beyond measure. The pen consists of a ball-point at one end and a highlighter at the other. Just right! Sadly, some of the delegates were all too used to pushing ball-points – this one twists – and many could be seen repeatedly trying to get their pens to work. But so far as an understanding of task is concerned, I can't fault it.

Figure 3.3 The HCI '98 pen

3.5.2 Procedure for task analysis

Each task is a hierarchy of task and subtask. In other words tasks can be broken down to their simplest level of task. It is not always necessary or desirable to break tasks down to their lowest or most fundamental level. The usability engineer should simply stop at the level that is required.

A task consists of an input and output and a process which transforms the input to the output. Figure 3.4 shows this as a diagram.

Figure 3.4 A typical task

For example, supposing the task was to receive invoices and payments from a customer and then issue the receipt, the task could be represented as in Figure 3.5.

Figure 3.5 Receiving payment and issuing receipt

In order to break down each task to its constituent parts it is necessary to ask a series of questions about the task. For each task it is necessary to define the inputs to the task. These are:

- ▶ **What information is needed?** This simply looks at what information the task performer needs in order to carry out the task.
- ▶ **What are the characteristics of the information sources?** The information source will have characteristics. For example, it might, or might not, be reliable. The information might not be in the form in which it is finally needed for the task to be performed.
- ▶ **What is the availability of information?** The information might not be freely available to the task performer. It might be affected by outside influences.
- ▶ **What possible errors might occur?** It is important to know what errors might occur so that they can be designed out of the system.
- ▶ **Who or what initiates the task?** The task might depend on a process that occurs beforehand. This might be initiated by another person or by a machine or by the task performer. For example, if two people are washing up, it is not possible for the person drying the dishes to do that before the person doing the washing up has done that. What causes the task to begin is important since it will have an effect on the task itself. For example, it might not be possible to optimise the speed at which a task is done if the initiation of the task is dictated by an outside process that is unpredictable or slow.

The outputs from the task will also be considered:

- ▶ **What are the performance criteria?** The measure of how well the task has to be done is important. It is necessary to see whether a range of outputs is acceptable or if the task has to achieve a certain level.
- ▶ **What happens to the output?** The destination of the output is important because the system may need to pass the output on to another process.
- ▶ **How does the task performer get feedback about task performance?** Workers like to have feedback about how well they are doing. It is important to know about any methods for gathering information about task performance.

The task itself will have been affected by the process of transformation. It will be necessary to ask questions about those transformations:

- ▶ **What is the nature of the decision making?** It is important to know what kinds of decisions need to be made by the task performer so that these decision making processes can be supported.
- ▶ **What strategies exist for decision making?** Any strategies that are in place to help with decision making need to be examined and made available in the new system. Some of these might be automated.
- ▶ **What skills are needed?** It is important to know what skills are needed because those skills will need to exist in the workforce and

they will need to be maintained. A system will need a strategy for providing those skills through training and for updating them.

▶ **What interruptions are likely to occur and when?** Interruptions may cause error. It is important to know what might cause errors and, if possible, when they may occur.

Finally, it is necessary to look at the task composition of each particular job:

▶ **How often is the task done and when?** The frequency of the task is important. This might have implications for the design of a system. A task that is done frequently will be learned rapidly. A task that is done infrequently may not be remembered. It might be necessary to offer much more support for someone performing an infrequent task.

▶ **Does the task depend on any other task?** The task may depend upon something else. This may well affect the timing of the task and its accuracy or performance level.

▶ **What is normal/abnormal workload?** It is important to find out what the normal workload is so that the system can cope with it. However, there is likely to be an abnormal workload (either much more or much less than usual). How does the worker cope when there is more than the usual amount of work? What happens when there are low levels of work?

▶ **What control does the task performer have over workload?** Some workers are able to schedule their work. However, quite clearly some tasks cannot be put off. It may not matter if a bill is sent out today or tomorrow but it would not be feasible to put off a blood transfusion until tomorrow.

It would be useful at this stage to examine a small task in some detail in order to see how task analysis will help us to elicit the goal and to understand the problems.

3.6 A small task...

The task I want to look at is to remove nail varnish from the user's two hands (each has four fingers and one thumb) and to paint all fingers and thumbs with nail varnish. I recognise that, as yet, a computerised nail-varnish machine hasn't been invented but again – as in the example of hole-digging – I should like the reader to pretend… it's just a matter of time!

Box 3.1 shows a complete interview with someone who is describing the task of painting-on nail varnish. This is a very small task but it generates a huge amount of talk which then has to be converted into information that constructs a clear picture of what the user means to do. It should be evident that task analysis is time-consuming and does generate information that can be difficult to incorporate into a system. The information required for task analysis is shown in square brackets – '[]'.

Box 3.2 and Table 3.1 show an interview with the same task-performer using the semi-structured format introduced in the last chapter.

Figure 3.6 The nail-polishing machine

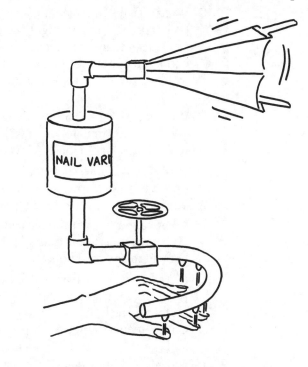

Figure 3.7 The nail-drying machine

Box 3.1 Interview with the user to elicit details about task

> **Q** What do you need to know if you're about to put on nail varnish?
> [What information do you need to perform the task?]
>
> **A** I suppose I need to know what I'm wearing and when I'm going out and what colours of nail varnish I have.
>
> **Q** How does that decision get made?
> [Where do you get that information?]
>
> **A** Well, I suppose I have to decide what I'm wearing but the availability of the varnishes will be what's in the box. The time I'm going out might be down to me or to someone else.
>
> **Q** Is that information easily found out?

[Is that information freely available?]

A Yes, it mostly is.

Q What mistakes might you make?
[What possible errors might occur?]

A I might smudge the nail varnish so it doesn't dry smoothly, or perhaps it doesn't dry properly or perhaps it's become sticky and won't go on smoothly. Sometimes in correcting a badly painted nail I spoil the others.

Q Who decides when you should do the nail varnishing?
[Who or what initiates the task?]

A Always me. But obviously, I'm affected by what I'm doing.

Q How do you know when you've painted your nails properly?
[What is the performance criteria?]

A The nails have to look the same and they need to all be painted.

Q What happens when you have finished?
[What happens to the output?]

A I go out to a party, I hope!

Q How do you know that you've done the job well?
[How does the task performer get feedback about task performance?]

A Compliments I suppose. Or perhaps I'm just pleased at how they look.

Q What sort of decisions do you have to make about painting-on nail varnish?
[What is the nature of the decision making?]

A There are really about time and whether I have an alternative.

Q How do you decide whether to paint-on nail varnish and what colour to choose?
[What strategies exist for decision making?]

A Checking what's available; what I'm going to wear will depend on where I'm going and what the weather is. That dictates the nail varnish colour. These are simple decisions based on availability of the nail varnish; if I have time to do it and whether or not the old varnish won't go, or is untidy. I suppose it depends if I'm trying to impress someone too!

Q What skills do you need to be able to do this?
[What skills are needed?]

A The ability to remove nail varnish, the ability to paint it and the ability to choose the colour in the first place.

Q What interrupts you when you are doing the task?

[What interruptions are likely to occur and when?]

A The phone could ring, I suppose, or someone could call round, or a dog could want something.

Q How often do you do this and when do you do it?

[How often is the task done and when?]

A That depends on how quickly the varnish gets chipped or if the colour I'm wearing isn't suitable. Or I'm bored with it. Perhaps three or four times a week. Mostly before I go out but sometimes I might do it when I have some time to spare.

Q Do you have to do anything first?
[Does the task depend on any other task?]

A Yes, I have to file them first. The nails that is.

Q What is the normal amount of time you can give to this?
[What is normal/abnormal workload?]

A Three times a week is normal. More than that would be abnormal! I'm awfully busy and it's tedious waiting for the stuff to dry.

Q Can you decide whether this is to be done or not?
[What control does the task performer have over workload?]

A I suppose I can decide not to do it! But I hate not having my nails painted!

Box 3.2 An interview to elicit information about task

Interviewer:	What do you do?
Subject:	I put on new nail varnish.
Interviewer:	How do you do that?
Subject:	I paint-on new nail varnish after I have removed the old.
Interviewer:	What happens to make you do that?
Subject:	Well the old nail varnish might be chipped, or it might be the wrong colour, or maybe I'm bored with it. Or perhaps I'm going out.
Interviewer:	What do you do to remove old nail varnish?
Subject:	I get some acetone on a cotton wool ball and rub it over each of the nails in turn to remove the old varnish. Sometimes I need more than one cotton ball. It depends on how thick the varnish is and the colour it was. Some nail varnishes are more difficult to remove than others.
Interviewer:	What do you need to do this?
Subject:	I need acetone and cotton wool.
Interviewer:	What are the results of doing this?
Subject:	The nail varnish is removed.
Interviewer:	What errors occur?

Subject:	They don't often. I suppose, occasionally, I don't clean the nail properly. Or someone interrupts me and the acetone evaporates from the cotton wool.
Interviewer:	What do you do if mistakes happen?
Subject:	I clean it again with fresh acetone.
Interviewer:	How do you get the new nail varnish on?
Subject:	I paint-on new nail varnish.
Interviewer:	When would you do that?
Subject:	If I wanted fresh nail varnish and the old was removed. I might have to file my nails first. I would need nail varnish to apply.
Interviewer:	What is the final result?
Subject:	The nails are covered with nail varnish.
Interviewer:	What errors occur?
Subject:	I might smudge one, or put the varnish on too thick, or accidentally touch it before it is dry. Sometimes, in cleaning one off after it has been smudged, I accidentally remove polish from nails that were perfect.
Interviewer:	What do you do if mistakes have occurred?
Subject:	I clean it again with fresh acetone. I paint it again.

Table 3.1 Elicitation of task details from subject

Questions	Answer
1 What do you do?	Put on new nail varnish.
2 How do you do it?	I remove the old nail varnish.
	Task a
	I put on new nail varnish.
	Task b
3 What do you do to remove old nail varnish?	I get some acetone on a cotton wool ball and rub it over each of the nails in turn to remove the old varnish.
Task a	
4 What are the preconditions for doing this?	I need acetone and cotton wool.
5 What are the results of doing this?	The nail varnish is removed.
6 What errors occur?	I don't clean the nail properly.
7 How do you correct them?	I clean it again with fresh acetone.
8 How do you get the new nail varnish on?	I paint-on new nail varnish.

Task b	The old nail varnish has been removed.
9 What are the preconditions for doing this?	There is fresh nail varnish to apply.
10 What are the results of doing this?	The nails are covered with one coat of nail varnish.
11 What errors occur?	a) I smudge one. b) Sometimes in cleaning one off after it has been smudged I accidentally remove polish from nails that were perfect.
12 How do you correct them?	a) I clean it again with fresh acetone. I paint it again. b) I paint them again.

Box 3.3 shows the task as a series of actions. The errors likely to occur are also shown.

Box 3.3 A simple task

Applying nail varnish...

1   A cotton wool ball is soaked in acetone and the ball is then used to wipe off the varnish from each finger and thumb. The acetone is replenished as necessary. A second or even third cotton wool ball may be necessary.

2   Once all fingers and thumbs are cleaned of the old nail varnish a new colour is applied on each fingernail in turn.

3   The task performer waits for several minutes while the varnish dries. A second coat of varnish might be necessary.

Error

The varnish is applied badly and it is necessary to remove it from one or more nails. In doing so it frequently happens that holding the cotton wool ball soaked in acetone removes varnish from fingernails that were perfect.

Using task analysis we have the goal, we have the way in which the task is done at present and we have the errors.

This can be shown diagrammatically as in Figure 3.8 or as an outline as in Figure 3.9.

In Figure 3.8 the tasks are decomposed to the desired level. A single line after a box means there are no further decompositions. An arrow indicates that there is further decomposition though this isn't shown in this example. The plan expresses the expected performance of the tasks and allows for alternatives. Repetitions and conditions can also be shown using HTA.

Figure 3.8 Task model for applying nail varnish using HTA

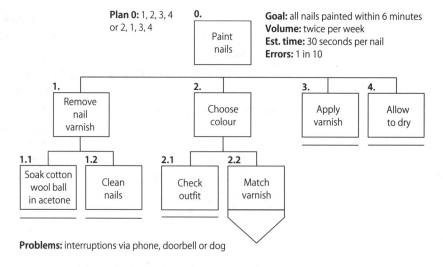

Plan 0: 1, 2, 3, 4 or 2, 1, 3, 4

Goal: all nails painted within 6 minutes
Volume: twice per week
Est. time: 30 seconds per nail
Errors: 1 in 10

Problems: interruptions via phone, doorbell or dog

Figure 3.9 Task model for applying nail varnish using outline

Painting nails

☐ Remove nail varnish
☐ Choose colour
☐ Apply nail varnish
☐ Dry

This can also be expressed in the form of structured English as in Figure 3.10.

Figure 3.10 The task as structured English

> **Applying nail varnish:**
> soak cotton wool ball in acetone
> wipe off the varnish from a nail
> repeat until all nails are clean
>
> apply varnish to nail
> repeat until all nails are painted
> allow to dry
>
> **Error:**
> if smudged then
> soak cotton wool ball in acetone
> remove smudge
> allow to dry

Unfortunately, there is no method, at present, for ensuring a better solution using task analysis. In order to provide a solution which rules out error we have to resort to what I call magic. A better word might be inspiration. There are solutions to the nail varnish problem but they depend upon the usability engineer working them out from the description of the goal and the occurrence of error.

1   Get someone else to paint your nails for you.
2   Wear a glove on the hand that is using the acetone.
3   Dip the fingers in an acetone coated sponge.
4   Don't paint your nails.

But task analysis cannot and does not give you those solutions of itself. What it does do is to allow the usability engineer to concentrate on the problem and that concentration is of itself quite likely to lead to a solution. These sudden flashes of inspiration which solve problems that seem quite knotty and difficult are often described with reference to Archimedes and his cry of 'Eureka!' Inspiration is often viewed as being sudden, almost baseless but the truth is that it is follows a period of careful and concentrated thought. For example, Newton, in describing his discovery of the law of gravity said that he had reached that conclusion by 'Thinking on it continually.' Lewis Wolpert, writing about finding solutions to difficult scientific problems, sums up the nature of illumination rather succinctly:

> In every case where scientific illumination occurs suddenly, it is preceded by a long period of intensive conscious study. The need for rest, for a new start, may give a false impression of sudden discovery…
>
> Wolpert; 1993, p62

Although task analysis does not provide a solution, by focusing thought it is more likely to lead to one – particularly if the usability engineer follows the lead of the ergonomists and concentrates on the problems of the current system.

In actual fact though, in this case, a computerised system would undoubtedly fix the error. However, the usability engineer cannot bank on the fact that errors in the manual system will simply go away once the task is computerised.

The other problem that usability engineers using task analysis will face when eliciting information from users about their task is that users do not always remember what they do. It has to be remembered that the interviewee is very likely to be an expert performer of the task being described. Experts are very bad at explaining exactly what they do because they tend to lump activities into procedures and they fail to break tasks down into simple components. For example, take the activity of logging on to a VAX/VMS from my home via modem. The steps required are shown in Table 3.2.

Table 3.2 The steps required to log on to the VAX/VMS by remote connection

1	I start up the appropriate software.
2	I select the appropriate dialling code and issue the command to dial.
3	The system dials the appropriate number and connects. The system informs me that connection has taken place via a confirm box.
4	I type in my username followed by return.
5	I type in my password followed by return.
6	I select the appropriate menu choice and type the number in followed by return.
7	Type in my username followed by return.
8	I type in my password followed by return.

I frequently ask students to list all of the actions required to log into the VAX remotely. They tell me the following:

1 I log on to system.
2 I make a menu choice for the VAX.
3 I log on to the VAX.

Figure 3.11 shows the 'real' interactions with the system as I log on to VAX/VMS.

Figure 3.11 Logging on to VAX/VMS via modem

```
AT&F E1 V1
OK
CONNECT sbu
Annex Command Line Interpreter    *    Copyright (C) 1988, 1995
Xylogics, Inc.

Checking authorization, Please wait...
Annex username: xristine
Annex password:

Permission granted
Welcome To South Bank University dialup service.

We are using an Annex 2000 terminal server and 15 Sonix modems.

The modems are connected to the terminal server at 115200 and
have hardware flow control enabled. X-on/X-off is set to pass
through.
Please check you modem is set to use hardware flow control and
X-on/X-off is set to passthrough.

The Modems support the following speeds.
V21      300bps        V22    1200bps      V22bis  2400bps
V32bis   4800bps       V32bis 7200bps      V32bis  9600bps
V32bis   14400bps      V32bis 19200bps     V34     28800bps
```

```
Welcome to South Bank University Dialup Service

        1)      Connect to Vax
        2)      Connect to unix
        3)      Connect to library
        4)      Connect to niss.ac.uk
        5)      Show Annex users
        6)      Exit

        Enter Number:  1
Local Session to vax established
Welcome to the South Bank University Alpha cluster

Username: xristine
Password:
        Welcome to the South Bank University Alpha Cluster

Last interactive login on Sunday, 17-MAY-1998 01:14:40.08
Last non-interactive login on Thursday, 5-MAR-1998 14:28:02.68
```

A spanner in the works...

One of the problems with using interviews and questionnaires with users as a way of eliciting information about their task, seems to be that away from the task they do not appear to be particularly adept at remembering what they really do. Mayes *et al* (Mayes, 1990) in their study of users' ability to recall MacWrite screens suggested that:

'…the striking point remains that overall recall performance of even our frequent users was surprisingly poor… it is apparent that away from the computer, or outside the context provided by a task, the knowledge is simply less accessible.'

Holtzblatt and Jones (1995) make a similar observation about one subject, asked for her opinions about a word processing package she used frequently:

'Outside of the context of actually doing work with the editor, she was unable to recall this problem. It was the experience of encountering the problem that brought it to memory.'

All of this implies that it is far better to interview or question the user in the environment of the task if it is necessary to find out how a task is really performed and what the problems are.

3.7   The ethnographical approach

The ethnographical approach is not as well developed in the field of HCI as the other methods examined in this chapter. It is a method of study very much in evidence in the social sciences, and particularly in anthropology, where it is well developed as a research method. In HCI, there is growing interest in ethnography and the way in which it might allow a better understanding of the social context of task. As we have seen in the last chapter this is probably a direct result of the rise in importance of CSCW (Computer Supported Cooperative Work) systems.

Ethnographical interviews can be seen as a means of developing the sort of knowledge about users, their working practices and the environment in which they are operating that is needed to develop relevant systems. Grudin suggests that the aim of design now is to 'incorporate organisational and social knowledge' (Grudin, 1990).

Ethnography is directed at studying the social character and activity of groups in their natural setting. Because it concentrates on the sociological aspects it views the tasks as part of a social organisation between the participants in their natural environment. The ethnographer attempts to discover how cooperation and collaboration take place within the context of the activities. This is done by working along side the group. Monk *et al* suggest that the ethnographer needs to act as

> ...an uninformed outsider whose job it is to understand as much as possible about the "natives" from their own point of view.
>
> Monk *et al*, 1993

The ethnographer needs to be immersed in the culture and practices of the people being studied. Ethnography may use a variety of techniques with which to gather information. It might use video, interviews, questionnaire or observation. The difference is not so much in the tools but the way in which the material is gathered and the attitude to the users. Monk *et al* go so far as to say that what is achieved by this method is:

> ...the holistic perspective, in which everything – belief systems, rituals, institutions, artefacts, texts etc – is grist for the analytical mill...
>
> Monk *et al*, 1993

A spanner in the works...

An ethnographical approach was used in a study by Hughes *et al*. Their study was of air traffic control and it took place over a year (Hughes *et al*, 1993). What emerges from their study is an interesting difference in the perspective of designers and the sociologists who were conducting the study. Hughes *et al* comment that what the designers expected from the study was a list of core activities that air traffic controllers undertook but ethnography is not able to deliver such a list in the form the designers wanted:

'After more than a year of working together, we now realise that the expectations of the systems designers were unrealistic. While the system designers continue to maintain that there are 'core' air traffic control activities, there is a greater realisation that ethnography does not present its analyses in ways to furnish such a description. The sociologists, for their part, did not see the need for such a distinction, or more accurately, felt that any such description of 'core' activities could only be a gloss for the complex work of controlling.'

Hughes *et al*, 1993

Hughes *et al* concluded that:

'While we are confident that the ethnographic studies have been valuable in the context of the system design, we must admit this is as much a matter of faith as it is backed up by evidence… The nature of ethnography and (we stress that this is very much from the point of view of system design) its 'unstructured' observations is such that it has been difficult to organise and direct the ethnographic record so that we can co-relate observations and systems requirements.'

One of the biggest problems Hughes *et al* faced with their ethnographical approach was that their paperwork was insufficient. It is all too easy to watch people doing things and to forget that there must be a record of what actually happened. Dix *et al* remark that ethnographers:

…report and do not like to speculate. So, it is not yet clear how well their approach can contribute to the design of new systems.

Dix *et al*; 1998, p543

To a certain extent, Dix *et al* are echoing misgivings about ethnography that has been voiced by sociologists concerned about the lack of methodology in the approach (Maynard, 1989).

The ethnographical approach may be insufficiently tried and tested in HCI but there is no doubt that it could help to imbue systems with a sense of the culture and social makeup that were inherent in the system that is being replaced. Just as systems failed in the early days because unsuitable keyboards and computers were placed on unsuitable desks and secretaries found them impossible to use, so CSCW systems will fail if they neglect to take into account the nature of social intercourse.

However, Scott Kim suggests that:

Different disciplines have different priorities, different thinking styles, different values. When people from different disciplines get together, their values collide. What one person finds valuable others do not even notice. And they do not notice that they do not notice.

Kim, 1995

This may account for the differing perspectives that Hughes *et al* found they had with the sociologists they worked with in their ethnographical study.

I questioned John Hughes about the 'distance' between the ethnographers and the software engineers on his study (Hughes *et al*, 1993) and he summed this up rather nicely for me:

> The 'distance' we refer to is really a difference in 'mentality' rather than anything more serious. Part of it is the difference in focus. Engineers need to focus on details that can be made to integrate together and, perhaps not unnaturally, are attracted to methods of describing human social behaviour which 'look like' engineering. The rationale of ethnography, of course, rejects this idea as at least premature. Once the software engineers get the point, then the 'distance' is no more [than] simply a division of labour.
>
> Hughes, 1998

A further problem is, of course, the time factor. This is a real problem and nicely summed up by another spanner, this time courtesy of Ben Shneiderman.

> ***A spanner in the works...***
> Ben Shneiderman says that:
> 'Whereas traditional ethnographers immerse themselves in cultures for weeks or months, user-interface designers need to limit this process to a period of days or even hours, and still to obtain the relevant data needed to influence a redesign...'
>
> Shneiderman, 1998

The ethnographical approach is therefore not without its problems but its solutions may make the development of acceptable and therefore usable systems much more likely. Like task analysis, there are problems and perhaps what is needed is a closer integration of the two approaches.

Finally, Henry Petroski suggests that 'engineers do their best job when they interact with those who will be the customers of their product...' (Petroski, 1996). Perhaps this is the best spur we can have to find a place for ethnography.

3.8   Adopting the right attitude for design...

The aim of a design is to create something that fits. But creating something that fits and fits comfortably and naturally is not easy. Socio-technical design is a response to the desire to create systems that are useful and apt. The aim of socio-technical design is to fit the process of design into the framework of the needs of the particular organisation. Socio-technical design takes the idea of designing for the user and the task a stage further than we have seen so far and endeavours to design within the structure of the organisation and the way in which it operates. This finished product is thus more closely associated with, and more suited to, the needs of the organisation because it has been designed and built with that in mind. The social aspects of an organisation are very important and account for the way in which an organisation operates and views itself. It would be extraordinary if everyone was expected to buy exactly the same colour, size and design of clothes but all too often we try to give very different organisations the same solution and then wonder why they fail to work effectively.

Socio-technical design takes into account the work carried out by the organisation. It considers the social composition and structure and the way in which the organisation carries out its activities. In order to do that it is necessary to pay close attention to the user and the needs of the user. Thus, socio-technical design encourages the user to have a significant part in the development of the system.

3.8.1 The principles of socio-technical design

The principles of socio-technical design are concerned with providing a framework for the production of applications that are truly in step with the organisation and its users (Mumford and Sutton, 1991). The Tavistock Institute was formed in 1946 by a group of psychologists concerned with the mental health and development of the individual. The following were identified:

Compatibility
The design process must be compatible with its objectives. The objectives need to be compatible with the work of the organisation. Inevitably, end-users will need to be involved in this process since they will be clear what those objectives are.

Minimum critical specifications
The specification drawn up for the system will consist of the minimal possible solution. Functionality that is not required simply clutters a system and makes it more difficult to use, more complicated for the user and slower in operation. If future functionality is seen as necessary then this should be hidden until it is required.

Socio-technical criterion
A problem should be controlled as closely as possible to the site of its origin. Problems that are passed on to be solved by someone else are problems that will increase in size – like a snowball going downhill. Where the problem occurs is also where the best understanding of the problem is likely to exist. Although others might be consulted in the process of solving the problem, it is seen as belonging to the place where it originated. This gives the individuals concerned with it, feelings of responsibility and control.

Multifunction

Employees should not be expected to perform fractions of tasks because this reduces job satisfaction and does not allow them to see their task through to the end. The work of Frederick Winslow Taylor led to the development of what was later known as *Taylorism*. This is the idea that tasks should be broken down into discrete activities which are then performed by individuals – one worker to each complete, discrete, activity. For example, one of my students explained that he spent the summer making sandwiches and that his task was to put the ham onto the already buttered bread! Unlike Taylorism, socio-technical design seeks to place workers in control of processes. It teaches that partial tasks are unfulfilling for the individual worker doing them. People take pride and pleasure in work that makes sense to them and is seen as a whole. An organisation whose workers are content is much more likely to be successful so the current trend is to add coherence and meaning to work in order to make it more enjoyable. Socio-technical design, therefore, is concerned with the design of suitable tasks that will give the worker the sense of seeing the task through to the end.

Boundary location

The work boundaries separating one group from another must be chosen with care. It is important that tasks are seen as being entire and it is equally important that groups see themselves as entire groups that are quite distinct from any other group.

Information flow

Information should go to the place where it is used. It should not involve others as this can overcomplicate a process and lead to error. This is the same reasoning we met earlier when we looked at problems.

Support congruence

Systems should reinforce the behaviour of the organisation. The nature of the organisation should dictate the structure of the system and not the other way round.

Design and human values

Human Computer System design should concentrate on providing a high quality of working life. The quality of working life is important since if an individual feels happy and content the quality of work produced will be higher. Happy employees are less likely to take time off work, and are less error-prone.

The principle of incompletion

Design is iterative and continuous. The process of design consists of design, evaluate and then re-design. Usability metrics will provide a means to bring this process to a close. We will examine usability metrics in Chapter 5.

Socio-technical design is a framework in which user centred-design can take place. It is almost like a mind-set but it has a series of guidelines. The concepts go beyond what is presented here but this should give sufficient flavour to the ideas put forward by the exponents.

CHAPTER SUMMARY

▶ The Action Cycle is formed of seven stages: one stage for goals, then three for execution and three for evaluation.

▶ Many everyday tasks are opportunistic, that is they are not planned but occur if the person finds that it is appropriate and convenient to carry out a particular task at that time.

▶ People do not always behave in a logical fashion! System designers need to remember that and design for it.

▶ Norman suggests that a large number of the difficulties that people experience when they perform everyday tasks are due to a poor relationship between the intention of the actor and the physical actions that can be performed on the object they are working with, and the state of that object.

▶ The Gulf of Execution shows the difference between what the user wants to do and what can actually be done using the controls that are available.

▶ The Gulf of Evaluation shows the mismatch between the real state of the system and the intentions and expectations of the user.

▶ Usability engineers must look at the user's goals more intently than they look at the user's task since the computer solution might not need to perform the same actions as the one it is replacing.

▶ The process of task analysis should produce a clear understanding of what it is that the system must do.

▶ HTA is a Hierarchical Task Analysis which has the advantage that it can be represented diagrammatically or in the form of outlines.

▶ A task consists of an input and output and a process that transforms the input to the output.

▶ There is no method, at present, for ensuring a better solution using task analysis; that requires inspiration!

▶ Users do not always remember what they do when they are away from the task. It is important to interview them in context.

▶ The ethnographical approach is not as well developed in the field of HCI but there is growing interest in it because of the rise of CSCW.

▶ Ethnographical interviews can be seen as a means of developing the sort of knowledge about users, their working practices and the environment in which they are operating.

▶ Socio-technical design provides a user centred-framework for usability engineering.

SELF TEST LIST

- action
- Action Cycle
- ethnography
- goal
- Gulf of Evaluation
- Gulf of Execution
- Hierarchical Task Analysis
- Jackson Structured Programming
- socio-technical design
- task
- Taylorism
- transformation

EXERCISES

1   Using the interview you carried out in Chapter 2, try to convert your findings about the task into an HTA diagram.

2   Why would an ethnographical approach be suitable for the development of systems designed for the general public?

3   Read Draper's paper 'The Notion of task in HCI' (details of how to obtain this paper can be found below). Consider a package that you know well. Think of a task you might carry out and produce a task list. Examine the task list for activities that do not actually lead to the goal – for example, Draper gives the example of 'saving' in case of accidents. Now for the same task produce an ideal process for getting the job done. What differences are there between the two lists?

4   Carefully examine the interface below. An extract from the user manual is also given.

a) This system is a knowledge in the head system. Explain what that means. Convert it into a knowledge in the world system and explain what that means.

b) How effective would Norman's model be for predicting problems with this system? Give reasons for your answer.

User manual

The temperature of the shower can be set from Very Hot to Cold. The water pressure can be set from 1 to 5. At 5 it is at its highest and at 1 at its lowest. The heat of the water affects the water pressure. Choose your setting from A to E. Allow 5 minutes for the temperature of the shower to take effect.

Water temperature	Water pressure	Shower setting
Very Hot	Very Low	A
Hot	Low	B
Warm	Average	C
Cool	High	D
Cold	Very High	E

Actual interface

REFERENCES

Dix A *et al* (1998) *Human Computer Interaction*. Prentice Hall, Hemel Hempstead.

Draper S W (1993) 'The notion of Task in HCI' in Ashland S, Henderson A, Holland E and White T (eds) *Adjunct Proceedings of INTERCHI '93*.

Grudin J (1990) 'The computer reaches out: the historical continuities in interface design' in Chew and Whiteside (eds) *Empowering People*, conference proceedings of CHI '90, pp. 261–8. ACM, New York.

Holtzblatt K and Jones S (1995) 'Conducting and Analyzing a Contextual Interview' in Baecker, Grudin, Buxton and Greenberg (eds) *Readings in HCI: Towards the Year 2000*. Morgan Kaufmann, San Francisco.

Hughes J A, Sommerville I, Bentley R and Randall D (1993) 'Designing with ethnography: making work visible.' *Interacting with Computers*, vol. 5, no. 2, pp. 239–53.

Hughes J (1998) Personal communication to the author.

Kim, Scott (1995) 'Interdisciplinary Cooperation' in Baecker, Grudin, Buxton and Greenberg (eds) *Readings in HCI: Towards the Year 2000*. Morgan Kaufmann, San Francisco.

Mayes *et al* (1990) 'Information Flow in a User Interface: The Effect of Experience and Context on the Recall of MacWrite Screens' in Preece J and Keller L (eds) *Human Computer Interaction*. Prentice Hall, Hemel Hempstead.

Maynard, Mary (1989) *Sociological Theory*. Longman, London.

Monk A, Wright P, Haber J and Davenport L (1993) *Improving your Human Computer Interface*. Prentice Hall, Hemel Hempstead.

Monk A *et al* (1993) 'Mixing Oil and Water' in Ashland S, Henderson A, Holland E and White T (eds) INTERCHI '93 Adjunct Proceedings.

Mumford E and Sutton D (1991) 'Designing Organisational Harmony' in *The Computer Bulletin*. August 1991, pp. 12–14.

Norman D (1988) *The Psychology of Everyday Things*. Basic Books, New York.

Petroski H (1996) *Invention by Design*. Harvard University Press, Cambridge, Massachusetts.

Preece J *et al* (1994) *Human-Computer Interaction*. Addison Wesley, Wokingham, England.

Shneiderman B (1998) *Designing the User Interface*, 3rd edition. Addison Wesley, Reading, Massachusetts.

Wolpert, Lewis (1993) *The Unnatural Nature of Science*. Faber and Faber, London.

FURTHER READING

Draper S W (1993) 'The Notion of task in HCI' in Ashland S, Henderson A, Holland E and White T (eds) INTERCHI '93 Adjunct Proceedings.

This is a short paper – two sides – and is well worth reading. The ideas are challenging not just on task but also on the role of psychological investigation. If I say any more, I'll be more long-winded than the paper. Read it! It's fun too… The paper can be obtained from Steve Draper's Web site:

```
http://www.psy.gla.ac.uk/~steve/task.html
```

much more easily than trying to track down the Adjunct Proceedings which, incidentally, cost an arm and a leg. I am still recovering from the shock – financial and emotional – of buying a copy. Steve's site is a bit of a distraction though – a sort of electronic Aladdin's Cave – so if you are less than purposeful put aside some time in which to be pleasantly distracted.

Norman D (1988) *The Psychology of Everyday Things*. Basic Books, New York.

Don Norman's book needs to be read for his insights and wisdom and the fact that he is such marvellous fun. This book has been renamed *The Design of Everyday Things*. It is well worth reading, and rereading…

Petroski H (1996) *Invention by Design*. Harvard University Press, Cambridge, Massachusetts.

I found this useful for understanding how engineers and designers think. I would suggest dipping into it rather than reading the whole thing.

Redmond-Pyle D and Moore A (1995) *Graphical User Interface Design and Evaluation*. Prentice Hall, Hemel Hempstead.

This has excellent chapters on HTA and loads of examples. It is truly an impressive manual.

Making usable products

CHAPTER OVERVIEW

This chapter:

▶ looks at the problems of gathering user requirements and producing a user requirements specification;

▶ suggests suitable questions that will need to be addressed by the feasibility study;

▶ looks at methods of supporting design so that these can be made available to the end-users for evaluation and thus involve them in the design process.

4.1 The importance of design

Getting the design right is all about understanding user requirements and the environment in which the product operates. Sometimes that might mean that designers have to try to understand a process or tool that they have little or no experience of. I want to start off this chapter by looking at an impressive but simple piece of design which I came across whilst on a weekend break in the Lake District.[1] Those of you who have walked in the Lake District will know that it is full of gates, sties and rain – hence the lakes! If you are taking a dog for a walk then gates have to be opened in order to get the dog on the right side or the dog needs to be lifted over the gate. Gates in the countryside are frequently difficult to open and close so it is preferable to avoid this. Lifting a dog over a gate can be problematic though. If the dog is small it can be accomplished readily enough although they tend to wriggle. A large dog is difficult to lift and doesn't always assist with the process; the wriggling is more difficult to handle. Figure 4.1a shows me lifting Clarrie over a gate – easy! But even after serious weight training lifting a neighbour's dog – Emily – over the gate is a problem. See Figure 4.1b.

Sties are a real problem therefore. Little dogs may be able to squeeze under them (especially if you don't want them to…) but large dogs will

---

1. For readers outside the UK, the Lake District is a mountainous area of northern England famous for its lakes and the poet William Wordsworth.

have to be lifted or if they are agile they may jump. Figure 4.2 shows an ideal solution to the problem of getting a dog over the right side of an obstacle. Figure 4.2 shows a panel with a hand-hole cut into the top so that it can be raised in order to allow the dog to pass through to the other side. Here is a solution that understands the needs of the dog and the dog walker. It is an example of appropriate design. (Incidentally, no dogs were harmed during this photo-shoot; the same cannot be said to be true of the author!)

Figure 4.1a The author lifting Clarrie over a gate

Figure 4.1b Attempting to lift Emily over a gate

Figure 4.2 Dog passing place in a field in the Lake District

Designers have the ability to understand problems. They talk to people about the tasks they are carrying out and ask them what the problems are. They suggest solutions and listen to user's comments. This process could be seen in action in a wonderful series shown on Channel 4[2] during the summer of 1998. The series was called *Designs on your…* and consisted of three programmes about redesigning three products – the bra, the loo and the electric car. The two designers – Richard Seymour and Dick Powell – solved their design problems by going to the people who needed the products whether it was bras, loos or cars. Richard and Dick had no idea what women wanted their bras to do until it was explained to them. They had no idea what it felt like to wear one but they had the ability to listen and to interpret those desires and complaints into a product. When the first one failed, they listened again and designed again. Their commitment was total and they were disappointed when their first attempt did not translate into what the user really wanted. Sometimes, Richard and Dick had no idea how their designs would be realised. In the case of *Designs on your Bra* they researched the available materials and produced the appropriate material for the finished product. But in the case of *Designs on your Car* they admitted that they had left the engineering solutions to their designs for other engineers to solve – although they insisted that given time they could

2.   For non-UK readers, Channel 4 is a UK television channel.

realise those designs themselves. They knew what needed to be done and what is more to the point they knew it could be done and even how to do it.

Ben Shneiderman describes design as:

> [blending] a thorough knowledge of technical feasibility with a mystical esthetic sense of what attracts users.
>
> Shneiderman; 1998, p99

In other words, in order to design you have to know what can be done along with the ability to make it look nice too. Getting a design right isn't about being complicated either. It is about understanding exactly what the user wants to do and catering for just those needs. Figure 4.3 shows the one and only ashtray my household contains. Even a non-smoker like me can appreciate the thought that went into that particular design. It contains grooves along each of the edges: two thin ones for cigarettes and two wide ones for those fat cigars. All you need is one ashtray designed with a bit of thought.

Figure 4.3 An ashtray

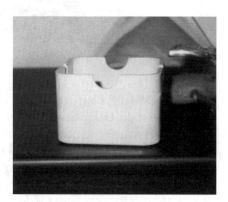

Since software development has emerged from the early days when programmers did everything, software design has consisted of a process that involved different types of expertise and has tended to stay that way. The people who gather information about the user and turn that information into requirements would not be those who did the programming. These user requirements would be translated into system functionality and software performance by the software engineers. There is, all too often, a mismatch between the two, simply because it is going through layers of interpretation. It is a bit like the children's game of Chinese Whispers which I can remember playing as a child – although my students, in an attempt to make me feel very ancient, deny all knowledge of it. Those of you who have played it will need no description but in case it did not form part of your childhood repertoire of games, or you have forgotten how it was played, then I will describe the game. One person at the end of a line whispers something to the next person and so on until the last person yells out what they heard. It is usually obscene and quite unlike what was said originally. Because the person gathering information from the user wasn't involved in developing the system, what was said by the user had a tendency to be distorted in the same way that what the first person in Chinese Whispers says is inevitably distorted by being passed on.

An aside...

When I was reading over sections of this chapter with my father, he reminded me of the apocryphal story of the message sent down the line of soldiers. The message was: 'Send reinforcements we're going to advance.' But it was received as 'Send three and four pence we're going to a dance.' It's a nice example of exactly what I mean by the Chinese Whispers effect.

Incidentally, three and four pence is old currency and means three shillings and four pence – about 17 pence today.

Figure 4.4 shows an interpretation of Chinese Whispers in picture form. Neil Vinall, an artist friend of mine, used the idea in a series of pictures and has kindly reproduced the effect here.

Figure 4.4 Chinese Whispers represented as pictures

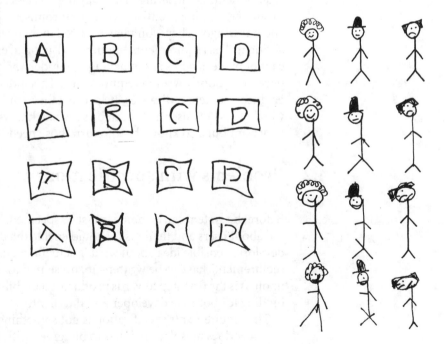

This tendency to separate out the tasks has made requirements gathering and specification very difficult. This is perhaps best expressed by Roger Pressman wielding a fairly hefty spanner in the direction of requirements specification.

A spanner in the works...

Pressman states that requirements specification appears to be simple on the surface but in actual fact is fraught with difficulties. He sums these up thus:

'The dilemma that confronts a software engineer may be best understood by repeating the statement of an anonymous (infamous?) customer: "I know you believe you understood what you think I said, but I am not sure you realise that what you heard is not what I meant."'

Pressman, 1987

Or, to put this more succinctly, one of my first-year students, writing an answer under the tensions of an examination, suggested that:

'The user provides the gap between the systems analyst and the programmer.'

Quite! I couldn't put it better myself.

We can agree that there is a gap between the end-user and the programmer. The problem really is how do we bridge it? Suppose that the person engineering the software was also responsible for carrying out the requirements engineering? That way there is less chance of a misunderstanding occurring. Any compromises will be made in the open – and knowingly. They won't have arrived there by misinterpretation or accident. The requirements engineer will go on to engineer the product and cannot make excuses about having not understood what was needed because of poorly written requirements. This individual is a usability engineer; someone who sees the process through from beginning to end, who knows how user needs can be satisfied, knows how to find out what they want but also knows how to turn those needs into software systems.

4.2   Problems with specification

Before the system can be built it must be specified. The processes of finding out about users and their tasks should enable the usability engineer to develop a sensible idea about what is actually required by the user. The requirements have to be written-up, presented to the users and agreed upon. It is the first step towards producing a usability contract which will be binding for both the developer and the client.

The requirements specification is not something that the usability engineer does in isolation; it has to be agreed with the customer so it must be carried out with the end-users and in terms that the customer and the end-users can understand. It is an iterative process like much of User Centred Design and Development and it requires user involvement. It is important that the requirements as understood by the customer are the same as those interpreted by the software development team.

> **A spanner in the works...**
> Dix *et al* suggest that:
>
> 'Though the requirements are from the customer's perspective, if they are to be met by the software product they must be formulated in a language suitable for implementation.'
>
> Dix *et al*, 1998

Obviously, when there is translation from one representation to another there is room for ambiguity and differences to creep in (remember the Chinese Whispers). This may account for some of the problems that software development teams have experienced when trying to meet the requirements of the user. Again, having one individual – the usability engineer – who talks to the customer and is part of the development team, will help to avoid these pitfalls.

In order that there should be no misunderstanding it would be best if the requirements were understood to mean the same by both the customer and the development team. That is why it is so important that the requirements are drawn up by the usability engineer and the customer. The usability engineer understands the language of the customer because the process of requirements gathering will have involved close encounters with the customer's organisation and language. The usability engineer is by definition a software engineer and part of the development team so can understand what is required there too. No promises will be made that cannot be kept because the usability engineer understands, and is part of, the software engineering processes. No system will be built that is not what the customer wants because the usability engineer understands user requirements and likely levels of performance. The usability engineer blends the skills of software engineering and Human Computer Interaction.

> **A spanner in the works...**
> BIUSEM commenting on the efficacy of the Method for Usability Engineering (MUSE) explain that:
>
> 'The MUSE method expects the requirements to be defined and furthermore to be defined early on in the course of a project. In practice this is rarely the case; indeed human factors methods such as task analysis may also be seen as requirements elicitation methods...'
>
> BIUSEM; 1995, p15

Requirements capture is not easy. As we have seen in the previous chapter, task analysis is not perfect as a means of capturing what it is that the user actually needs to do in order to accomplish the goal. The problem is that if the usability engineer simply replicates what the system does already it may not be sufficient. It could be that the reason that the system is being changed is that it was inadequate in the first place.

4.3   What does the customer want?

Before the requirements document can be drawn up it is necessary to elicit the requirements for the system. This is no easy task. Often, the customer does not know what is really required of the new system or they may have expressed their requirements in the vaguest of terms. Customers will also tend to express their requirements in their own language and this has to be interpreted into functionality for the system. The customer may well have particular expertise and the requirements will mean something to them but the usability engineer may not have much experience in that field and therefore may not understand what the customer means. It could be that the requirements of the new system are being gathered from various disparate sources and these will have to be brought together to make sense in the requirements documentation. Furthermore, business is not static and it could be that the goal post moves during the elicitation process.

It is therefore important to ensure that the proper requirements of the user are actually gathered since it is not always clear what the customer actually wants.

A commercial software developer summed-up this problem for me when I asked a group of software developers how they went about the task of eliciting requirements:

> Ask them and nag them but then don't believe a word. Expect failure and disappointment, don't expect too much till you have built them something that they can look at. They usually get the idea then.

4.4   The initial stages

In order to understand what is required it is first necessary to understand the environment in which the system will be operating. Before detailed requirements can be drawn up the usability engineer should have spent some time understanding the business. The ethnographical approach may well be appropriate at this stage. It could be that the complaints made about the approach by Hughes *et al* (Hughes *et al*, 1993) would not be so critical at this point. During this very early stage, the usability engineer is trying to get a feel for the environment in order to ensure that the system fits in with the ideals of socio-technical design (which we examined at the end of the last chapter). At this 'look and feel' stage, hard documentation is not required. The usability engineer is learning about the organisation and gaining the trust and cooperation of the employees. It could well be that too great a reliance on paper and tape recorders would get in the way; although eventually, of course, the usability engineer will have to do this work. This stage need not be very long and could take the form of an introduction to the organisation and an initial examination of the processes. As Shneiderman quite rightly says this needs to be accomplished in a 'period of days or even hours' (Shneiderman; 1998, p108). Norman suggests that the traditional timescale for an ethnographical study is inappropriate. What is needed, he suggests, is 'rapid ethnography'. He describes this as an observational technique that allows data to be gathered. He goes on to say that perhaps contextual inquiry might provide the necessary structure for rapid ethnography (Norman, 1998).

Once this introductory phase is over it will be possible to approach requirements gathering with a better understanding of the socio-technical makeup of the organisation and therefore the type of environment that the new system will be fitting into.

Usually, the process of developing a system will start off with a project proposal. This will be a brief and general description of what is wanted from the proposed system. It might be quite vague and incomplete. From this brief document it should be possible to start the gathering of information that will go towards the requirements document. Typically, this will consist of:

- ▶ **The needs of the organisation** This might be in terms of feasibility (from the commercial aspect). For example, the system may have to sell a given number of units within a time-frame or perhaps it is hoped to maintain current staffing levels at the same time as increasing staff productivity.
- ▶ **The system requirements** This will specify how the system is expected to achieve its objectives in terms of its required functionality and the nature of its internal software structures. For example, there will be a statement of how data will be structured. The technical constraints of the system should also be addressed.
- ▶ **User requirements and functionality** This will involve a specification of user requirements and system functionality from a user-centred perspective. There should be an indication of all supporting functions for the users including help systems, hardware, and user interfaces.

4.5 The feasibility study

Before requirements gathering can be completed it is important to carry out a proper feasibility study. Some of the answers to the questions about feasibility will be helpful in understanding the environment in which the system will operate. It will also give the usability engineer the chance to get to know the business organisation and its social make-up. Feasibility studies concentrate on whether or not the system is needed, what it will do, what it won't do and whether or not it can be developed within the constraints of the time and budget available and whether there is the technology to support the system.

The feasibility study will provide answers to the following questions:

1 **Why is the system needed?** If the present system is adequate and there is no need for expansion then it is best to leave things alone. Sometimes customers perceive a need for the wrong system. It is important to attempt to look at this question without bias. It is very easy to go in with the attitude that there is a need to prove how necessary a system is. The old adage: 'If it's not broken don't fix it' is a good one to apply here.

2 **What would happen to the organisation if the system was not developed?** If the answer to this question is 'nothing' then the likelihood is that the system is not required. However, we need to be careful here – the history of technology is full of cases where people have failed to predict how useful a new invention will be![3]

3 **How will the system help to improve the organisation?** Again, the answer to this question will help to prove the need for the system. There must be benefits to the organisation.

4 **Are there critical processes that need to be supported by the system? If so, what are they?** This will give the scope of the projected system and will identify possible trouble spots at an early stage.

5 **Are there critical processes which need *not* be supported by the system? If so, which are they?** Again, this is useful for identifying scope and for preventing the system from taking on areas that can be safely left out.

6 **What, if any, are the knock-on effects of the new system?** It is important to ensure that any side effects from the new system are identified. If there are other systems in place that will be affected by the new system that needs to be identified at an early stage.

7 **What are the technological implications for the system?** All too often customers have insufficient understanding of technical implications, although, of course, there is no reason why they *should* have such an understanding. It is the job of the usability engineer to ensure that the technology is available and used appropriately. Customers quite often hold two contradictory positions. Some customers can have unreasonable expectations of computer systems and the technology to facilitate their aims may not, as yet, exist – they may want something akin to *Star Trek's* computer… Other customers underestimate what can be done or want to use a technology in ways it wasn't designed for. I know of at least two organisations where spreadsheets were used for formatting and calculations were done by hand because the users did not understand that the spreadsheet could do those calculations. One

---

3. Don Norman discusses this regarding computers in *The Invisible Computer*.

group of users used a spreadsheet for word processing so the output was rather odd!

8 **Can the system be produced within the given budget?** It is important to budget at an appropriate level. Anything less than complete honesty about such matters is unprofessional and unacceptable.

9 **Is there a timescale for the development of the system? If so, is it possible to develop the system within that time-frame?** Again, it is important to be realistic and honest.

The answers to these questions will produce a feasibility report which is then made available to the customer.

An aside...

Student projects all too often overlook feasibility studies because the student wants to get down to the task in hand, I suppose. I know my project students quite often get irritable with me because I insist we carry out feasibility studies first. One student told me that he would simply ensure that the product was produced and that resources were therefore not finite. I tactfully pointed out that time was finite and there wasn't much he could do about that one! It is important that all proposals – even for small systems – look at how feasible it is to produce them. Where small systems are concerned this isn't time-consuming but it can save a lot of embarrassment and problems later.

4.6   Requirements

Software requirements analysis is about focusing on what the system should do rather than how the software will work. Pressman suggests that requirements analysis:

> ...enables the system engineer to specify software function and performance, indicate software's interface with other system elements, and establish design constraints that software must meet... [it] provides the developer and the customer with the means to assess quality once software is built.
>
> Pressman; 1987, p137

The first task in requirements specification is to recognise the goal of the system and the problems that exist within the system at present. The requirements will address all of the three areas considered above – namely business requirements, technical requirements and user requirements.

In order to understand the nature of the business requirements and the needs of the organisation it is necessary to gather information about how the system is to be used and who will use it. The first stage of requirements gathering will be to profile user types (as has been discussed in Chapter 2).

The technical requirements will be specified by what the system has to do, its performance levels and how it has to fit in with what is already present in the organisation.

The user requirements will be dictated by the profiles of the users that emerge from studying the organisation, what the nature of their tasks are and what the levels of performance for the system need to be. These levels of performance will help to produce the usability specification.

In order to consider how this would operate in reality we need to look at a real manual task that needs to be turned into an automated system. Box 4.1 shows a description of a proposed new system.

Box 4.1 The proposed system

> *Proposal for the development of the Breakfast Buddy Toaster*
> The proposed system is for an automated toaster which can store the individual toast-making requirements for four people. The proposed system must dispense with the need for the user to be present during toasting and must deliver hot toast.

To start with, we need to examine the task as it is carried out at present, identify the user types and look at the structure of the environment the system is operating in. Box 4.2 shows a description of the current manual task.

Box 4.2 The current manual task

> *Making toast for four people*
>
> 1 The bread has to be sliced.
> 2 The bread has to be placed under the lighted grill.
> 3 Once the first side has been toasted the bread has to be turned and the other side toasted.
> 4 When the toasting is complete the toast is removed.
> 5 The grill is switched off.
> 6 The toast is ready to eat.
>
> *Possible error*
>
> 1 The toast may not be toasted to the individual requirements of the diners. Not everyone likes toast the same but to produce different levels of toasting would take more effort.
> 2 The task is boring. It is easy to forget about, or to become distracted, so that the toast is burned.
> 3 The toast can grow cold before it is needed.

From an examination of all of the above it is now possible to bring together the outline of our requirements.

From this proposal we can develop the first stages of our requirements document. This is shown as Box 4.3.

Box 4.3 The first stages of requirements gathering

> ### Organisational, technical and user requirements
>
> ▶ *Organisational and business requirements* The Breakfast Buddy is a proposed system to be used by up to four people. It will be necessary for the product to sell at least 20 000 units within a three-year period.
>
> ▶ *System technical requirements* The toaster will contain a smart chip that will enable the storage of up to four sets of toast requirements data. The system will operate from normal household electrical power sources and will be a modified version of a conventional toaster. The toasting elements will use current technology.
>
> ▶ *User requirements and functionality* The system will recognise up to four separate user identities. It will accept definitions of the level of toasting required from each. This will be done via voice input to the system. The user will give the command to toast and the system will recognise the voice and produce the level of toasting that has already been programmed into the system. A ready signal will be given when toasting is complete.

Box 4.4 shows the process for an automatic toaster that gets rid of the problems and errors encountered in the manual system. This would act as a description of the proposed new system.

Box 4.4 The automated system

> ### The Breakfast Buddy Toaster – functionality and description
>
> 1 The bread has to be sliced.
> 2 The bread has to be placed in the toaster and the level of toasting is selected.
> 3 The toaster will recognise up to four individual preferences of toasting level. It can be pre-set to always toast to any of those four given levels.
> 4 Each diner has to set the level of toasting they require. Future interactions with the toaster simply require the toaster to recognise the individual. It will then toast to the required level.
> 5 Any amount of toast, up to four slices, can be done at the same time and to different levels of toasting.
> 6 The toast can be served hot to each individual.
> 7 It is possible to set other levels outside the four personalised ones.

Once requirements have been agreed, no further changes should be made without a signed agreement between the parties concerned. I say this with good reason. It is very easy to make promises when users are reeling off a list of problems that a system seems to have. But promises made under such circumstances are all too easy to forget. Or even worse, they can be fulfilled without the proper documentation being applied.

I once came across this rather plaintive plea. I have no idea where, but I vaguely remember that it is Martial addressing a drinking companion:

Omnia promittis cum tota nocte bibisti;
Mane nihil praestas, Pollio, mane bibe.

For those of you who, like me, have 'small Latin and less Greek' here it is again in English:

You promise me everything when you've been drinking all night. But in the morning you don't keep your promises. Drink in the morning.

Never promise users anything on-the-fly. Any promises must be properly agreed and added to the requirements and the usability specification. These act as part of the contract. They must not be changed lightly nor be seen to be easily dispensed with. If they are 'right and just' and the team has done its work properly there should be no need for changes.

That might sound very 'hard-nosed' – particularly as everything presented thus far has been very much from a user- centred perspective. I believe there is no conflict between this seemingly 'tough' perspective and the earlier chapters of this book. I don't believe it is in the interests of either the end-user or the usability engineer to make promises without firm agreements.

Perhaps it would be sensible to see what happens when users suggest changes and developers agree and carry out those changes on-the-fly. The LAS CAD mentioned earlier in this book had, amongst its many problems that of changes taking place on-the-fly.

> SO [Systems Options], in their eagerness to please users, often put through software changes on the fly thus circumventing the official Project Issues Report (PIR) procedures whereby all such changes should be controlled. These on the fly changes also reduced the effectiveness of the testing procedures as previously tested software would be amended without the knowledge of the project group. Such changes could, and did, introduce further bugs.
>
> LAS 3082, 1993

In their report on MUSE, BIUSEM noted that requirements documentation had several problems:

> There are no guidelines on the assumed level of rigour and formality in the requirements document nor clear directions on the appropriate form and detail of user information. There are no procedures or handshakes for incorporating new 'requirements' unearthed during analysis, nor, in the occasional cases where requirements are available and rigid, any guidelines on how to reject new suggestions and thereby prevent 'requirements creep'.
>
> BIUSEM, 1995

It is of paramount importance that the requirements document is done, done early and is taken seriously. If it is known that requirements will change and the specification for the system will alter during development – and at the frontiers of technology this will inevitably be the case – then this must be built into the requirements document so that all parties are aware of their obligations. Requirements are not static and specifications may well need to move with them but this must be a controlled and documented process.

BIUSEM go on to note that 'the effects go beyond design and specification through to testing' (BIUSEM, 1995). Of course they do! How can you test a system if you don't know how it was required to perform in the first place. Usability metrics need a specification to work from in order to operate properly and effectively. However, it could be that the metrics themselves are used to modify or perhaps even to firm-up the specification; and I see no problem with this.

4.7 Strategies for representing design

There are several methods for representing designs, either for the end-user to examine prior to the development of the system or as a means of allowing the design team to check the design, keep a record of the design or to evaluate the design so far. There are specialist books on the subject so all that can be offered here is a brief look at some of the more accessible strategies that are particularly effective for involving end-users in the design process. The design tools covered in this section are:

- ▶ storyboards;
- ▶ state transition diagrams;
- ▶ simulations;
- ▶ scenarios;
- ▶ rapid prototyping using an interface builder;
- ▶ Wizard of Oz.

However, there is a lot to be said for paper and pencil and whiteboard and marker. My students regularly produce small designs using overhead projector (OHP) slides within a very tight time-frame. Once the time is up I start yelling that their product is late and behind schedule! They then put their design on the projector, talk us through it and the class picks holes and asks for clarification. This means that by the end of a session the design can be modified. Designs produced like this are cheaper because they require no special knowledge of a system and they are quite fast to produce. Also, they are easily modified and anyone has the skill to do the modifications. It also seems to be the case that there is nothing like an overhead projector for allowing the designers themselves to find faults!

Figure 4.5 shows an example interface created in this way by a group of students at South Bank University.

Figure 4.5 An OHP slide design for an interface

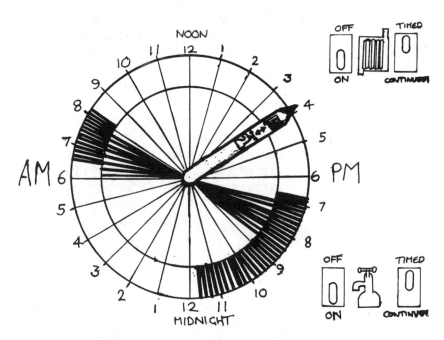

4.7.1 Storyboards

The initial designs for the system can most conveniently be presented in the form of storyboards. At the simplest level the design team might sketch a design for the user to look at. This design might be very temporal in that it could be drawn and modified on a whiteboard; sometimes end-users are happy to make suggestions themselves when interfaces are presented in this way. However, when the design is beyond the embryonic stage and a little more concrete, it is useful to present the end-user with a storyboard in order that the design might be evaluated.

A storyboard consists of parts of the interface mounted onto card or paper. At South Bank, human factors students are encouraged to use either screen dumps produced from a drawing package or scale drawings. These are placed on the board and can be moved around by the user and the design team until a suitable and comfortable design emerges. We have found that users prefer to move paper around rather than point to elements on a screen since they cannot easily move screen items around for themselves. Therefore, a paper interface is a lot less intimidating than an on-screen version. It does not require any particular expertise to move paper about whereas an on-screen prototype would require a usability engineer to make the changes for the user. This would mean that the user's ideas have to be properly interpreted and the user is not directly involved in the way that moving paper elements around on a card encourages user participation. Psychologically, given a choice between the two, the user is more likely to suggest changes to a paper-based rather than on-screen system prototype.

The storyboard can consist of mock-ups of the screens with the various elements being movable around each screen. Re-usable adhesives can be used to hold the elements into place once the users are pleased with the final appearance.

The other advantage of the storyboard is that it can be used to trace progression from one part of the screen to another and to check understanding of the various commands, dialogs and so on. The storyboard is literally hard copy of the interface so that each action leads to another part of the storyboard. Users can make choices and see what dialogues they would be dealing with.

The storyboard is a cheap and effective way of checking the design of the system in the very early stages. It is useful for the way in which it allows designers and end-users to discuss the system together and to try out their various ideas. It has the advantage that those end-users who are nervous of computers are not subjected to on-screen interfaces straight away. However, storyboards cannot capture a system's performance and sometimes it is very hard to convey detail with them since it would be too time-consuming to run through a computerised process that involved many screens. Where this is necessary a simulation would be a much better choice.

Figure 4.6 shows a set of storyboards created for a telephone helpline and logger. Figure 4.7 shows a photograph of part of the series of storyboards. This would be shown to the end-users.

Figure 4.6 A photograph of the actual set

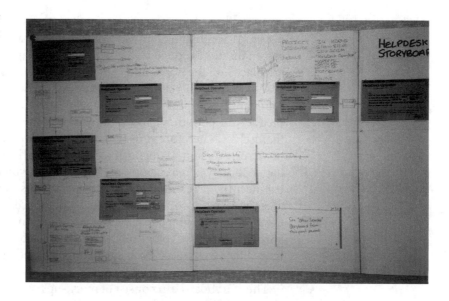

Figure 4.7 Part of a set of storyboards created for a telephone helpline system

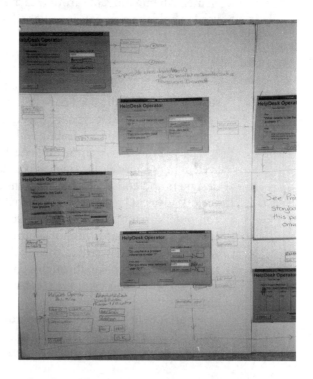

However, there is nothing to prevent the use of an on-screen storyboard. Presentation software can be used in this way so that the system appears to be working but, in reality, all that is being demonstrated is a slide show. There are many presentation systems which would be suitable for this type of activity. Again, the design can be produced relatively cheaply.

Some of the hypertext systems can be used in this way in order to produce a simulation – most often with limited functionality. Figure 4.8 shows a mock-up interface produced with a graphics package.

Figure 4.8 An interface mocked-up in a graphics package

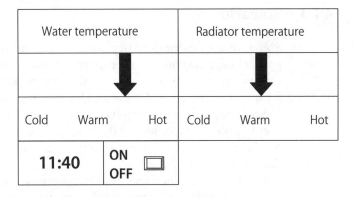

4.7.2   Simulations

Before the advent of visual programming tools, which can make the development of the user interface a lot easier, application tools such as HyperCard or ToolBook could be used for the development of a simulation interface. HyperCard is easy to use and can easily produce a simulation of a system that appears to have functionality. However, it is important to realise that such simulations are created in order to be thrown away. Far too many limited functionality simulations and throw-away prototypes have managed to outlive their sell-by dates and have appeared masquerading as real applications. Since they were never developed as real applications they all too frequently have not been engineered.

Figure 4.9 shows the interface to the prototype of a system built in ToolBook.

Figure 4.9 A prototype built in ToolBook

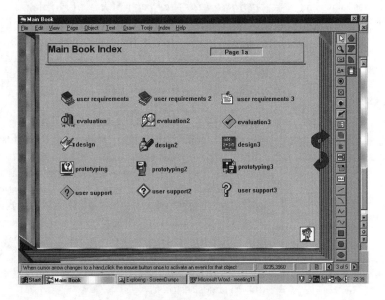

4.7.3   Scenarios

Scenarios are descriptions of possible interactions with a system. They enable designers and end-users to ensure that processes which need to be carried out can actually be done using the proposed system. They are useful for understanding users' tasks and for spotting problems.

Scenarios can be used in several ways. They can be written by the end-user in order to explain what it is that is done at present or they can be produced by the usability engineer in order to allow the end-user to see how the new system will operate.

Scenarios are a good way of putting end-user and usability engineer on the same wavelength. However, they are time-consuming to produce and assume a good knowledge of what actually needs to be done. However, since the system cannot be designed until the usability engineer understands the end-user's task, scenarios are a good way of confirming that knowledge.

Some authorities suggest that scenarios are very useful for requirements gathering in that they enable developers to see exactly what tasks need to be performed. If the method is used to understand the current system, it is wise for users to be involved in the process otherwise it is easy for misconceptions about the current system to creep in. If it is used as a method of working through the proposed system then users will undoubtedly be involved as part of the evaluation process.

Scenarios for the nail-painting system introduced in Chapter 3 and the toast-maker introduced in this chapter are shown in Box 4.5.

Box 4.5 Scenarios for the Pretty Slik Nail Painter and Breakfast Buddy Toaster

> *Scenario 1 for the Pretty Slik Nail Painter*
> A very busy lecturer needs to attend a party but is wearing the wrong nail varnish to go with the dress she wishes to wear. Being a lecturer and therefore too poor to own a car she is relying on a software engineer friend to pick her up. She has only ten minutes available for changing her nail colour from green to pink.
>
> *Scenario 2 for the Breakfast Buddy Toaster*
> Sam, Jackie, Chris and Alex are eating breakfast cereal. They will follow breakfast cereal with toast. Sam has almost finished eating the cereal and wants the toast in a few minutes. Sam likes toast that is well done, almost black. Alex and Chris want toast much later after a cup of coffee. Alex likes toast that is golden brown but done on one side only. Chris likes toast golden brown and toasted on both sides. Sam likes toast that is slightly brown. Alex is ready for toast now.
>
> Sam pushes the first selector to the label 'Sam' and feeds in a slice of bread. Alex pushes the second selector to the label 'Alex' and feeds in two slices of toast.

> After a few moments Alex's toast is ready; a light next to Alex's name on the toaster flashes and a tone sounds. Alex removes the toast.
> After two minutes the light next to Sam's name flashes and a different tone sounds. Sam removes the toast.

The first scenario, for the Pretty Slik Nail Painter, simply states a problem scenario. It does not explain how the task would be carried out. A scenario like that could be developed by the end-user to describe the sorts of problems they have to deal with at present. The usability engineer would then use the scenario in order to consider the design. But such a scenario could also be developed by the usability engineer and shown to the end-user in order to ensure that the problems really have been understood. This type of technique has been used in the development of expert systems for some time and is well established in that field. In fact, HCI can learn a lot from how practitioners operate in the field of artificial intelligence. The interviewing techniques are also well developed there.

The second scenario walks through the process of using the Breakfast Buddy Toaster and shows how various interactions with it will take place. Using that scenario it would be possible to criticise the way in which it functions and to consider the problems there might be.

Scenarios are cheap. They require limited resources and they do not require a deep understanding of human factors in order to implement them. However, they do require a sound understanding of the system they are replicating.

4.7.4   State transition diagrams

The state transition diagram (STD) is a means of representing the design. It can be used to ensure that all parts of the interface have been accounted for and it can be used as a means of checking potential user inputs and their outcomes.

Figure 4.10 A state transition diagram for the interface shown in Figure 4.11

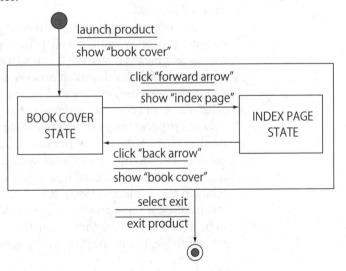

The STD is a vital tool to the developer of GUIs but it is far from easy for a non-computer literate user to understand. However, some of my students have used a simplified STD and the storyboard to represent designs so that they are suitable for the user to look at.

Figure 4.10 shows a state transition diagram for the interface shown in Figure 4.11.

Figure 4.11 The interface represented by the state transition diagram shown in Figure 4.10

4.7.5 Rapid Prototyping

Rapid prototyping is useful when the user is unsure what the system should be like, or is liable to lose interest. It is also very useful when the user is a novice. This is because the prototyping stage can then act as a means of training the users to a particular standard prior to the introduction of the finished product.

Some software engineers frown on rapid prototyping as they believe it encourages sloppy habits. Rapid prototyping of the interface should be seen merely as a means of getting the design right. The system will still have to undergo the full development process; it will have to be designed from a programming point of view and must be properly represented at all stages otherwise it will become impossible to maintain.

Some programming environments are particularly adept at being used for the rapid production of interfaces. Sadly, the ease at which these can be produced all too often causes the systems to be a mishmash of hacked-together code which would be a nightmare to verify and to maintain (Culwin and Faulkner, 1997). Rapid prototyping must not be seen as a means of escaping a properly engineered product. If software is to be seen to be fit for its purpose then it must be properly documented and maintainable. It must be properly designed and code must not be written by the seat of the pants. If the interface is to be produced using one of the modern visual development tools then it must be properly engineered. Unfortunately, far too many interfaces are hacked together as a demonstration for the user and modified according to the user's needs. Then, instead of acting as a pattern for the real design, the system is built either using the rapid prototyping tool which was used to develop the demonstration interface, or the interface is bolted onto the system's functionality. Any software produced for an end-user must be engineered.

The rapid prototype allows the user to evaluate the system as it develops and user feedback can then be used in the further development of the system. This is known as the design–build–evaluate cycle (Ashworth, 1991). Figure 4.12 shows this process.

Figure 4.12 Rapid prototyping using user feedback to drive the product

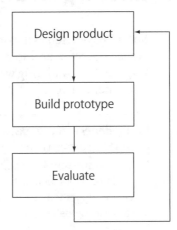

4.7.6 Wizard of Oz

The Wizard of Oz is a method by which a system can be tested without first having to build it. The user is presented with what appears to be a working system but in actual fact the role of the system is taken on by a human being who is situated somewhere else – sometimes unbeknown to the user.

The advantages of the Wizard of Oz method are apparent. The system does not have to be built so this type of prototyping can be done quite cheaply. Secondly, the 'wizard' – who is on the design team – is able to examine the functionality of the system by intercepting the user's commands. Thirdly, examination of the wizard's output to the user can also be used as an indication of how the system will need to operate.

The method has been used to good effect in the evaluation and examination of natural language systems. For example, Gould *et al* simulated a listening typewriter by using a hidden typist to type in what the user said (Gould, 1995). Kelley supplemented his natural language calendar by taking over the parts it could not deal with (Gould, 1995). Dan Diaper used the Wizard of Oz in his analysis of requirements for a natural language enquiry system (Diaper, 1989). The Wizard of Oz method is most appropriate in systems with intelligence – especially where the proposed system goes beyond what is technically feasible or where the appropriate technology is not readily available.

One of the problems of the Wizard of Oz method is that analysing the dialogues produced by interactions between user and wizard can be time-consuming and therefore expensive. It does require that the wizard knows and understands the limitations and extent of the functionality that is to be provided in the new system. However, it is an extremely effective way of gathering information for a proposed system and has been used to great effect for requirement's gathering for natural language systems (Diaper; 1986, 1989).

4.8   Involving the user – some problems

So far I have acted as if working with users and involving them in the design is such good fun and so rewarding that anyone reading this could be forgiven for wondering why it doesn't always happen that way. It is time for a spanner or two…

A spanner in the works…   Ben Shneiderman reminds us that: '…extensive user involvement may be costly and may lengthen the implementation period, build antagonism with people who are not involved or whose suggestions are rejected, force designers to compromise their design to satisfy incompetent participants, and simply build opposition to implementation…'   <div align="right">Shneiderman; 1998, pp. 109–110</div>

It would be wrong of me to argue that working with users isn't without its problems. Users are people and so are designers. People can be tiresome as well as interesting and fun. Sometimes, working with users is problematic but the alternative – to ignore them – would be foolhardy. I don't believe it is an option. Richard Seymour and Dick Powell in the programme *Designs on your Car* (Channel 4) saw their designs rejected. They watched the customer make, what they believed to be, the wrong decision but they accepted that decision with dignity.

When we work with people we need to remember that we won't always be right and even if we are, sometimes right won't prevail. As Stephen Jay Gould says:

A potential for inherent "progress" provides no guarantee of realization in actuality.   <div align="right">Gould, 1997</div>

I remain optimistic, however, and take the view that losing the battle doesn't mean losing the war. Like Dick Powell and Richard Seymour, usability engineers will undoubtedly see decisions made on the basis of economics not on the basis of good design; however, the task of developing usable systems for everyone is too important to allow our personal feelings to get in the way. Richard Seymour said in *Designs on your Car* (Channel 4) that a designer wakes up every day to see things that need improving and fixing. Usability engineers need to adopt that same positive attitude towards systems and must not be dismayed by rejection.

> **A spanner in the works…**
> John Karat argues that:
> 'developing usable software involves more than involving users…'
>
> Karat, 1996

But software isn't just about producing a system which the user can easily and effectively operate. It has to be engineered and tested. It requires people skilled in its production. A usability engineer is well placed to produce software and involve users in the process.

CHAPTER SUMMARY

- ▶ Getting the design right is all about understanding user requirements and catering for just those needs.
- ▶ The usability engineer gathers the requirements and develops the software so there is less chance of misunderstanding.
- ▶ The requirements specification is drawn up between the usability engineer and the customer. It is the first step in producing a binding contract.
- ▶ It is important that the requirements understood by the customer are the same as the requirements interpreted by the software development team.
- ▶ Customers will also tend to express their requirements in their own language and this has to be interpreted into functionality for the system.
- ▶ Before requirements gathering takes place it is important to carry out a proper feasibility study. Some of the answers to the questions about feasibility will be helpful in understanding the environment in which the system will operate.
- ▶ Software requirements analysis is about focusing on what the system should do rather than how the software will work.
- ▶ The first stage of requirements specification is to recognise the goal of the system and the problems that exist within the system at present.

▶ Once requirements have been agreed, any changes must be properly agreed and added to the requirements and the usability specification. These act as part of the contract. They must not be changed lightly nor seen to be easily dispensed with.

▶ There are several methods for representing designs: either for the end-user to examine prior to the development of the system or as a means of allowing the design team to examine the design.

▶ The initial designs for the system can most conveniently be presented in the form of storyboards since this is a cheap and effective way of checking the design of the system in the very early stages.

▶ Simulations are another good way of allowing the user to examine the design.

▶ The state transition diagram (STD) is a means of representing the design. It can be used to ensure that all parts of the interface have been accounted for as well as being a means of checking potential user inputs and their outcomes. However, it is not easy for non-specialists to understand.

▶ Rapid prototyping is useful when the user is unsure what the system should be like, or is liable to lose interest, or is a novice user and the prototyping stage is intended to act as a means of training the users.

▶ The rapid prototype allows the user to evaluate the system as it develops and user feedback can then be used during further development of the system. This is known as the design–build–evaluate cycle.

▶ The Wizard of Oz is a method by which the user is presented with what appears to be a working system, but in actual fact the role of the system is played by a human being who is a member of the design team.

SELF TEST LIST

- design–build–evaluate cycle
- feasibility study
- prototyping
- rapid prototyping
- requirements specification
- scenarios
- simulations
- state transition diagrams
- storyboards
- Wizard of Oz

EXERCISES

1 Produce a suitable requirements specification for the Pretty Slik Nail Painter. Use the interviews from Chapter 3. Get a friend to examine your requirements (preferably someone who, like me, is obsessed with nail varnish!) and refine them if necessary.

2 From the requirements list you have produced for the Pretty Slik Nail
   Painter, produce a suitable interface to satisfy the requirements you
   have developed. Check the interface with a friend.

3 Produce a suitable scenario for the interface you have just produced. It
   should be a scenario which describes actual interaction with the system.
   Again, get a friend to go through the scenario with you. Now develop a
   scenario where something goes wrong. Perhaps the user changes his or
   her mind about the nail colour. Perhaps the phone rings. How does
   your system cope with these problems?

4 Using the scenario for the Breakfast Buddy Toaster, design a suitable
   interface for the system. Turn the interface into a series of storyboards
   and get a friend to try to operate it. Fix the problems and try again!

REFERENCES

Ashworth G (1991) 'Evaluation case study II: a voice-operated database
    enquiry service' in Andy Downton (ed.) *Engineering the User Interface*.
    McGraw-Hill, London.

BIUSEM (1995) *Benefits of Integrating Usability and Software Engineering
    Methods*. ESSI project 10290. See also:

    `http://www.esi.es/ESSI/Reports/All/10290/Objectives.html`

Culwin F and Faulkner C (1997) 'Integration of Usability Considerations
    within the CS/SE Curriculum' in the proceedings of the Thirteenth
    Annual Eastern Small College Computing Conference, October 24–25,
    New Jersey, pp 169–278.

Diaper D 1986 'Identifying the Knowledge Requirements of an Expert
    System's Natural Language Processing Interface.' Proceedings of the
    Second Conference of the BCS HCI Specialist Group, September 1986.

Diaper D (1989) 'Bridging the Gulf Between Requirements and Design' in
    the proceedings of the *Ergonomics Society Conference on Simulation in
    the Development of User Interfaces*, pp. 129–145. Brighton, 18–19 May,
    1989.

Dix A *et al* (1998) *Human Computer Interaction*. Prentice Hall, Hemel
    Hempstead.

Gould J (1995) 'How to Design Usable Systems' in Baecker, Grudin,
    Buxton and Greenberg (eds)*Readings in HCI: Towards the Year 2000*.
    Morgan Kaufmann, San Francisco.

Gould, Stephen Jay (1997) *Life's Grandeur*. Vintage, London.

Hughes J A, Sommerville I, Bentley R and Randall D (1993) 'Designing
    with ethnography: making work visible' in *Interacting with Computers*,
    vol. 5, no. 2, pp. 239–53.

Karat J (1996) 'User Centred Design: Quality or Quackery?' in *Interactions*,
    vol. 11.4, ACM.

LAS (1993) *Report of the Inquiry into the London Ambulance Service.* London: LAS.

Norman D (1998) *The Invisible Computer.* MIT Press, Cambridge, Massachusetts.

Pressman R (1987) *Software Engineering: A Practitioner's Approach,* 2nd edition. McGraw Hill, New York.

Shneiderman B (1998) *Designing the User Interface*, 3rd edition. Addison Wesley, Reading, Massachusetts.

FURTHER READING

BIUSEM (1995) *Benefits of Integrating Usability and Software Engineering Methods.* ESSI project 10290. See also:

`http://www.esi.es/ESSI/Reports/All/10290/Objectives.html`

A highly readable report on MUSE with some interesting incidental comments on the way. MUSE raises some interesting questions – one of which is its exclusion of information about the user except as an incidental.

Karat J (1996) 'User Centred Design: Quality or Quackery?' in *Interactions*, vol. 11.4, ACM.

John Karat's short paper is a report back on a panel he organised and moderated at ACM SIGCHI. He deals a couple of body-blows to User Centred Design and, on the way, a swipe or two in the direction of usability and usability engineering. It is two pages long, highly readable and thought-provoking. It also outlines some of the opinions of other panellists.

Sommerville, Ian and Sawyer, Pete (1997) *Requirements Engineering.* John Wiley, Chichester.

This is a good, thorough text and easy to read. It is written as a text for practitioners as well as students, so it is very practical. It is also very honest and Sommerville and Sawyer point out where problems are likely to happen or where their methods won't work.

Usability metrics

This chapter:

▶ introduces usability metrics – the measurements that can be taken to judge the usability of a system;

▶ looks at ways in which the criteria offered by the ISO can be turned into attributes to be measured using the metrics;

▶ introduces the idea of a usability specification and looks at the extensions to usability engineering that have been suggested by Whiteside, Bennett and Holtzblatt (Whiteside *et al*, 1988).

5.1 So how do I know it's usable?

So far, this book may seem a bit like reading a thriller and waiting for the murder to happen so that you can start working out who the murderer is. This chapter though gets to the heart of the matter and looks at how we can say whether or not a product is truly usable. At this stage I shall admit that some of what follows is rather contentious.

Paul Booth characterises the usability approach as addressing the practical issues first. He is adamant that usability is not just something related to information technology (IT) and its products but to other systems, machinery and products too (Booth, 1988). This position is more than amply proven today in that manufacturing industries have taken up the usability cause with some degree of enthusiasm. There are textbooks available cataloguing the attempts of manufacturers to operate from a usability perspective (Jordan, 1998; Trenner and Bowa, 1998).

Booth points out that usability problems can account for the abandoning of software products simply because users could not use them. He argues that the usability approach is a two-pronged attack: firstly on education and secondly on incorporating human factors into the process of design (Booth, 1988). So far as education is concerned both the ACM (Association of Computing Machinery) and the BCS (British Computer Society) have submitted HCI syllabuses which attempt to integrate HCI considerations throughout the computer science/computer studies curriculum (ACM, 1992; BCS, 1995).

Ensuring that a product is usable is not easy and guaranteeing usability is even more difficult. Usability engineering seeks to solve the problem of ensuring that the product is what the user really wants and will actually use. It does this by:

- defining usability through metrics;
- setting planned levels for usability attributes;
- incorporating user-derived feedback into the design process;
- repeating all of the above until usability levels are met or amended by agreement with the user;

Let's return to the definitions of usability we examined in the first chapter. The International Organization for Standardization (ISO) defines usability as:

> …the effectiveness, efficiency and satisfaction with which specified users can achieve specified goals in particular environments…
>
> ISO DIS 9241-11

On the face of it the ISO would seem to give a fair amount of guidance in helping us to decide whether or not a product can be described as fitting the criteria for usability. Systems should be:

- **effective** – they should accomplish the task;
- **efficient** – they should accomplish the task in the least time and with as little effort as possible;
- **satisfying** – they should be a pleasure to use!

But in reality, how can usability engineers say whether or not a system is effective, efficient or, even worse, satisfying? User satisfaction with a product is a very subjective measure. How can we measure individual user satisfaction let alone compare various users levels of satisfaction with a product?

Let's look at the ISO definition once again in a little more detail. The ISO definition of effectiveness includes the idea that effectiveness is:

'the accuracy and completeness with which users achieve specific goals'

In terms of the original definition this would mean the degree that the task could be accomplished with the specified tool and by a particular user working in a particular environment. Again, on the face of it, this doesn't give us too much of a problem. It should be possible to say that a particular user, working in a particular environment and doing a particular task should be able to accomplish that task. All we need to do is to give the users the task and see if they can accomplish it. That's easy enough, on the surface, at least. If the task is simple then it is comparatively easy to judge whether or not it has been completed. Where the task is complex it may be more problematic. Complex tasks may be partially completed. It might then be advisable to break those tasks down into subtasks so that each one can be examined individually. For example, if we take the production of a letter on a word processing package we could view the creation of the letter as hard copy as a complete task. If the user failed to produce a hard copy of the letter we could say that the task was not completed. However, that might not be very useful when we were trying to evaluate our system. So, we could break down the task of producing a letter as hard copy into several subtasks or stages:

▶ typing in the text;
▶ spell-checking the text;
▶ formatting the text;
▶ saving the file;
▶ printing out a hard copy.

Quite clearly, all of those subtasks can be further broken-down into lower-level tasks – as we saw in Chapter 3 when we examined the user's task and looked at task analysis. For example, spell-checking the text might consist of invoking the spell-checker and either consenting to or rejecting suggested changes to the words in the document. By breaking-down the tasks further still, we can reduce them to keystrokes and mouse-clicks! On occasion, this might be a useful exercise but for most of the time such a detailed level of analysis won't be necessary.

Efficiency is slightly more problematic. Efficiency is defined by the ISO as:

'the accuracy and completeness of goals in relation to resources expended'

We could, at one level, simply view this as the time taken to accomplish the task. However, resources might well be more complex than time; we could also examine concepts such as effort, for example. In this definition not only would the task have to be done but it would have to be done within a given time-frame and with a specified amount of effort. There is again no problem about deciding on a time-frame and measuring whether or not our system achieves those goals. Again, the user performs the task and if it is done within the time-frame we can say our system was efficient. We may again have to face the problem of incomplete tasks but we can circumvent that difficulty by breaking down tasks to a lower level until we are satisfied that we are looking at a discrete task. Specifying effort is problematic. Do we take the amount of effort as a measurement of time or do we break down the various actions to the level of keystrokes and mouse-clicks in order to see how much physical effort the system demands? Or do we simply take a subjective measure of effort from the perspective of the user? Obviously, this is a moment for discretion and it may well be that the solution chosen will be dictated by the problem under consideration.

Satisfaction is a real problem though. The ISO defines satisfaction as:

'the comfort and acceptability of the system'.

Dogs wag their tails when they are pleased. Perhaps the wag-rate is related to how pleased they are? A fast-wagging tail belongs to a very pleased dog, a slower wag indicates less pleasure. Measure the wag and you know how happy the dog is. For years now I have tried to persuade engineering friends to build a wagometer to make this easier. It would be nice if we had a satisfaction-meter to measure user's happiness with the systems we give them. We could just try it out on them and know how pleased they were. But we don't have that either. However, we can ask them to tell us how content they are with the system and the way in which it operates and try to convert that into some sort of overall measure of satisfaction with the system.

Again, this is not without its problems. In an effort to demonstrate how varied human response is, I once asked students to rate their liking of chocolate on a scale of 1 to 10 with 1 being dislike intensely and 10 being like more than anything else in the world. Some students were so enamoured with chocolate that they begged me to allow them to say 11! However, we still had no guarantee that one person's 10 wasn't another person's 7 or 11!

Comfort is difficult to judge too. Some of my students and I have attempted to measure physical comfort by developing what I have called a 'fidget-rate' – a measure of how much fidgeting and movement takes place within a given time-frame. We have used this measure as a means of trying to compare the user's subjective experience of comfort/discomfort with our objective measures. We are as yet a long way off coming to any useful conclusions! Comfort is very difficult to describe and assess.

Using all of the definitions of usability provided by the ISO we can then, with some degree of confidence, say that it is possible to measure the usability of a product. Provided, of course, that the ISO's definition is the correct one – that is, efficiency, effectiveness and satisfaction are the sum total of usability and providing that we can think of sufficient means to measure them!

The next sections will endeavour to present suitable attributes that should allow reasonable measurements to be taken.

5.2   Usability attributes

The ISO provides us with a starting point. On the surface it may seem to be quite narrow in its suppositions – after all it specifies that the system must be usable by a specified user, in a specified environment performing a specified task (Draper, 1993). On the surface at least it would seem to be quite difficult to be more limited and circumspect than that! In actual fact, it is quite the opposite. It is a broad and sweeping statement about producing usable products and, if anything, its lack of discrimination gives the usability engineer something of a problem when interpreting what is actually meant. If a product was efficient, effective and satisfied the user then it is probably likely that it is usable as well. But the problem is, the ISO doesn't suggest how efficient, how effective or how satisfying the system must be. It acts as if 'efficiency', 'effectiveness' and 'satisfaction' are absolutes – like 'roundness' – and therefore easy to spot. Or better still we have some sort of meter to place on the system with which to test its usability levels. It doesn't suggest what sort of range usability has to cover whether in terms of those definitions or in terms of the user population. All of that is down to the interpreter – the usability engineer. We shall look at this problem in more detail in Chapter 8. But for the time being I want to ignore these objections and present an overview of the processes involved. Later on we can look at the problems and objections and perhaps consider some solutions and answers to the criticisms levelled at usability engineering – particularly the metrics.

However, even with the above problems, those three categories for judging software – efficiency, effectiveness and satisfaction – are not sufficient for our needs in usability engineering and we need to explain them in terms we can interpret and measure. Otherwise usability is on a par with user friendliness – it does not have a real and quantifiable meaning in the real world. We therefore need to apply attributes to each of the categories defined by the ISO for deciding whether a system is usable in order to have more material with which to judge our system. These attributes must be measurable. If a system achieves the measurements we set then we can say that the product is usable. Also, it has to be remembered that while usability engineers must ensure their products conform to ISO standards, at the same time the role of the usability engineer is to forge better standards for the future. We don't just want to finish the race – we want to finish first!

The following sections examine possible ways of looking at the attributes of software and measuring those software attributes against predefined criteria. In each case suitable metrics – things to measure – will be suggested and their purposes explained.

The attributes of usability can be couched in all sorts of terms depending upon the preferences of the writer. My own preference tends towards Shackel's original definitions though I have been influenced by Hix and Hartson (1993) and Booth (1988).

Shackel's definitions, if you remember, were couched in far more humane terms and there were more classes. Shackel defined usability in terms of effectiveness, learnability, flexibility and attitude. Incidentally, this is sometimes described as LEAF: Learnability, Effectiveness, Attitude, Flexibility.

However, for the time being I intend to examine the ISO recommendations and to comment on the appropriateness later.

5.2.1 Effectiveness

The effectiveness of a system from Shackel's point of view was about whether a task could be accomplished with the specified system and within a given time-frame. For the ISO, effectiveness is about whether or not the task can be accomplished. It has no concept of time.

We can break down the concept of effectiveness into the following categories for close examination and measurement.

▶ The success to failure ratio in completing the task.

▶ The frequency of use of various commands or of particular language features/functions.

▶ The measurements of user problems.

▶ The quality of the output.

Obviously, at a simple level, the task is either completed or not completed but as we have seen above we can view the entire task as a series of subtasks and then look at the ratio of success to failure either overall or between the sections of the task.

The frequency of use of the various commands or the evidence of use of particular aspects of an interface might well give us information about how effective the system is. If there is redundant functionality then we want to know about that. Why are the commands not being used? Are they necessary? Is there another, more efficient, way of doing the task that the user has worked out? Or are there seemingly ways of doing the task that don't actually achieve success?

Notice that effectiveness is all about task completion: success to failure rate, problems experienced, use of commands. But there is also a measure of just how successful 'success' really is: by an examination of output quality. In other words, is there a range of acceptable performances? How is success measured? Or is the output either right or wrong? This would be equivalent to saying that for a particular job candidates had to have a given range of qualifications or be of a certain height. The exact qualification or the exact height would not be given. A range of people might be able to fulfil the criteria. In the same way it might be that output can be tolerated within a given range. For example, it might be acceptable for an address to have mistakes in capitalisation or have the post code missing; a letter sent to such an address will very likely get to its destination. However, a telephone number with a wrong digit would probably be useless though it may well be someone's telephone number.

5.2.2 Efficiency

The ISO definition is about how much effort is required in order to accomplish the task. Some people refer to this as throughput. This sense of efficiency could contain ideas of how much time was spent on the task but effort could also be measured. An efficient system ought to require as little effort as possible:

▶ The time required to perform selected tasks.

▶ The number of actions required in order to perform a task.

- ▸ The time spent looking for information in documentation.
- ▸ The time spent using on-line help.
- ▸ The time spent dealing with error.

The first two metrics would give a measurement of how much time and effort needed to be expended on a particular task. Obviously, we can measure both the number of actions needed to perform the task and the time it takes. There may well be a correlation between the time and the number of actions though this will not always be the case. Some actions will take less time than others. If necessary these can be broken down to the lowest level that is to a series of keystrokes and mouse clicks. Cognitive models can be used to break down the task to a series of cognitive events. However, it is unlikely that such high level detail would be needed. For example, the GOMS methodology can be used in just this way (Card, Moran and Newell, 1983).

Time spent trying to figure out how to use the system needs to be measured since it will affect, at least initially, the efficiency of the system. If the system is not used regularly it could well be that the user has to constantly re-learn how to use it and this time will never be drastically reduced.

Notice that there is not a separate, nor formal, requirement for learnability in the ISO though arguably this is where that attribute would be considered. At this stage, however, we will simply move on to consider user satisfaction and then return to the idea of learnability later.

5.2.3 User satisfaction

It might seem unlikely that it would be possible to measure the satisfaction a user feels whilst using a system. Such a measurement would seem to be too subjective. However, a useful measurement of user satisfaction can be made if the evaluation team's measurement is based on observations of user attitudes towards the system.

The aim in designing the system is to promote continued and enhanced use of the system by the user. Thus the aim of usability engineering is to ensure that the user has positive feelings towards the system. It is possible to measure user attitudes using a questionnaire, for example:

How would you rate your overall opinion of the system?
1 = very bad to 5 = very good

It might be sensible to specify in advance that the aim is to achieve a user response of at least 90 per cent of users responding with scores of 4 or 5. In this way, it is possible to provide a reasonably objective measurement of what would otherwise be a very subjective response.

This then completes the factors that need to be considered directly for the ISO. However, Shackel separated learnability from efficiency, added a separate category – flexibility – and had a final category of attitude which is partially replaced by the ISO's satisfaction.

As the aim of usability engineering is to produce truly usable products, I want to push the ISO definition a little harder and look at the additional features offered by Shackel's original definition.

5.2.4 Learnability

A system should be easy for the user to learn so that it is possible to use the system effectively as quickly as possible.

In fact when users come to new systems this is the first attribute they will become aware of since they will be endeavouring to learn how to use the system. How easy it is to learn will undoubtedly colour their attitudes towards the system. It is necessary for systems to be learned quickly because the cost of training is high and employers would like their employees to be productive with a system as quickly as possible. However much we might value education from the point of view of economics if a degree in computer science could be obtained via a needle in the arm then universities would be out of business tomorrow! Furthermore, extended learning times reduce the advantages of changing to a new system because training costs money and may render adopting a new system unprofitable in the short term or even in the long term if there is a high turnover of staff.

How easy a system is to learn can be measured in terms of a novice user's experience of learning how to operate it. A system that is easy to learn will cause the user to be able to carry out a large amount of tasks in a short space of time, thus reflecting how the user quickly learns to operate some areas of the system. It could be that this learning curve flattens out as the user achieves the required level of competence and then gradually adds knowledge of more functions to their initial understanding of the system. It might be that all of the functionality of the system is never learned. Indeed, it is unlikely that all functionality will ever be necessary for all users. Even if it does become necessary, some tasks are rarely done and how to do them is never really learned. Other strategies might be resorted to.

However, some systems[1] can be said to aim for zero learning time. These systems will be highly usable and transparent and will endeavour to use the user's 'knowledge in the world' in order to make them easy to learn. In other words they will build on what the user already knows or provide clear cues as to what needs to be done. Norman defines 'knowledge in the world systems' as systems that do not require any learning. They provide all of the information that a user needs in order to operate them (Norman, 1988). This can easily be illustrated by Figures 5.1 and 5.2. Figure 5.1 is a recycling bin; it tells you exactly what sorts of material you can throw into it. Figure 5.2 is a rubbish bin but if you didn't know that you might not be able to

---

1. Such as those designed to be used by the general public and operating on the principle that the user will walk up to the system and use it immediately.

deduce it. Knowledge in the world systems frequently show signs of clutter because they provide lots of clues about what would be suitable activities to carry out with them. Knowledge in the head systems are sleek and information-free. Figure 5.1 shows all the signs of clutter I would expect to see on a knowledge in the world system. And Figure 5.2 shows the sleek, sexy lines of knowledge in the head; if a rubbish bin can be sexy that is! Knowledge in the world systems are always easy to use, no matter how much time elapses between use, you return to them and can use them again without difficulty. The same cannot be said to be true of knowledge in the head systems which require the user to learn how to use them and remember that information about operation.

Figure 5.1 Knowledge in the world

Figure 5.2 Knowledge in the head

My kitchen has a variety of storage containers. Some are glass and the contents obvious. But others are delightfully patterned tins. In April 1998 I had the outside of my house painted and left tea and coffee for the painter, along with a note saying sugar was in the pig tin. Alan, the painter, was bemused to find some very peculiar golden brown objects which he thought might be some sort of weird sugar that vegetarians went in for. So he tried one – an apricot! My knowledge of my knowledge in the head system had failed me somewhat.

5.2.5 Flexibility and attitude

Shackel defined flexibility as allowing adaptation to some percentage variation in the task, and/or the environment specified. What he means by this is that although the usability of the product should be defined in terms of specified users, specified tasks and specified environments there should be some leeway so that the product could be used outside those original targets. Although Shackel talks about adaptation he seems to be referring to task and environment rather than user. Quite clearly he means that the product should adapt to the environment and the task rather than the other way round. He doesn't seem to be implying that different users might want to use the product in a different way – which might be a nice way of defining a flexible product.

When examining Shackel's definition it is important to realise that he didn't have the ISO to guide him! Otherwise, defining a specified set of usability criteria which you then insist should be able to be surpassed may seem a little odd.

Certainly Paul Booth had problems with Shackel's definition of flexibility and I can sympathise. Booth suggests that it is:

> ...particularly difficult to specify, communicate and test in a real product development environment...
>
> Booth, 1988

I suspect it is an attribute that would work well when applied to a manufactured product rather than a piece of software. In fact, if you look at Shackel's paper 'Ergonomics in Design for Usability' (Shackel, 1986) all becomes clear. Shackel's concept of usability is very much geared to an ergonomic perspective. He seems to have manufactured products very much in mind. These criteria would work very well on a video recorder, for example. Booth then goes on to replace 'flexibility' with 'usefulness' and excludes flexibility altogether. I suspect that flexibility is actually quite a good attribute for a manufactured product and a software product to have. However, perhaps it ought to mean a little more than Shackel implied and to suggest that users are able to use the product in a way most suited to them or in different ways according to how they feel or what they are doing. A lot of software does provide this flexibility. For example, the word processing package Microsoft Word allows you to create a new document by:

- ▶ selecting new from the file menu;
- ▶ pressing the shortcut keys;
- ▶ selecting a template and opening it;
- ▶ selecting an existing document and deleting the entire contents and then saving under a new file name using 'Save As'.

An aside…

Incidentally, 'Save As' is my preferred method and is something like Russian roulette for excitement. I inevitably forget to select 'Save As' and use the shortcut keys for 'Save' instead, thus overwriting the file. No matter how many times I make that error I never learn – despite having lost some quite important files. I've become quite expert at using the file-recovery facilities!

The early versions of Microsoft Word were quite happy to let me do that. The latest version nags a bit in a querulous sort of way – 'Are you sure you want to delete the selected text?' Alas, of course I'm sure. I want the document set-up I've selected. What I don't want to do is to save it and overwrite the original but Word has done its bit and doesn't stop me from being very silly…

Why the system itself can't simply keep versions of your document defeats me. I know I could set this up myself but it never dawns on me that I ought to until disaster strikes and then I'm too busy with the problem to take the necessary precautions for the next time. Instead, like everyone else with good intentions I resolve to behave differently tomorrow!

Quite clearly, almost any system will require some amount of time for a user to learn how to use it; even if this time is minimal. But other things can be measured as well. For example, it might be decided that the learnability of a particular application is best measured by examining all or some of the following criteria:

- ▶ The time required to learn the system.
- ▶ The time required to achieve a stated performance criterion.
- ▶ The difficulties observed in acquiring the necessary skill.
- ▶ The time spent looking for information in documentation.
- ▶ The time spent using on-line help.
- ▶ The time spent dealing with error.
- ▶ The time required to maintain knowledge of the system.
- ▶ The time required to re-learn the system after time away from it.

The measurement of learnability will also involve an objective measurement of just how easy the system is to learn. This can be done in a number of ways but the following would make acceptable objective indicators; although, again, it might be necessary for the team to add others as required:

- ▶ The frequency of error messages.
- ▶ The frequency of particular error messages.
- ▶ The frequency of use of on-line help.
- ▶ The number of times the user needed help on a specific problem.

Some people like learning new things. Some people regard learning as a challenge. But that isn't true for everyone. Some people hate learning new systems. Learning ought to be fun but it isn't always seen like that. Many learners want to do things and can sometimes seem quite reckless in their attempts at operating parts of a system that is less than transparent. Carroll and Mazur have a suitable spanner to toss into the learnability works...

> *A spanner in the works...*
> Carroll and Mazur noted that one user operating the Lisa said:
> 'I'm getting impatient. I want to do something, not learn how to do everything.'
> Carroll and Mazur, 1986

It is unlikely that users will learn all of the system at once. It must be possible for learning to occur in discrete packages whenever possible.

Learnability also contains the idea of how much effort and training are required to maintain the skills and the concept of re-learnability given time away from the system.

Finally, Shackel's definition of usability included attitude which is a much richer criterion than the ISO's 'satisfaction'. Incidentally, Fintan Culwin (Culwin, 1998; Faulkner and Culwin, 1999) believes this should be 'enjoyment'; he likes the idea of the alliteration but there is a serious statement there too in that systems really should be fun to use. For me, Shackel captures this in his concept of attitude. Not only does he define it in terms of how much wear and tear on the user is acceptable but he believes that continual encounters with the system should bring about enhanced satisfaction. In other words, people should enjoy using the system; they should have fun. If usability criteria are to be applied to products as well as software then 'attitude' is a far better criterion to be looking at than 'satisfaction'.

Fun is something that computerised systems can often be short of. It is also so very subjective. The same concept presented in a different way can lead to ideas of fun or not fun.

An aside...

For example, when I first moved to a PC platform – when I was about three-quarters of the way through this book – I came across the Microsoft Office Assistant which defaults to 'Clippit' – a sort of bendy paperclip. This assistant followed me for a day but annoyed me beyond measure. Sometimes, it appeared to scribble things and make notes; it also tapped on the glass of the VDU to attract my attention. And I wondered what it was writing and whether I needed to know what it was writing. I couldn't work; it appeared to be watching me. Was this stuff it wrote about me being sent off to Bill Gates and Microsoft? Then I found out I could change the appearance of the assistant to 'Power Pup' – a cartoon dog. When Power Pup is 'idle' or 'animated' it wags its tail and makes doggy noises. My two dogs were constant companions as I worked on this book so I am accustomed to 'doggy noises' at home. I found Power Pup comforting and reassuring when I wasn't working at home. I was amused by her antics and enjoyed watching her do things like looking words up in the dictionary as I spell checked or – most usefully – feeding pages through the printer. For me Clippit wasn't fun at all but Power Pup is.

5.3 More on attributes

So far we have looked at the criteria for judging the usability of a product and have suggested metrics which would allow us to determine the usability of our system. However, we now need to examine the nature of the attributes we are assigning these metrics to and to consider just what they may reveal about the system. Learnability and flexibility have already been considered. We shall now go on to look at:

▶ error and error rates;
▶ time taken to perform the task.

5.3.1 Error and error rate

Error and error rate are the classic measures of efficiency. The argument is that if a user can carry out a task without making errors then the system will be faster and more efficient to use since it requires less effort. It has to be remembered that errors have to be corrected and this takes time. But above that, errors can cause frustration and annoyance, leading to more errors and time lost in this sometimes vicious circle.

James Reason provides the following working definition for error:

Error will be taken as a generic term to encompass all those occasions in which a planned sequence of mental or physical activities fails to achieve its intended outcome, and when these failures cannot be attributed to the intervention of some chance agency.

Reason, 1991

An error is the term we give when an action goes wrong. It can be caused by a wrong decision or a physical mishap and it cannot be accounted for by a chance act by something or someone else. For example, if I press the wrong button on my telephone and thereby accidentally terminate a call that is an error but if one of my dogs pulls the lead from the telephone and terminates the call then I would not classify that as an error. Though I may well be less than happy at what she did!

Lewis and Norman in a witty and thought-provoking paper on error suggested that a distinction needed to be made between 'slips' and 'mistakes'. A slip occurs when a user knows how to carry out a task but does something wrong during the task performance. For example, selecting the wrong door-key to your house would be a slip as would taking the wrong turning on a well-known journey.

A mistake is where the user does not understand how a system really works. In other words, the user has a model of the system which does not reflect the true operation of the system. Lewis and Norman differentiate between slips and mistakes by explaining that:

> A person establishes an intention to act. If the intention was not appropriate, this is a mistake. If the action was not was intended, this is a slip.
>
> Lewis and Norman, 1986

In other words, if you intend to put your socks in the washing machine but put them in the fridge instead then this is a slip. But if you thought that putting them in the fridge would get them clean that would be a mistake.

Obviously, in examining error for the purpose of usability metrics we are more interested in mistakes than slips; although it could be that slips occur because of too much similarity between two operations, in which case it would be important to examine the causes. Sometimes slips occur as a direct result of bad design because recalling the correct procedure requires effort or because two actions are very similar.

An aside...

For example, my office PC has its CD-eject button and system power on/off switch in close proximity and, on occasion, I have been known to choose the wrong one... Trying to open the CD drive when I intend to switch off is not too much of a problem but turning the system off when all I want to do is replace 'The Verve' with Shostakovich is a little sadder. Especially as the system tells me I have closed down without going through the proper procedure and then wants to check everything for me! When I purchased a PC for home I made sure those buttons were not close together and were a different shape.

Jordan adds to this classification of error with a scale of severity from minor to catastrophic (Jordan, 1998). He suggests that errors can be scaled thus:

> ► **Minor errors** For Jordan, this is an error that is quickly spotted and can be easily rectified although it may well be irritating. Jordan

points out that although minor errors may have minimal impact in terms of time and irritation, they do have a cumulative effect and that several minor errors can cause considerable loss of time and patience. We need to remember that errors cause annoyance and that users who have been irritated by error are likely to work less well and make further errors.

Minor errors affect efficiency but they do not prevent a task from being completed although they may impact on time factors.

▶ **Major errors** Jordan again defines this error type as one which the user will be able to spot and rectify but the cost in terms of both time and irritation is obviously larger than for minor errors. I suppose my example of overwriting a file I needed is a good example of a major error.

Again, as with minor errors, major errors affect efficiency but they do not prevent a task from being completed.

▶ **Fatal errors** Jordan defines a fatal error as one which prevents the user from completing the task in hand. Obviously, fatal errors affect effectiveness and efficiency since they actually prevent the task from being completed.

▶ **Catastrophic errors** Jordan defines catastrophic errors as those which not only prevent the task from being completed but also cause other knock-on effects. These effects have to be severe. Interestingly, catastrophes quite often start off with quite small errors but the effects snowball and eventually lead to something very severe. A catastrophic error is not one that can be easily rectified. Indeed, it may well change the state of the system to such an extent that recovery is not actually possible in terms of returning to a previous state.

5.3.2 Time

Time is another classic measure and one that is unproblematic. The measurements of how much time a task takes to complete and how much time is spent on error (accessing help and so on) is also used to judge the efficiency of a system.

Time is a measurement from the beginning to the end of whatever action or activity is being observed.

5.4 The aims of usability engineering

All decisions about the usability of the interface should always be made by the usability engineer. These will be conscious and explicit and the usability engineer will know the reasons for them since they will have been made consciously. However, all too often decisions are not made like this and some will be hidden, or unconscious and implicit. Some will be made for reasons that have nothing to do with the usability of the system or the needs of the user; for example, some decisions might be made on the basis of economics or by accident. To avoid the latter it is important that goals are visible, and effective collaboration between members of the design team is supported. In this way, when design decisions are made the design team is in control of them. Decisions are not made by default or unconsciously. The idea of usability engineering is to help make this process of design open and apparent and to have ways of measuring that result against criteria that have been agreed on well in advance. The inclusion of usability engineers on the development team can help to guarantee the visibility of decisions because they will be aware of the user's needs and the problems of developing the system.

5.5 Defining objectives in usability engineering

The aim of the usability approach is to identify exactly what success is and decide how it might be measured. Obviously, this will involve the recognition and adoption of a series of attributes that are measurable and fulfil the needs of the user. These attributes might not be the same for different users working in different environments and on different tasks. It is also likely that even where only one category is changed, the need for attributes might not be the same.

5.6 Usability engineering as a process

To produce an application using the usability engineering approach it is necessary to first produce a *usability specification* (see Table 5.1). This is a statement of usability attributes that will be examined. It states:

- ▶ which set or subset of users it applies to;
- ▶ what the preconditions for measurement are;
- ▶ how the criteria will be measured;
- ▶ what the criteria for representing the attainment is.

Table 5.1 Usability specification

user population: all users
pre-conditions: measurements to be taken after one week of use
attribute: throughput

This specification will then be used as a basis for the evaluation of the application. The process of evaluation, redesign and re-evaluation can then be carried out until the required levels are met or some alternative agreement is reached between the customer and the development team. Incidentally, having a usability specification to drive the development means that it is easy to know when to stop developing. One of the problems of rapid prototyping is that it is hard to know when to stop. Usually, developers decide that there will be a fixed number of iterations. The ideal moment to stop would be when the system was perfect or when the customer was completely satisfied. But judging both of these is incredibly difficult without a usability specification.

5.7 Extensions to the usability specification

Whiteside, Bennett and Holtzblatt (Whiteside *et al*, 1988) have suggested that the usability specification should be expanded in order to specify more detailed performance criteria. These extensions add to the effectiveness of the metrics as a tool. The additions are as follows:

- ▶ **Worst case** This is the worst possible scenario for the system and one that will possibly make it unacceptable to the customer. It is actually useful to have a sense of what the worst-case scenario is before the project begins.
- ▶ **Lowest acceptable level** This is the lowest level of performance that is acceptable by the user.
- ▶ **Planned case** This is the level that the system is expected to achieve.
- ▶ **Best case** This is the best possible scenario; notice it might not be what the system is expected to achieve.
- ▶ **Now level** This is the state of the current system – the system that is to be replaced. This acts as a base level to measure the new system against. Sometimes it can be difficult to decide upon appropriate metrics but the existence of the now level as the base level can help this process since users can decide just how acceptable current levels are. It can be quite difficult to project into the future what you might feel about a new system.

These additions by Whiteside *et al* would seem to be very useful augmentations because they allow the application to be measured against a scale of performance. It might be that this will make the task of evaluating between various systems much easier since real measurements can be put on the attributes and these compared. Also, it is much easier to set levels and make comparisons before development starts if they are specified within a range and this may well solve some of the criticisms levelled at usability engineering. We will look at some of these later in this chapter and again in the final chapter of the book. The temptation is that once a system is developed its level of performance becomes what was expected. If the levels of performance are set down at the outset then there is a clear goal.

Table 5.2 shows an example of this extended specification. These extensions to usability allow some trade-off. It could be that, on reflection, the end-user is willing to tolerate a poorer performance in one category because of a better than expected performance in another category.

Incidentally, getting the levels of the metrics is relatively easy and painless. The now levels can be used to set the worst case and the lowest acceptable levels. Quite often the users will have a clear idea of what they want for an improvement to the system so this can be used for setting lowest acceptable levels. Planned levels and best levels will easily emerge from these.

Table 5.2 Extended usability specification

Usability specification						
user population: all users						
pre-conditions: measurements to be taken after 1 week of use						
		Worst case	Lowest acceptable level	Planned level	Best level	Now level
Attribute:	Measurement:					
throughput	errors for task	5 or more	2	1	0	5
throughput	time taken	10 or more	5 minutes	3 minutes	1 minute	10 minutes

5.8 Checklist for developing a usability specification

To carry out the measurements required by the usability approach, a suitable checklist is required. This might consist of the following:

- ▶ the time taken to complete task;
- ▶ percentage of task completed;
- ▶ percentage of task completed per unit of time;
- ▶ ratio of success to failure;
- ▶ time spent dealing with errors;
- ▶ the frequency of use of on-line help and documentation;
- ▶ the amount of time spent using help and documentation;
- ▶ the percentage of favourable/unfavourable user comments;
- ▶ the number of repetitions or failed commands;
- ▶ the number of good features recalled by user;
- ▶ the number of commands not used.

This checklist would be worked through and then the results could be compared with the expectations which have already been specified in the usability specification.

5.9 How to obtain the usability metrics

The usability specification is drawn up once the customer requirements for the system are known. When the customer and the usability engineer are satisfied that the requirements are the ones that are really needed, and that the usability specification will address those requirements, then both can go towards forming part of the contract which will be binding for both parties. Any subsequent changes have to be agreed by both parties.

The system will be developed using any of the typical user-centred design techniques. For example, perhaps it will be produced using rapid prototyping with user involvement driving the prototypes. However, whatever method is used, the user will be involved in the development and refinements can take place, with agreement!

Once the system is built, or the part of a system is built, then the metrics can be applied and the results analysed to test for conformance with the specification.

Usability engineering requires that the users perform the task or tasks. This performance has to be evaluated and this can be done in a number of ways.

First, the user could perform the task. The evaluation team can then measure the performance in terms of the checklist given above. For example, the evaluation team can measure how much time was taken, how many errors were made or how much help was needed before the task was completed.

Secondly, it is possible to monitor users during evaluation trials, when they are using the system. This allows observation of difficulties encountered and how they are solved. This monitoring can be done in any of the ways suggested in the previous chapter.

Thirdly, the evaluation team can carry out interviews and obtain the necessary material that way. This might be a good way of obtaining information about user satisfaction with the system. A similar approach is to use questionnaires.

Usability metrics are part of the process of evaluation. Perhaps in some ways they are akin to the more rigorous and scientific approach of software testing. They do not replace testing with users. These are measurements to gather information about performance. They do not gather the sort of data about user's preferences and attitudes that might be needed. That has to be done using the methods discussed in the next chapter.

A spanner in the works...
Paul Booth agrees that measuring the acceptability of a system is a wise and just activity. However, he is concerned about how the targets are set and who sets them.

'The usability approach has been characterized as one that begins by analyzing the user's needs and setting usability goals for the intended system (or product). The idea of setting usability goals for products has been well accepted within both academia and industry. Unfortunately, the question of who sets usability goals and how they are set, has received less attention.'

Booth, 1988

I would prefer to talk about usability targets rather than usability goals since the term 'goal' tends to be used when talking about user's actions and tasks. However, the question about who should decide what the target should be, is a sensible one. If you view usability engineering as a process that involves usability engineers from start to finish then the answer is painfully obvious – it has to be the usability engineer in conjunction with the user. The usability engineer understands the user's problems, knows what level of performance is required from the system and can produce these as targets.

When Paul Booth wrote his criticism of usability there was still a lot of software development taking place that was replacing a manual system for the first time. In contrast, I have been amused by the latest edition of Shneiderman's book which, rather than point to design, quite frequently refers to 'redesign' (Shneiderman, 1998). Shneiderman is responding to the fact that a lot of what gets built by software development teams today is a replacement for an old computerised system and the engineers and designers are quite often redesigning rather than designing for the first time around.

I could, therefore, suggest that the problem has gone away and choose to ignore Booth's remarks. But that isn't my belief. We are on the edge of watching computerised systems and software wriggle their way into all sorts of products that a while ago we would not have thought possible. This reminds me of Norman's comment that he was amongst a group of experts who couldn't imagine what the average person would do with a computer in the home. It just wouldn't be useful to them. Norman adds wryly that they had not considered such things as games and the Web (Norman, 1998) – see page 94. Paul Booth's criticism may not be valid now but it was valid then and will probably be valid again in the not too distant future. However, Booth's criticism stems from the idea that the targets will be set *for* the user rather than *by* the user. The usability engineer must agree levels of performance *with* the user before the usability specification is agreed. If the usability engineer sets the targets for system performance without the agreement of the end-user then there can be no guarantee that the system will be what the end-user wants. This would be tantamount to setting up a blind date. Some of them work and some of them don't. Metrics on their own do not produce usable systems. Usability engineering is part of the user-centred design approach.

> **A spanner in the works...**
> Paul Booth goes on to suggest that:
> 'The usability approach suggests how we can measure the usability of a system, but does not say how a system might be changed in order to improve its usability.'
> Booth; 1988, p128

Booth himself replies to this criticism saying that improvements have to come via a design and redesign process and that this is essentially a creative process.

However, supposing the system fails to achieve its performance criteria then quite clearly it is known how the system has failed. For example, perhaps throughput is too slow or the system takes longer to learn than is acceptable. The problem area will be pinpointed by the failure. Usability engineers can then focus on those areas and hopefully affect an improvement.

Also, Booth assumes that the usability evaluation and production of the metrics will be done without having adhered to a user-centred approach; he treats it as an alternative to, or a substitute for, user-centred design. But a usability engineering approach implies user-centred design. User feedback will have been incorporated into the design in the early stages so that all the metrics will do is to confirm, or otherwise, the measurements which allow the usability stamp to go onto the system.

CHAPTER SUMMARY

▶ Usability addresses the practical first and the theoretical second.

▶ Ensuring product usability is not easy but usability engineering seeks to solve the problem of ensuring that the product is what the user really wants – and will actually use – by defining usability through metrics, setting those metrics and then testing to see they have been reached.

▶ Usability engineering also uses user-derived comments in order to drive the development process.

▶ The ISO provides us with a broad and sweeping statement about producing usable products. If a product was efficient, effective and satisfied the user then it is probably likely that it is usable as well.

▶ The three categories for judging software – efficiency, effectiveness and satisfaction – need to be defined in terms of measurable attributes.

▶ A system can be judged to be effective if the task is completed. However, this might be difficult to attest so tasks can be broken down into subtasks. The quality of the output might also need to be measured.

▶ A system can said to be efficient if the user can accomplish the task as quickly as possible and with least effort. Measurements can be taken of time and error rate to confirm this efficiency.

▶ User satisfaction can be measured by turning subjective measures into a percentage of user responses.

▶ The learnability of a system might affect its efficiency and effectiveness so it needs to be included in the usability specification. Learnability also implies re-learnability.

▶ All the decisions regarding an interface should be made by the usability engineer.

▶ The aim of the usability approach is to identify what success is and decide how it might be measured.

▶ To produce an application using the usability engineering approach it is first necessary to produce a usability specification which is a statement of usability attributes that will be examined.

▶ Whiteside, Bennett and Holtzblatt (Whiteside *et al*, 1988) have suggested that the usability specification should be expanded in order to specify performance criteria. These additions should be included in the usability specification as they create a better tool for judging the usability of a system. They also enable comparisons and trade-offs to be made.

▶ The usability specification is drawn up by the usability engineer and the customer once the requirements of the system are known. Usability metrics are part of the process of evaluation. They are not the entire process.

SELF TEST LIST

- attitude
- catastrophic errors
- effectiveness
- efficiency
- error rate
- fatal errors
- flexibility
- knowledge in the world
- knowledge in the head
- LEAF
- learnability
- minor errors
- major errors
- usability attributes
- usability engineer
- usability metrics
- usability specification

EXERCISES

1 Choose a small application, piece of equipment or perhaps a small section of something large. Draw up a suitable usability specification for the system and decide how you can carry out the necessary measurements.

2 How can requirements and usability specifications be used together to confirm the importance of each?

3 Make a list of examples of when performance levels would be critical to the acceptability of a system.

4 What problems do you think there might be in specifying time-frames for a product? How can these problems be overcome?

5 What sort of activities might you build into a system to make it enjoyable? How would you measure enjoyment?

REFERENCES

ACM SIGCHI (1992) *Curricula for Human-Computer Interaction*. ACM Press, New York.

BCS HCI (1995) BCS Model Syllabus 'Challenging Computing Curricula'. *Interface,* no. 28.

Booth, Paul (1988) *An Introduction to Human Computer Interaction*. LEA, Hove.

Card S, Moran T and Newell A (1983) *The Psychology of Human Computer Interaction*. LEA, Hillsdale, New Jersey.

Carroll J M and Mazur S A (1986) 'Lisa Learning'. *IEEE Computer,* 19(10), November 1986, pp. 35–49.

Culwin F (1998) Private communication with the author.

Draper S W (1993) 'The notion of Task in HCI' in Ashland S, Henderson A, Holland E and White T (eds) *Adjunct Proceedings of INTERCHI '93.*

Faulkner C and Culwin F (1999) 'Integration of Usability Issues within Initial Software Development Education' in *Proceedings of the Thirtieth SIGCSE Technical Symposium on Computer Science Education*, March 1999.

Hix D and Hartson R (1993) *Developing User Interfaces*. John Wiley, New York.

Jordan P (1998) *An Introduction to Usability*. Taylor and Francis, London.

Lewis C and Norman N (1986) 'Designing for Error' in Norman D and Draper S (1986) *User Centred System Design*. LEA, Hillsdale, New Jersey.

Norman D (1988) *The Psychology of Everyday Things*. Basic Books, New York.

Norman D (1998) *The Invisible Computer*. MIT Press, Cambridge, Massachusetts.

Reason J (1991) *Human Error*. Cambridge University Press, Cambridge.

Shackel B (1986) 'Ergonomics in Design for Usability' in Harrison M D and Monk A F (eds) *People and Computers: Designing for Usability*, Proceedings of the Second Conference of the BCS HCI Specialist Group, September 1986.

Shneiderman B (1998) *Designing the User Interface*, 3rd edition. Addison Wesley, Reading, Massachusetts.

Whiteside, Bennett and Holtzblatt (1988) 'Usability Engineering: our experience and evolution' in *Handbook of Human-Computer Interaction*. North-Holland, Amsterdam.

FURTHER READING

Hix D and Hartson R (1993) *Developing User Interfaces.* John Wiley, New York.

> If you don't intend to read much more than one book on developing effective systems then this is the one to read. It really is about engineering. It's a pity that the title doesn't make that clear. It's a super book, great fun and very easy to read. It is also meticulous. It's getting a tad ancient so let's hope they go to a second edition soon…

Jordan P (1998) *An Introduction to Usability*. Taylor and Francis, London.

> A short, easy to read introduction with the emphasis away from software. The earlier collection of essays edited by Jordan is excellent too and fascinating.

Whiteside, Bennett and Holtzblatt (1988) 'Usability Engineering: our experience and evolution' in *Handbook of Human-Computer Interaction*. North-Holland, Amsterdam.

> This has to be read because it was ground-breaking stuff.

Usability evaluation

CHAPTER OVERVIEW

This chapter:

▶ looks at methods of evaluating systems during the design process – prior and during building and after the system has been completed;

▶ examines the idea of summative and formative evaluation and looks at suitable methods for each of the stages of development;

▶ examines the ideas of empirical and analytical evaluation methods;

▶ looks at ways in which the user can be involved in the design and usability engineers can build processes in an effective and active way.

6.1   Evaluating systems

The usability metrics discussed in the previous chapter still require methods of gaining details of the measurements and many of the techniques available for data collection can be used for other evaluative purposes as well. For some of the data gathering the system itself can be used to log interactions between it and the user.

However, despite carrying out the measurements and testing these against the usability specification it will still be necessary to carry out other forms of user evaluation. Metrics are useful for testing system performance; the information thus gained tends to be quantitative. However, in order to evaluate a system thoroughly it is necessary to gain qualitative information as well. Producing a good human computer system is not just about ensuring that both the computer and the human perform as efficiently as possible; in order to be usable it has to conform to ISO standards for user satisfaction.

Hewitt in a useful and thorough paper on evaluation points out that evaluation will inevitably set the direction for design and redesign. Therefore, it is very important that there is a clear set of project goals for the system to achieve or, as he believes, the system can get lost in its own development process (Hewitt, 1986). What he means by this that it is easy to forget what the aims of the system really were when faced with the results of an evaluation. Solving the problems raised by evaluation can mean that the project goal becomes overlooked. Hewitt goes on to say that, like system design, evaluation is iterative and should take place as each design stage occurs. Just as the system will change with each evaluation–design cycle so too will the nature of the evaluation change. It is important to note this and it cannot be stressed too highly. Different types of evaluation are valid and useful at different points during the development.

6.2   Formative and summative evaluation

Hewitt suggests that it is essential to recognise two types of evaluation: formative and summative (Hewitt, 1986).

6.2.1   Formative evaluation

The purpose of formative evaluation is to help the design process. It is used to refine and to formulate the design. It will involve working closely with users and gathering feedback about their opinions of the system. Obviously, the nature of these opinions will depend on what development method is being used. The opinions offered about a prototype might be of a different nature from the opinions offered about a paper-based system or a storyboard. This form of evaluation should start at a very early stage since changes are cheaper the sooner they are taken onboard. Also, users need to be involved in the design process as soon as possible.

The type of evaluative method used for formative evaluation will concentrate on qualitative information about the system. That is, the evaluation method will elicit opinions about how users feel about the system; what problems they are experiencing; any changes they feel might be needed; what the strengths of the system are and so on. Quite clearly, this type of qualitative data will need to be collected in quite a different way from how quantitative data might be collected.

6.2.2   Summative evaluation

Summative evaluation, on the other hand, is much more likely to require quantitative data. Hewitt describes the purpose of summative evaluation as being about:

> …assessing the impact, usability and effectiveness of the system – the overall performance of user and system.
>
> Hewitt, 1986

This is the sort of data that we were keen to collect in the previous chapter when we looked at usability metrics. Summative evaluation is therefore more useful when the design is complete. A complete design might consist of a completed section of the system; it might not be the entire system.

Formative evaluation will therefore drive the design–evaluate–redesign cycle. It will produce the sort of information that designers need to know about the way in which users are interacting with the system. It will provide designers with information about misunderstandings, errors and difficulties in operating the system. But summative evaluation will give a measurement of what the improvements in performance of the system actually are. It is not possible to ignore one form of evaluation in favour of another. It would be like driving a car with only forward or reverse gear – but not both! Hewitt sums this up rather nicely:

> These two types of evaluation have very different goals, and different stages in the design process require different types of evaluation, or they require mixes of the two in different proportions.
>
> Hewitt, 1986

6.3 Analytical and empirical evaluation

Basically, there are two quite different approaches that can be adopted in the evaluation of a system. However, it is also possible to combine the two techniques and this is probably a more sensible approach because each method can yield different findings. The first method is the analytical evaluation method and consists of a formal pencil-and-paper evaluation of tasks and goal – for example, the GOMS methodology suggested by Card, Moran and Newell (Card *et al*, 1983). These analytical methods can be applied to the system by a usability engineer. They might consist of using a model in order to work out how complex a system is, how long a task might take to perform or how many ways there are to perform a different task. Some methods of evaluation conducted by experts will be examined in the next chapter.

The second method is the empirical method and consists of an analysis of user performance in relation to the proposed system. It might consist of tasks to be performed with the system, observation, questionnaires or experiments and interviews. Empirical methods involve working with users and gathering data that will have to be analysed.

Sometimes analytical methods work well and can be used to compare two designs prior to developing a more costly prototype. Analytical methods can also be used in evaluating systems after they are complete. Empirical methods can be costly both in terms of money and time so it is important to be quite clear about what the aim of the evaluation is.

6.4   How to carry out evaluations

Any evaluation method will have a basic structure and requirements:

- ▶ identifying the target group;
- ▶ recruiting users;
- ▶ establishing the task;
- ▶ carrying out the evaluation;
- ▶ reporting on the findings.

Identifying the target group

The target group may be obvious because it may well be the same as that identified during the process of requirements gathering and specification. However, some designs may require targeting different types of user at different points so it is advisable to check that the correct target group has indeed been identified.

Recruiting users

Recruiting users is frequently time-consuming. If the system is being developed in-house or for a specific customer then the task is easier but it is important to allow sufficient time. It is not simply that a number of users have to be recruited to carry out the task; it will also be necessary to ensure that they are the appropriate user-type with the necessary range of skills. It is always better to recruit more users than seem to be necessary so that if there is a problem a reserve user can be called upon to step in. It is wise to try to avoid using users who have already been involved in aspects of the design process. Sometimes, this just might not be possible.

Some evaluation methods have recommendations for the numbers of user that are necessary. Bruce Tognazinni suggests that three users can give the designer a good idea of what users in general might think about the system (Tognazinni, 1993). Redmond-Pyle and Moore suggest that 'after three there are diminishing returns from testing with additional participants' (Redmond-Pyle and Moore, 1995). Monk *et al* suggest five users for cooperative evaluation (Monk, 1993). Some problems and some evaluation methods are more demanding of subject numbers than others.

Redmond-Pyle and Moore suggest administering a questionnaire to possible evaluation subjects so that it is possible to identify specific people to use in the evaluation. The questionnaire can also be used to produce information about usability problems (Redmond-Pyle and Moore, 1995).

Establishing the task

Most evaluation methods will very likely involve some form of task. In the early stages of evaluation it is better for this to be very specific and concentrated rather than broad-based. The task will need to be worked out as appropriate and a task list produced for the user. This task list will need to be tested before it is used in a proper evaluation. A task list that appears to be clear to the writer may not be clear to the reader!

The form the task list takes will depend on what the usability engineer hopes to establish from the evaluation.

At the same time as establishing the form of the task and the nature of the instructions to be given to the user, it is also necessary to decide how much, if any, instruction is to be given to the user prior to attempting the task. This will need to be specified as part of the session protocol.

Preparing for the evaluation

Before the evaluation can be conducted, further preparation needs to be carried out. The users will need to be introduced to the system and it has to be decided just what will be said to them. It is best that this information is written down so that all eventualities are covered. The prototype or the completed system itself will need to be prepared and arranged in an appropriate area for the evaluation. The usability engineer will need to ensure that a suitable method for recording the evaluation has been considered and is ready. This might mean installing and testing video cameras or tape recorders. A dry run is always a sensible precaution as machinery and evaluation procedures can fail.

It will also be necessary to ensure that any documents for recording information are ready and have been tested. These might include a questionnaire for the subjects to fill in. It may also include instructions for conducting the evaluation exercise if more than one person is involved in this. Figure 6.1 shows a document we used in the Brewsers project in order to ensure that all of our evaluators did exactly the same thing. Figure 6.2 shows guidelines issued to the evaluators and Figure 6.3 describes the logging procedure we adopted. Even for a small-scale evaluation exercise the documentation can be quite extensive.

Figure 6.1 Instructions to the evaluators

INSTRUCTIONS FOR EVALUATOR

1. Before the start of the investigation, ensure everything is in full working order. This must include:

   - a properly working keyboard, computer, monitor etc;
   - a properly functioning browser;
   - home page displaying;
   - links are correct and functional;
   - log file is ready to be used, follow the 'LOGGING Procedure';
   - task sheet, observation sheet and questionnaire ready;
   - blank copy of Agreement.

2. Introduce the user to the computer. Ensure that the user is fully comfortable with the seating, the positioning of keyboard and mouse, monitor brightness etc.

3. Once the user is comfortable, and not before, ensure that they are aware of the purpose of the investigation, along with the task they are to do.

---

4. Once this is understood, the user will be asked to sign an agreement stating what is to be expected of them, plus a statement that the user can terminate the investigation at any time.

5. After all previous conditions have been satisfied, the investigation may begin. The user is not to be prompted from this stage onwards.

6. During the investigation, notes should be taken on the physical actions of the user. Check for signs of frustration or boredom, for example the drumming of fingers or yawning, and time when this happens (this could be checked against the log book).

7. When the user has completed the investigation, they must be thanked for their time and effort. The user should be made aware that the results obtained from them are to be made available on request.

8. Once the user has left the room, the logging process must be stopped. To do this, follow the LOGGING PROCEDURE as highlighted below. Once this has been stopped (through checking), record the time when the logging was stopped.

Figure 6.2 Evaluator guidelines

EVALUATOR BEHAVIOURAL GUIDELINES

1. A friendly approach to the user should be adopted at all times. However, care must be taken not to become 'over-friendly' – a degree of formality must be maintained. Refer to the user by their first name, or any other preferred name given by them.

2. The Evaluator must be open and 'honest' within reason. No question should be ignored, and the Evaluator should treat the user with respect at all times.

3. The Evaluator should avoid making the user feel uncomfortable in any way whatsoever.

4. If the user wishes to terminate the investigation, at any time, or for whatever reason, the Evaluator must not prevent this. The Evaluator should not 'force' the user to remain in the investigation if the user does not wish to continue.

5. During the investigation, the Evaluator must resist all temptations to distract the user. This will include, but not limited to, unnecessary or unavoidable noise, physical distraction, movement or excessive 'fidgeting', consuming food or drink.

6. The Evaluator must keep the order of events (as defined in the INSTRUCTIONS FOR EVALUATOR section) the same for each user – a divergence will ensure inconsistent results.

7. The Evaluator should make clear to the user exactly what the task is to be performed. This will prevent the user from forming 'incorrect' conceptualisations about the task in hand.

Figure 6.3 Logging instructions

LOGGING PROCEDURE

While the subject is carrying out the investigation, the system will record the following actions in the log file:

- Page Request;
- Cancel Request;
- Home Request;
- Page Served.

For each subject the logging must be initiated by pressing a set of specified buttons before the subject starts. The logging must be stopped after the subject leaves the room by pressing the same set of buttons.

Note: The log file does not have to be opened, cleared, saved, etc., for each subject.

To make the logging process active or idle press the same combination of buttons:
<**ALT**> + **L** in the brewser (**note**: The HOME button should be in focus to function).

(IN ORDER TO ENSURE that the logging process is active (system is ready to record subject's actions) the title bar in the brewser will display a capital letter 'B'. Therefore, the title bar will display 'Brewser'.)

To stop the logging make sure the log file is initiated and terminated without the subject being aware of it. For each subject record the time when the log was initiated and stopped on the questionnaire sheet corresponding to that subject.

Once the evaluation is complete it is necessary to debrief the subject. Material for the debriefing will need to be prepared. This might include a questionnaire. It will certainly include answering any of the subjects' questions.

Carrying out the evaluation

The users should be welcomed into the evaluation area and made to feel comfortable. It is important to ensure that they know exactly what will happen and what is expected of them. The evaluator must ensure that the user knows that it is the system and not them that is being tested. It is also important to stress that whatever happens is useful for gaining insights into how the system works. The user must not be made to feel responsible or inadequate if things go wrong. It is also necessary to explain what will happen with any recordings, questionnaires or other evaluation material.

Figure 6.4 shows an agreement we used in the recent Brewsers project at the School of Computing, South Bank University.

Figure 6.4 Agreement with the user

AGREEMENT

I agree to the conditions set out below, concerning the evaluation:

- I am physically comfortable with the use of this computer and its related facilities.
- I am aware of the task expected of me, and find the instructions acceptable.
- I can quit the evaluation at any time.
- I am satisfied with the conduct of the Evaluator.

Signed:

_____ user's signature   _____ date

_____ evaluator's signature _____ date

Once the user is comfortable and knows what to expect and that they can quit the evaluation at any point, then the task list can be presented and the evaluation can commence.

When the user has finished the evaluation there should be a debriefing when questions can be asked of the user. The user should also be encouraged to ask questions of the evaluator and should be thanked for helping. The user should be told that findings will be made available on request.

Reporting on the findings

At this stage any problems encountered during the evaluations should be listed so that they can be examined for possible causes and solutions.

Not all problems have solutions. Some problems may be ignored because of other factors but each problem should be considered and possible causes examined and solutions sought.

6.4.1 Code of conduct

Anyone involved in evaluating a system has to remember that they are working with people, not objects, and will need to take care that they do not do anything that might cause the subjects harm either emotionally, physically or psychologically. Experiments have to be thought out with care and the team needs to make sure that there are no adverse effects upon the subjects.

Many organisations have a code of conduct and recommendations for carrying out work with subjects. However, the following list should provide a suitable starting point if no existing guidelines are available – although this is becoming increasing unlikely:

▶ Explain to the subject what is expected.

▶ Explain that the subject is free to leave or quit the experiment at any time.

▶ Explain what the purpose of the experiment is.

▶ Make sure the subject understands that the system is being tested and not them.

▶ Make sure that the subject is comfortable.

▶ Explain that the results are confidential and how they will be used.

▶ Where possible get the subject to agree, in writing, to the guidelines you have set.

▶ Never at any time do anything to embarrass, hurt or otherwise distress the subject.

6.5 Experiments

Experimental method is part of the armoury of HCI. It is perhaps one of the methods that is most problematic in that there is much argument about how, when and why it ought to be used in evaluating systems. The problem may stem from the fact that HCI has inherited (from psychology in particular) a leaning towards scientific experimental method. On the face of it, this would seem quite simple but the mere terminology gives us plenty of problems.

To start with, it is far from easy to reach a conclusion about what scientists really mean by 'scientific method'. Although scientists quite clearly know what they are doing when they go about the task of 'doing science' the adherence to a set procedure does not appear to happen (Wolpert, 1993; Shermer, 1997). Shermer suggests that although, quite clearly, scientists don't go through a set of clear-cut stages which progress from one to another, scientific theory can be described by the following (Shermer, 1997):

▶ **Induction** – forming a hypothesis. This hypothesis emerges from general observations made and conclusions drawn from existing data.

▶ **Deduction** – consists of making very specific predictions that are based on the hypothesis.

▶ **Observation** – working from the hypothesis, data is gathered which should confirm the hypothesis and allow accurate predictions to be made.

▶ **Verification** – this consists of testing the predictions against further observations. The original hypothesis will then be confirmed or disproved.

Experimentation can therefore be used for the processes of observation and verification.

There are two basic approaches to experimentation on the users of a new system:

1   Test the new system's performance in relation to an existing system – this is known as a *comparative experiment*.
2   Test the new system in isolation – this would be an example of an *absolute experiment*.

Comparative experimentation is useful when there are two or more designs or approaches and they need to be evaluated prior to building.

Techniques for the design of the interface can vary from the formal to the informal. The more formal methods, and experiments fall into this category, tend to be expensive because they require controlled environments and skilled personnel to administer them. The more informal methods tend to be cheaper. Because experimentation is expensive it is important to ensure that the purpose of the exercise is clearly understood and the experiment has been properly thought out and designed.

6.5.1   Experimental method

HCI uses experimental method as a means of attempting to verify its theories. This means that a cause and effect relationship has to be established through experimentation. In order to be able to say that the theory can be supported, the following processes have to be adhered to:

▸   The problem must be identified and a hypothetical cause and effect relationship among variables must be formulated.
▸   The experiment must be designed and executed.
▸   The data from the experiment must be examined.
▸   The results of the experiment must be communicated.

Before the experiment can be carried out the research question or hypothesis has to be formulated. Michael Shermer describes the emergence of scientific fact on the basis of three generalisations – hypothesis, theory and fact (Shermer, 1997). For him, the hypothesis is seen as a testable statement that will account for a given set of observations. From this will emerge a theory that is a well-supported and tested hypothesis. Finally, fact is a conclusion that is confirmed to such a degree that it would be reasonable to agree provisionally that this is so. Notice the use of the word 'provisionally'. A fact is only a fact for as long as it appears to be the 'right' explanation and interpretation! Charles Dickens' Gradgrind and his cry 'What we wants is facts!' has no real meaning in the scientific community for whom facts may have to change as knowledge about the world changes. Feynman puts this rather nicely: 'All scientific knowledge is uncertain.' (Feynman, 1998). Although I don't want to open a can of worms here and start wondering about the nature of facts, and therefore reality, it is probably politic to remember that many so-called facts depend on the point of view of the person viewing them. Steven Rose, a biologist who has spent his life studying memory, has a nice story to tell about that and I shall offer it up here as an appropriate spanner.

A spanner in the works…

Rose describes how he suggested to Rupert Sheldrake that they carried out a joint experiment to test Sheldrake's idea that memories are present in a universal 'ether'. This means that once something novel has happened somewhere it makes it easier for it to happen again somewhere else. Rose and Sheldrake agreed on the design of the experiment and made two rival predictions about outcome. Rose predicted that the behaviour of subsequent hatches of chicks would be no different after a novel experience by a previous hatch of chicks. Sheldrake predicted that later hatches would acquire a memory of the experience of the earlier hatches by 'morphic resonance'. They ran the experiment. Rose says: 'I was proved right… Sheldrake, however, was able to convince himself that, viewed in a particular way, the data supported his hypothesis of morphic resonance. We couldn't agree on how to write the joint paper, and instead published two alternative accounts side by side. This just goes to show how little facts 'speak for themselves'. We all cling tenaciously to our views of the world; rather than accept an interpretation which destroys our paradigm…'

Rose; 1997, p49

Rose is not alone in this type of observation.

The research question or hypothesis will direct the research and experimentation so it needs to be chosen with care. The experiment will be designed on the basis of the hypothesis formation and the independent and dependent variables will emerge from this. The dependent variable is the behaviour that is being observed and the independent variable is the factor that is being manipulated. At the same time, the target group will be identified. The appropriate target group often becomes apparent once the hypothesis has been formulated. In fact, if it doesn't that could well imply a problem with the hypothesis. Formulating a hypothesis is not easy. Indeed, it is probably the hardest part for most people (Pirsig, 1974).

6.5.2   Hypothesis formation

The experiment is considered the most rigorous method of testing a hypothesis. It involves the researcher testing out ideas in a controlled environment and setting the conditions to cause particular effects to happen.

The object of experimental methods is to show that only one factor can account for an observed effect. This means that all other factors have to be discounted by careful control of the experiment and all extraneous factors must be excluded. Suppose we want to test the effect of colour on user performance. The first task will be to develop a suitable hypothesis. For example:

> The choice of background and text colour will affect the user's ability to check a document.

In this example the important factor that has been isolated is background and text colour. This is what will affect the user's ability to perform with the system. This is known as the *independent variable*; in the United States, this is quite often referred to as the *test*. The independent variable can be manipulated by the experimenter. The hypothesis suggests that the independent variable – in this case colour – will affect the user's behaviour. Here, the behaviour is the user's performance in checking a document – this is the dependent variable. During the process of experimentation, the dependent variable is measured to see if it is influenced by the independent variable. The extent of this influence will possibly be measured. If the behaviour of the user is shown to be significantly affected by the independent variable then the hypothesis is proved and the theory is strengthened. However, it is necessary to emphasise that in this case there will need to be a significant difference in the user's ability to check the document for the hypothesis to be proved true and the theory strengthened. This significant difference would have to be shown to exist through the use of statistics. Obviously, there is insufficient space in a book of this nature to go into details about statistical method. However, there are many excellent books dealing with statistics and experiments such as we might want to carry out in HCI. There are also software packages that can help with the process. Scientists use pre-prepared tables for examining probabilities and statistical significance. They would not usually work out the results from scratch.

At the same time the null hypothesis is formed. At the simplest level this can be simply a statement that the independent variable will not affect the dependent variable. For example, the null hypothesis for the experiment we are looking at would be:

> The choice of background and text colour will not affect the user's ability to check a document.

6.5.3   Problems and solutions

One of the biggest problems in designing experiments is to ensure that all extraneous factors are ruled out or prevented from influencing the results. The experiment must prove that the independent variable is responsible for the observed behaviour and nothing else can account for it. One of the ways to ensure that the dependent variable is responsible for any effect upon behaviour is by using control groups. This method uses two groups of subjects; the first group is exposed to the independent variable and the second is not. Hopefully, this means that it can be deduced how users would have performed if they were not subjected to the independent variable at all. Performance can be compared with that of the group subjected to the independent variable. Providing that no other influences came into play, the only difference between the groups would be the independent variable. The control group is the group that is used to make the comparison and the experimental group is the group that experiences the independent variable.

In medicine this type of experiment is quite common in field trials where, for example, a new drug or treatment is tested. The drug will be assigned to a group of experimental patients and a placebo prescribed to the control group. Usually, the people carrying out the trials do not themselves know who is prescribed what since they might affect the outcome of the trial – simply by their attitudes. Once the trial is over, the assignment of the drug can be looked at and compared with the assignment of the placebo. In this way, possible confounding factors are avoided.

However, it is not always possible or desirable to design experiments which take this format.

It is also possible that other problems with the design of the experiment can still exist. It could be, for example, that one group of people has accidentally been chosen in such a way that they are, for some reason, already better at doing the tasks set. The evaluation team has to make sure that the groups are the same so far as their composition is concerned. This can be done by attempting to ensure that the groups are the same. This process is known as *matching* and it can give rise to several problems! It means that particular attributes have to be identified and must be present in both groups. For example, it might be necessary to ensure that both groups cover particular numbers of men and women, age groups and occupations. If the groups are not matched and the experimental group performs better it would be difficult to say what had caused that better performance. Problems like this are called *confounding variables* because they are things that can upset the findings.

Matching is not an easy process; the correct attributes have to be identified and people with matching attributes then have to be found. It can lead to some desperate searches; it might mean that the researcher has to find a 27 year-old dog-owning vegetarian artist who can play the flute and is colour blind. This can be time-consuming and expensive.

For this reason it might not be possible or desirable to have two groups and the evaluation team may decide that they want to control the variables in some other way. For example, they might decide to give each user a period of time with the system when they were not given feedback and then give them some time when they were. The results from each experiment could then be compared. In this case the performance of each individual with feedback will be compared with their performance without feedback and it could be assumed that individual differences had been controlled. This type of experimental design is called *related measures design* whereas when different people undergo each condition of the independent variable this is called *independent measures design*.

There are still some remaining problems, however. Sometimes performance can be affected by the order in which things are presented to the subjects. This is called the *order effect*. For example, if learnability was being tested then it could be that one task seemed to be easier to learn than another simply because it was tackled second.

The effect of practice, the *practice effect*, must also be ruled out. This is a problem that occurs in many different psychological tests and has been evident in memory experiments. The subject simply gets better at the task as the task is repeated. On the other hand, it is possible that subjects may become tired and do worse as the experiment progresses. This is known as the *fatigue effect*. All of these order effects can be controlled by counterbalancing. This is a technique by which one half of the subjects do one condition of the independent variable first and the other do the other condition of the independent variable first. The final results from the experiment will show the whole scores obtained from doing both tasks. This means that any effects should have been cancelled out since they will have affected the two conditions of the independent variable equally.

The whole purpose of experimental design is to control as many aspects of the process as possible. In the example examined here the evaluation team has to ensure that nothing other than the independent variable is affecting the user's performance. This means ruling out any environmental factors that might possibly influence the result. For example, if the room in which the experiment was carried out on one group was noisy this might affect the final results.

Modern experimental method probably owes a good deal to the work of Karl Popper. Although there is currently – and has been for some while – a debate amongst the scientific community about the usefulness of the Popper teachings, it is probably just as well to look at them here. Initially, I had hoped to steer clear of what I suspect might be yet another can of worms for the reader but I have resigned myself to the fact that like Macbeth we are so far steeped in blood that to turn back is as tedious as to plough on. So, I have another of Pandora's boxes to open.

Karl Popper formed the idea that hypothesis could not be proved. That really, the aim for science was to disprove rather than prove. His idea was that no matter how many incidents were found to support a hypothesis this didn't really prove its truth since the emergence of just one exception would disprove the hypothesis. The equivalent in HCI testing is probably the 'trying to break it' method that used to be popular in testing games. In *Lifelines* Rose argues that science, scientific thought and knowledge is all a product of its time and its society. Some developments depend on order. One cannot be developed before the emergence of something it rests on. In Popper's case, this is strikingly true. He was very much a child of his time. He was responding to a real problem that existed and had to be dealt with and his consequent assertion that scientific knowledge should proceed through falsification is a nice example of a response to a need.

Modern science does use falsification as a means of establishing theory but it would be wrong of me to assert that this is the only method used by science. Sometimes it is impossible to proceed using falsification and other methods have to be used.

6.5.4 More fundamental problems and criticisms

In attempting to emulate the 'hard' sciences, psychology and thus the psychological elements of HCI have attempted to use experimental method. But there are a number of problems with hypothesis formation and testing in the context of the social sciences. Lewis Wolpert expresses these doubts and problems rather succinctly.

> Hypotheses can be framed and tested as well as possible. But the problem lies in 'as well as possible': the peculiarity of the social sciences is the complexity of the subject-matter, and so the difficulty of disentangling causal relationships is immense. There is little possibility, for example, of doing experiments equivalent to those in physics, say, in which it is characteristic to try to vary just one variable at a time, keeping others constant, and so observe its effect on the system.
>
> Wolpert; 1993, p125

One problem with experimental method as applied to the social sciences is that somewhat dubious hypotheses are formed, and then treated as if they have the same weight as hypotheses formed for the hard sciences. For example, stating that the temperature at which ice melts is 0 degrees Celsius might be easy enough to prove or disprove and to replicate. But in the social sciences this is rather more difficult. All too often, in HCI, hypothesis are formed which make statements like:

Users prefer to use A rather than B.

On the surface of it, this might be a fair concept to test. It might appear as if it can be tested and it would even be useful to do so. Showing that A is used more than B surely proves preference? Alas, a moment's thought will show some of the problems. Using A rather than B – even if it *indicates* preference – does not *show* that A is *the* answer and that all we need to do is substitute A for B and we will have happy users. How many tests do we do? What are the alternatives to A and B? Does it always hold true? What do we mean by 'preference'? How much leaning towards A rather than B indicates 'preference'? Such hypotheses try to align themselves with the rigours of scientific method as if there is some sort of final measure that can be made over what is really subjective and rather dubious material. Although we do have methods for converting these very subjective measures into more objective indicators, at the end of the day they aren't in the same league as experimental methods applied within the hard sciences. I have no objections to the testing of such ideas. I do have objections to the use of 'experiment' to describe them and the waving of the ideas of 'scientific method' as a justification for them. Again, Feynman has a wry remark to make about the way in which psychology is all too often forced to work:

> And it's a general principle of psychologists that in these tests they arrange so that the odds that the things that happen by chance is small, in fact, less than one in twenty. That means that one in twenty of their laws is probably wrong.
>
> Feynman, 1998

In areas like physics and chemistry the kind of controls that are necessary to change one variable at a time are relatively easy. Steven Rose sometimes abandons the label 'hard science' for physics and replaces it with 'simple'. By this, Rose means that physics more easily lends itself to reductionism – reducing large questions to scaled-down smaller versions. Even in biology, Rose has severe doubts about how efficacious reductionism might be. Indeed, he questions his own use of the method. He suggests that the 'simple' sciences don't have this problem – that, possibly, they can be reduced to simplistic experimental methods; however, there is no guarantee that, in the more complex sciences, the theories which emerge from experimental method will scale up. In fact, even physicists whom Rose sees as facing fewer problems experience difficulties over reductionism. Again, it is a case of finding the right approach for the task in hand. Some things seem to reduce to levels that are manageable while other questions do not.

The problem of scaling up isn't the only one we have to grasp in applying reductionism and experimental method to user psychology. As we have seen, in HCI it is possible that extraneous factors will creep in without our realising that this has happened, or without our ability to control them. But the problems associated with hypothesis formation and the design of the experiment are not the only difficulties.

> **A spanner in the works...**
> Psychological experiments have come under criticism. The main problem appears to be that people taking part in experiments do not always act in the same way as they would if performing the task for themselves in real life. Several writers in the field of HCI and psychology have made quite forceful attacks on the aptness and validity of experiments. Draper (1993) in his paper on task mentioned in Chapter 3 of this book points to the idea that 'people will do far more for an experimenter than they would in other situations'.

Experimentation, therefore, has its disadvantages. The most obvious problem is that the laboratory is not the real world and no matter how carefully experimenters set up the environment and the task, they cannot capture the real world. Simply by selecting the task for the user to do, they are already constraining the subject's activity. The very nature of experimentation tends to force the experimenter into scaling down. In the case of HCI it is often the case that the task has to be small and contained and is often chosen by the experimenter. The subject concentrates on this small, selected task and nothing else. In the real world this is unlikely to occur and people are much more likely to multitask. However, multitasking would be very difficult for experimenters to observe.

However, scale is not the only problem. It is also impossible to control all variables that might affect behaviour (Wolpert, 1993). As Draper has pointed out, subjects may well do more in an experimental situation than they would do if it were real life (Draper, 1993). They have a sense of helping out in an experiment and they may well have quite different motivation from what they would have in real life. The mere fact that I have to make this distinction between the experimental situation and what I am referring to as 'real life' probably indicates the nature of the problem. But it is not simply the case that subjects may well do more in an experiment than they would normally; the converse probably applies too. For example, studies of vigilance or sustained attention – where someone monitors activity for long periods of time – have shown that people engaged in vigilance perform much better in a real situation than they do in the experimental one (Sanders and McCormick, 1992). The reasons for this are not really understood and although it is tempting to surmise I shall resist and leave the reader to do that!

Finally, one criticism quite often aimed at experiments is that they can all too often miss what people have to say about the task they are performing. Experiments do not, by their very nature, automatically gather opinions from subjects. The mere use of the term 'subject' to describe the participants in the study should offer an indication as to how far removed all this is from the real world.

There is another point too that it is easy to overlook. Some of the experiments set up by social scientists may seem to have little connection with reality. Subjects are asked to do tasks that they wouldn't really do in the course of everyday life. Draper in the same paper (Draper, 1993) suggests that this is because the real task is 'doing an experiment' and there are plenty of jokes about on the theme that psychology is the study of the behaviour of psychology students since they figure somewhat hugely in psychology 'experiments'. Don Norman has an amusing anecdote on just the theme of students 'doing an experiment':

> **A spanner in the works…**
> Don Norman once carried out a series of experiments on students who were asked to listen to lists of digits and then presented with a single digit and asked which digit followed. He noticed that one student was writing the list down and then providing the correct answer from the list. I shall let him tell the rest of the story:

'I was so upset that I immediately ordered her out of the room and out of my experiment: She was cheating! She was upset that I was upset: She was getting them all correct – I should have been pleased, she said, not upset.

Today I tend to agree with the student. After all, I had asked her to do a meaningless task, so she had adopted the sensible, intelligent response, Who but an experimental psychologist would expect anyone to remember anything as silly as unrelated digits without the aid of paper and pencil? Better yet, why would anyone ever have to remember such sorts of things without writing them down?'

Norman; 1993, p77

It is important to remember that isolating a task changes things. People in the real world do not have to act in the way in which we may ask them to perform for our studies and experiments. If we are lucky, they won't do our artificial tasks and will act naturally, as in the case of Norman's student, but in designing experiments we shouldn't bank on common sense prevailing it is all too easy to be overawed by the experimenter.

In order to redress these problems some researchers attempt to carry out experiments in the subject's real environment. But obviously, it is not always possible to carry out evaluations in this way. Some HCI researchers believe that ethnography provides a more suitable way of approaching the problems of how to gain information about people using systems.

Perhaps the almost final word on the subject needs to be left to Lewis Wolpert:

It can be argued that human behaviour and thought will never yield to the sort of explanations that are so successful in the physical and biological sciences. To try to reduce consciousness to physics or molecular biology, for example, is, it is claimed, simply impossible. This claim is without foundation, for we just do not know what we do not know and hence what the future will bring.

Wolpert; 1993, p135

Just because the methods we have at our disposal are problematic and perhaps flawed does not mean to say that the method cannot work for some things or that eventually this particular method will not yield for HCI what it does for the sciences. Or, as Luis Villazon has so wittily put it:

If one of the rooms in your house has a patch of damp on the wallpaper, do you brick up the doorway and resign yourself to living in a smaller house? No, you do not.

Villazon, 1998

A spanner in the works...

Landauer has this to say about some of the more 'scientific' inputs to the HCI effort:

'It is tempting to think that cognitive psychology, human factors and human engineering principles, and the newly emerging field of cognitive science might provide theory and fact to steer this effort. They can, but only to a modest extent. Psychological science has provided some real advances in understanding human behavior but only in limited domains, usually attached to narrow problems that have been brought to the laboratory.'

Landauer; 1993, p295

Experimental method does work for some aspects of testing the system. We need to accept there are problems and flaws and choose the best option for the particular aspect we are looking at. The task of the usability engineer is to do just that. Where there are clear-cut choices and the task is not too complex then an experiment can be useful. For example, at HCI '98, the annual United Kingdom conference of HCI, I heard a description of a series of experiments carried out on the size and shape of targets for an interface. This type of problem lent itself well to experimentation – though there were still problems with the experimental design (Ren and Morya, 1998). However, I have to say that for every paper I heard describing the results of an experiment there was at least one person in the audience who had an objection to either the way the experiment was designed or the way in which the results were interpreted. Quite often the person conducting the experiment was totally unaware of these alternative problems. Designing and interpreting experiments, especially for the social sciences, is far from easy. Richard Feynman argues that:

If you are doing an experiment, you should report everything that you think might make it invalid – not only what you think is right about it: other causes that could possibly explain your results

Feynman; 1988, p247

There are touching stories from physics and especially where quantum theory is concerned, where scientists have endeavoured to disprove their own findings (Lindley, 1997). None of us should become so attached to out theories that we are oblivious to their faults and weakness. Today's fact is simply the best explanation we have to date. It is no more or no less than that.

And that leads me on to the final word I have to say about experiments. Simply because an experiment seems to prove a theory that does not make that theory true. Science may use experimental method and appear to be rigorous – dare I say scientific? But the process of establishing scientific theory is long and arduous. It is quite possible for experiments in the 'hard' sciences to point to a theory that is later found to be untrue. The converse is also true (Wolpert, 1993; Shermer, 1997). If that is the case for the hard sciences then I leave it to the reader to surmise on how much more difficult the task is bound to be when we are working with people. Solutions are problems that have been resolved for the time being and they may well be superseded in the future as technology and our understanding of human behaviour advances. But, nonetheless, it is important to have a go for the present. I am always dismayed by those people who take a pessimistic view – everything we do is flawed, therefore should we cease to act? No scientific advance would occur without yesterday's flawed thinking. Feynman says that 'you must be willing to stick your neck out' (Feyman, 1998). And Rose, with that wonderful, disarming honesty points out how science never acts surprised by its mistakes. Instead, in his own field, each new discovery is treated as if it has just happened (Rose, 1998). There are no recriminations. This seems to me to be a healthy and necessary attitude if we are to progress. Experimental method is problematic. So is ethnography. But it is better to work with blunt instruments than to sit around waiting for what – a miracle? I doubt that a new methodology for our own discipline will spring fully formed from the head of anyone in the field without some serious groundwork. I have no doubt that our mistakes will appear amusing in the light of experience and knowledge but without our mistakes there can be no progress. The search for knowledge, like love, should not have any need to apologise and nor does it. Or, as Steve Jones puts it so aptly: 'Science is always taught with the benefit of hindsight.' (Jones, 1996).

6.6   Talk aloud, thinking out loud

In this evaluation method users are asked to think aloud while they carry out the activity with the system. This way valuable insights can be gathered about how people are operating with the system and their strategies for carrying out the task. This method can also be used on existing systems in order to find out how the task is done.

Talk aloud requires little expenditure and forms the basis for evaluation methods like cooperative evaluation. It does require the users to talk while they are working. It has to be said that some users find this difficult and need prompting whilst others are quite happy to chat about their task. The evaluator may need to intervene with questions and comments to encourage the subject to voice thoughts and opinions. Some users are excellent about voicing their thoughts though and need little prompting. Others may well become embarrassed.

The problem with talk aloud is that it may well affect the way in which users operate the system. It depends how alien the user finds talking about what is being done. The more comfortable end-users feel with the observer, the more likely this method will work.

One of my former students told me that he had to employ this method of talk aloud when being trained to drive a truck. He said that after practice talking about what you were doing came as second nature; so much so that when another vehicle on the road nearly caused an accident he was able to describe the evasive action he was taking as he did it!

However, evaluators need to be aware of the fact that talk aloud is not always easy and need to develop methods for getting the user to speak. Perhaps cooperative evaluation is better in this respect because it does have built in mechanism for allowing this to happen. Cooperative evaluation is described in the next section.

We once used a talk aloud evaluation method on some first-year student volunteers. We also wanted to use the exercise as a means of examining our own students and giving them feedback on how good they were as evaluators. Our first subject was scared. Not only did he have two students working with him but he also had two lecturers watching the two students. It required my intervention and an explanation that it was like a driving test with the examiner who examines examiners in the car as well. We weren't there to watch him, we were watching our students and anything that happened would be a useful learning exercise for them. Luckily, his own driving test had consisted of just that so he knew what I meant. Since then we have employed especially hardened subjects who are gaff-proof.

Cooperative evaluation is a development of the talk aloud, think aloud method and overcomes some of the problems by involving the observer in the process of evaluation and therefore creating a much less artificial situation.

6.7 Cooperative evaluation

Cooperative evaluation is a method of evaluation developed by Andrew Monk and his team at York University.

The aim of cooperative evaluation is quite simply to identify and rectify problems with the prototype. It aims to involve users by encouraging them to explain their behaviour at the level of the interface and whilst performing a task using the prototype. This task is set by the designer who may or may not be present when the user attempts to carry it out. Monk *et al* claim that the method requires very little training and is therefore comparatively cheap to carry out. However, they stress that it is for early designs and for prototypes that may not be complete.

The argument for cooperative evaluation is that the designer needs constructive criticism about the design in the very early stages. They believe that 'designers have a strong tendency to design for themselves' (Monk *et al*; 1993, p4) and that cooperative evaluation can help to overcome this tendency by ensuring close contact between user and designer.

Monk *et al* see cooperative evaluation as a means of refining the specification so that it meets the requirements for usability. It is a method of overcoming the difficulties of requirements gathering and the shortcomings that too often appear at that stage of system development. However, they do not believe it can be used to gather requirements since the tasks are set by the designer.

For the developers of cooperative evaluation, design is 'opportunistic' and software designers are not seen as having knowledge of human factors. Monk *et al* believe that explaining the problems back and forth will cause delays but that many of the difficulties can be fixed by cooperative evaluation since it involves users at the start of the design process.

Cooperative evaluation is impressive for its simplicity. The procedure consists of:

- ▶ **Recruiting users who will help in the evaluation** Monk *et al* suggest that five users are adequate and if there are resources for more than this they should be used for further evaluations rather than more users for the one evaluation. They believe that after the maximum of five users little else can be gained from further evaluations. The target group has to be identified and appropriate users for that group obtained.

- ▶ **Preparing tasks** Monk *et al* believe that the task should be reasonably specific – it should describe what the user must do. For example, a user might be asked to use a drawing package to draw a square and a circle. Asking a user to 'use the drawing package' would be too general. The task must be specified in detail and the processes for carrying out the task have therefore to be in place.

- ▶ **Interacting with the user and the system and recording what happens** Monk *et al* suggest that observers develop some method of recording what happens – what the users say and do. Additionally, observers should list problems and present a list of questions at the end of the session. Recording can be carried out in any of the ways already discussed – video, tape recorder and written notes for example.

- ▶ **Summarising the observations** At this stage Monk *et al* suggest that two broad categories of information are examined: unexpected behaviour and user comments. Unexpected behaviour is where the users do something that the designer did not intend them to do. Comments about the interface are useful for gathering information about what the user thinks about the performance of the system.

6.7.1 Strengths and limitations

Monk *et al* are insistent that cooperative evaluation is a method of involving users in the early stages. My own students have used it to good effect to gather information about prototypes but we have also used it to gather information about established systems with the view of ensuring that the next one is better and as a means of gathering information about required functionality. The method does seem to be very easy to learn and what is more, both subjects and observers appear to enjoy the process. We have never come across users who have become upset when systems fail or the task is difficult to finish. We suspect that is because they do have a sense of helping to find and fix problems rather than failing to do the task. Indeed, some of our evaluators have actually made comments to that effect.

It is difficult to think of a better way of involving users in the early design process and allowing designers to have close contact with the people who will use their systems.

Monk *et al* also insist that the method is only as good as the task that is chosen so that this does require some skill and care. They argue that because the task is set by the designer and because the designer is involved in the observation this means that cooperative evaluation is not suitable for quantitative measurements. They believe that it is not really possible for the designer to be impartial because there is too much at stake in the design. Other HCI experts have methods for allowing designers and software engineers to be present at evaluations but quite often they are not allowed to say anything.

It has dawned on me whilst re-reading *Improving Your Human Computer Interface*, that cooperative evaluation may well be the closest method of evaluation we have to the ideas and spirit of ethnomethodology which we examined in Chapter 2. The aim of ethnomethodology is that the researcher attempts to observe the lives of the subjects within their environment. Cooperative evaluation would be well within the scope of an ethnomethodology that admitted and allowed observers to take advantage of their intrusion into the environment. For example, the observers could use their ignorance of work practices to gain insights into behaviour. The problem we have in usability engineering is that we cannot simply sit back and observe. We have to build something at the end of the day so observation would be insufficient on its own. Observation without participation might well take too much time and as Shneiderman has noted we do not have vast quantities of time at our disposal (Shneiderman, 1998). Systems have to be built as quickly as possible if they are to be of any real use.

One of the criticisms of ethnomethodology is that it did not produce sufficient hard documentation (Hughes *et al*, 1993). However, the beauty of cooperative evaluation is that it does produce documentation almost as a matter of course and Monk *et al* give ample examples of this.

Box 6.1 contains part of the material used in a recent evaluation of a system. This material consists of a task list, the transcript from the evaluation exercise and the questionnaire filled in by the subject as a consequence of the evaluation exercise. Notice how much space is taken up by the transcript – a text description of a talk that lasted ten minutes but took me an hour and a half to transcribe! The participants in this exercise were two final-year students at South Bank University. One student (the evaluator) was evaluating a prototype he had built using ToolBook. The other student (the client) acted as the customer. Neither had carried out this type of evaluation exercise before. The problem we had with the client here was that he was also studying on my HCI course and had studied with me in the second year too, so he was rather more forthcoming and helpful in a practical way than we would expect most other users to be! This is because he understood what was intended and how this could be done. Notice his use of technical jargon during the interview. Notice too that the evaluator quite rightly makes assumptions about the client's grasp of the interface that he would not normally be able to. However, this was a real exercise and it is reproduced here warts and all.

Box 6.1 Evaluation exercise

This box shows all of the material used by two final-year students in an evaluation exercise on a prototype that one of them was building and for which the other was acting as the client. The original three prototypes had already been evaluated several times by other volunteers and the resultant interface was being evaluated by the client for the first time. The student who was building the system produced a task list and a questionnaire combined.

The first part of this box shows the interface to the prototype as Figures 6.5 and 6.6. After this there is the evaluation task list and questionnaire used by the client. This is then followed by a transcript of the session.

Figure 6.5 Interface to the Usability Engineering Courseware prototype

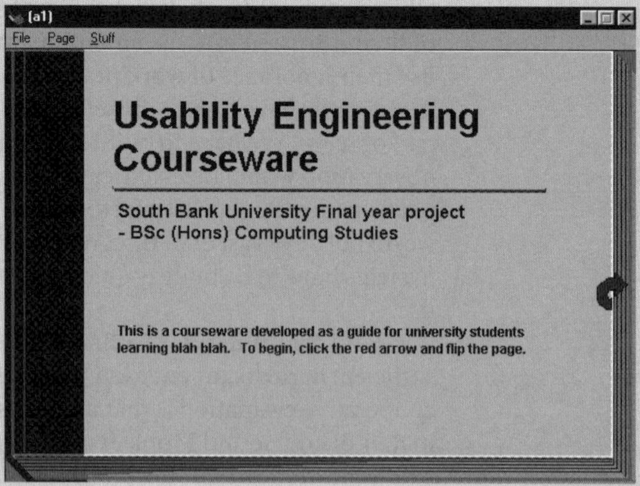

Figure 6.6 Interface to the Usability Engineering Courseware prototype

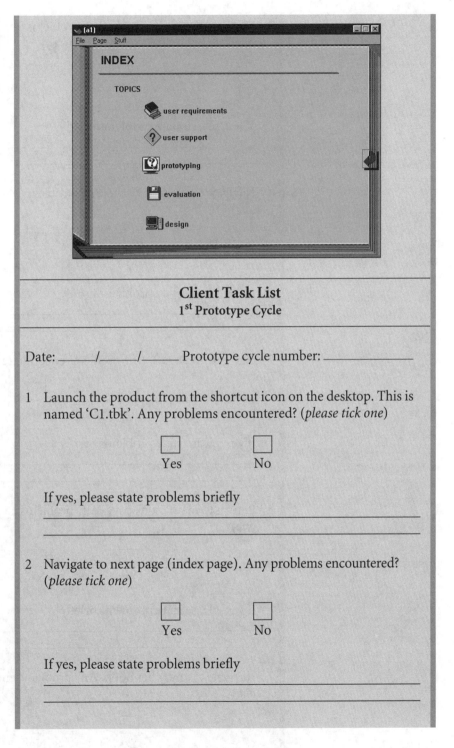

Client Task List
1st Prototype Cycle

Date: _____/_____/_____ Prototype cycle number: _____

1   Launch the product from the shortcut icon on the desktop. This is
    named 'C1.tbk'. Any problems encountered? (*please tick one*)

    ☐   ☐
    Yes   No

    If yes, please state problems briefly
    _____
    _____

2   Navigate to next page (index page). Any problems encountered?
    (*please tick one*)

    ☐   ☐
    Yes   No

    If yes, please state problems briefly
    _____
    _____

3   Navigate to another book. Any problems encountered? (*please tick one*)

☐ Yes   ☐ No

If yes, please state problems briefly

_____

_____

4   Navigate to the index page. Any problems encountered? (*please tick one*)

☐ Yes   ☐ No

If yes, please state problems briefly

_____

_____

5   Navigate to page 2. Any problems encountered? (*please tick one*)

☐ Yes   ☐ No

If yes, please state problems briefly

_____

_____

6   Return to main index page. Any problems encountered? (*please tick one*)

☐ Yes   ☐ No

If yes, please state problems briefly

_____

_____

7   Navigate to any other book. Any problems encountered? (*please tick one*)

☐ Yes   ☐ No

If yes, please state problems briefly

_____

_____

8   Close product. Any problems encountered? (*please tick one*)

☐   ☐
Yes   No

If yes, please state problems briefly

_____

_____

Evaluator: Right. Here's your task list. Um. Right. What we are going to do here is we are going to evaluate the interface, the prototype. We're doing something called cooperative evaluation which um is a method of looking at the interface to see whether there's problems. For example, in prototyping in the initial stages and what I'd like you to do is to give it a running commentary as you go along as part of cooperative evaluation. So you talk as you're going through about whatever you think is going on in the interface if you like it if you don't like it, whatever. Um. If you have any comments or any things you are unsure of then I'll try to point you in the right direction. I'll try not to give you a solution unless I need to because I just want to see how you're going to react. I have a task list. There are eight tasks that I'd like you to go through. Um. And don't worry about the date or the prototype cycle number at the top there. What I want you to do is to look through and tick yes or no. One of those two for each of the eight tasks. If you have any problems then just say them to me and I'll write them down. You don't need to write anything down. Right, that's that one over there. There's a pen for that. Um. And, OK so. Do you understand that?

Client: Yes.

Evaluator: Of course, you realise you're not being evaluated at all. It's the interface that we're looking at.

Client: Yes.

Evaluator: And if, you want to leave at any time you may. If you're uncomfortable then tell me.

Client: Yes, of course. Right.

Evaluator: We'll start off there then.

Client   So. Look at task one.

Evaluator: Yes, you need the task to start off with.

Client: Number one. Launch the product from the desktop. Any problems encountered. I'm going to try. I can see the icon just in the middle of the desktop so I'm going to double-click it. It seems to be working, opening something. And OK. It operates exactly. So, no problems with that one. I'll have a quick look at this. Looks quite good actually.

Evaluator: What things do you like about it?

Client: Well. It all looks quite professional. Um. There's the logo of the university. And it's not too cluttered which I think is nice for an opening page. And it's got the title which I think is an important thing.

Evaluator: Do you want to read what it says over there? See if you have got any problems with that?

Client: OK. This is a courseware evolved as a guide for university students learning either alone or collaboratively with other students. The aim of this courseware is to teach students the fundamentals of usability engineering. To begin click red arrow and flick to page. So there.

Evaluator: If you have a look at your next task.

Client: The next task is to navigate to next page. Which I guess is to by clicking on the red arrow. Which I'm going to do right now. That looks like. Looks fine. So no problems with task two.

Evaluator: Good.

Client: Um…

Evaluator: OK. So we just have a look at…

Client: Index. Urr. I like topics. I like the icons. Very simple. Urr. Third task. Navigate to another book. Um. So I take it that is any book I choose.

Evaluator: Yes. Any one you like.

Client: Any one I choose. The first one is requirements.

Evaluator: OK.

Client: Urr. That seems to be OK. There's no problems with this one.

Evaluator: Is there anything you like or dislike about this interface?

Client: It is nice that it kept the same layout as the main one.

Evaluator: So you like the continuity?

Client: That's right. It's consistent throughout. Um. Once again the red arrow to continue. So I guess that's task four to the index page. So I'm going to click on the red arrow again. So this is the index page for, for the requirements book. So I think that is OK. Task four.

Evaluator: So you like that continuity where um…

Client: So it's easy to understand because you have been through it before. I see. There are subsections within this topic.

Evaluator: Yes. That's what it's meant to be so…

Client: I can see a new red arrow which is pointing back to the cover of this book.

Evaluator: What's your next task?

Client: Task five. Navigate to page two. So I assume it's by clicking on this arrow as well. I've done that before. This is page two. It says that at the top. So, no problems with that. Ur… So next task is to look at content but that's OK. No problems with that. Return to main index page. That is understood. I'm going to try clicking the little arrow at the top of the page which is pointing up and see what this does. Yes. So this is the main book index. So, OK

Evaluator: OK. So what about that icon didn't you like. That you weren't sure about?

Client: Well, I wasn't sure it was going to take me to the particular book index where I was. I thought it was actually so I was quite surprised I got to the main book index even though that was the actual task, I guess. I was expecting to come back to the index book. The particular book index, then be able to return to the main book index. So even though I didn't have any troubles with this task it didn't happen as I expected it to happen.

Evaluator: OK. That's good.

Client: I don't know whether to say yes or no here. The task as… I think I should put no because it didn't quite happen as I expected it to happen. OK.

Evaluator: OK. Fine.

Client: I am however on the main index page. Um… so the next task is to navigate any other book. I choose another book. I choose the third one. Once again, back in the cover book. The cover is quite nice. So no problems with that. The interface… it's not part of that so I guess I'm not supposed to go into that.

Evaluator: Yes, you could do it.

Client: I'm looking at the index of this book and going into one of the subheadings. OK. This hasn't been implemented I guess…

Evaluator: Absolutely.

Client: I was expecting to see what pages it had.

> **Evaluator:** So when you clicked that button you expected it to do something?
>
> *Client:* Yes, I expected it to take me to whatever subheading I had chosen. I assume it hasn't been implemented yet. So I assume now that this arrow will take me to the main index which it does. So I guess that's OK. Next task then. Final. Close product. I assume that it's not that picture on the bottom. I'm going to try to get to the cover again.
>
> **Evaluator:** OK.
>
> *Client:* I still can't find the main cover where I find the exit. I'm back to the main index again.
>
> **Evaluator:** So you're a little unsure…
>
> *Client:* Yes, I can't find the icon to exit the application. I'm going as a last resort to choose to try to use the menu up top. I'm choosing the file menu and choosing the exit option. So I have exited the program even though I was a bit lost since I expected to find an icon in the main index that takes me back.
>
> **Evaluator:** Right thank you. That's that done. We need to have a debriefing now.

6.8   Wizard of Oz

The Wizard of Oz method was examined in Chapter 4 when we looked at design since it is quite frequently used as a design tool. It especially useful for mocking-up systems where the technology isn't easily available. However, it can also be used as an evaluation tool and as such needs to be examined again, briefly.

The Wizard of Oz can be used as an evaluation tool because the wizard (a member of the design team) is able to watch exactly what the user is doing. This information can be supplemented by a video camera watching the user or by an observer.

Many researchers using the Wizard of Oz method infer that the user must not know that the system is not real and that there is a wizard making the system work. However, I suspect that this is not always necessary. Some users are remarkably good at suspending disbelief and pretending. Some of my students and I used something like the Wizard of Oz method to show how a voice-controlled drawing package might work. A few students had argued that a voice-controlled drawing package would be easy to use. Having tried to convince them it had a number of problems, I gave up and decided to demonstrate my objections. So, I asked one person to be the computer and another to operate the system. It soon became clear that voice-controlled drawing is not easy, although the demonstration itself was one of the best bits of theatre I have every directed (Faulkner, 1991). The 'user' got seriously irritated with the 'computer' in much the same way that real users get irritated with real computers. The computer was inscrutable in the way that systems always manage to be! My students were finally convinced that voice-controlled systems were not as easy to use as they had hoped and certainly did not dispense with the need for precision.

Dan Diaper who has used the Wizard of Oz method of evaluation in natural language systems comments on the necessity or otherwise of the Wizard's anonymity. He had assumed that this was necessary but later came to believe that it wasn't (Diaper, 1989). It probably depends on the system being evaluated and the nature of the subjects helping with the evaluation. Some people are able to pretend much better than others and whether it is desirable to rely on that ability, or even to bring it in to play, is a matter of conjecture and debate.

6.9 Laboratory studies

Evaluation can take place in the laboratory. This may or may not involve end-users but obviously when the designer is trying to gain qualitative feedback for a formative study, it will be necessary to involve end-users. There is no harm in testing systems on anyone who happens to be available and passing by but sooner or later it is important to ensure that the system is tested on the sort of people who will be using it.

Some organisations have sophisticated and well-equipped usability laboratories which will contain audio/visual recording equipment, two way mirrors and computers set up to gather information about user performance. This equipment makes it very easy to observe users operating the system. All of this is unlikely to be available in the field!

However, usability laboratories lack the context of a working environment and in order to overcome this some organisations set out to replicate not just the immediate computerised system but its environment as well. Such set-ups will involve the introduction of filing cabinets, telephones and so on in an attempt to create a real working environment.

Sometimes, isolating the system and the task is necessary in order to allow a close and concentrated study of a particular aspect of the overall system. However, it must be remembered that this does, as a matter of course, change the nature of the task. A laboratory trial is not the same thing as seeing a system in a real working environment and such trials are limited in their usefulness.

Even the quietness of the laboratory could be a problem. The BBC recently introduced artificial background noise into an office because the environment was too quiet for people to work in (Harris, 1999).

6.10 Field studies and field trials

A field study is one that is conducted in the user's environment. It gives the usability engineer a much better idea about the context in which the system will be operating. However, it is not without its difficulties.

The user's environment will be full of the distractions and extraneous noise that a real working situation necessarily contains – this can make observation difficult. However, it does allow the usability engineer to view the system as part of the end-user's total environment. It will be possible to observe not just the immediate end-user using the computerised system but there will be other contacts and interactions that the laboratory studies cannot anticipate. For example, there will be interruptions to task and these may have effects on the way in which the system is able to perform.

However, even field studies cannot give a true picture of how the system will perform in reality because end-users are liable to be influenced by the presence of the observer, especially if recording equipment is used. If the usability engineers have built up a good relationship with the end-users then field studies are likely to be more useful since the observer will be less of a novelty and may well be ignored.

6.11 Functionality/feature checklists

Users can be given a list of a system's features or functions that can be performed by the system and asked to tick off those they have used. This sort of checklist is very useful during requirements gathering to see what features have to be incorporated into the system. It can also be used to evaluate a system to find out what features are not being used. It could be that users are unaware of the existence of features or go about tasks in a way that the design team had not considered and perhaps, therefore, do not need particular features. Complex systems quite often present multiple ways of carrying out tasks.

An aside...

For example, the VAX/VMS at South Bank University offers a command line mail system. A few years ago some students and I decided to carry out usability tests on the system. One of the tasks I wanted to look at was reading new mail when the user was already in the mail system. On the VAX/VMS there are folders. Mail is stored in a mail folder, deleted mail is moved automatically to the wastebasket folder and new mail goes automatically into a new mail folder. If a user is reading existing mail and a new mail arrives then the user needs to type one of the following commands:

```
mail> dir newmail
mail> select newmail
```

However, most users are unaware of the folders and have found that in order to read new mail they need to exit from the mail system then re-enter it. Entering the mail system automatically places you in the new mail folder! Even quite advanced users of the system were unaware of how this operated.

Asking users what features they have used will mean that they have to recall them and, as we have already seen, users away from the system are not always very good at recalling what they did. A checklist should offer a jog to the memory. However, the disadvantages are that users might tick features they have not used because they do not wish to appear ignorant. Some people can feel intimidated by a long list of features which they presume they ought to have been using. Simply finding what features a user uses doesn't tell the team anything about the operation of that feature or functionality – it simply says whether it is used or not. This approach also assumes that end-users do really know which features and functions they are actually using. It is all too easy to perform tasks but not to consider how they are done or what the names of the features or functions actually are. After all, this might not be relevant or useful or even interesting to the end-user. However, the method is cheap to administer and it does produce quantitative data that can be useful in evaluating the system.

6.12   Scenarios

Scenarios can be used as a method of gathering information about how users will use the system to deal with their tasks. A scenario can also reveal problem areas and errors. It enables users to look at the features and functions offered by a system and to talk the team through the processes involved in dealing with a particular scenario. In other words, before a system is built it is possible to work out whether or not it will cope with the sorts of problems that users face.

Scenarios require user participation for creating them in the first place or the design team has to have a very thorough understanding of the user's tasks if they are to produce the scenarios themselves. They can be very time-consuming to produce and to administer but they do yield useful insights into how users work with systems. If they are done thoroughly they can save a lot of time and energy elsewhere because the design team can be quite certain to have catered for every type of eventuality.

We examined scenarios in Chapter 4 when we were looking at design tools.

6.13   Valuation method

This method has been used to find out how important a feature is to a user. Users are asked to use a feature of the system and then to rate how much more they would pay for the feature if it performed in a particular way that the user deems important. This method is useful during requirements gathering to find out what users want and how they rate those wants.

The valuation method is a quick and easy method to administer to users and can produce useful quantitative data. However, it should not be taken too seriously as a measure of real prices that people are willing to pay. It probably delivers a list of priorities and should be treated as such. It should also be remembered that people can rate functionality differently according to what they are doing at the time. A can opener might seem to be very important if you want to open a can but it may seem less important when there are no cans to be opened! When users rate functionality this has to be put into context. It might be wise to gather this information in more than one way and to simply use the various methods as a means of checking what might really be wanted.

6.14 Incident diaries

Users can be asked to keep diaries of their interactions with a system. Typically these take the form of noting down when a problem occurs. They might be asked to note the problem, when and how it occurred and what actions they took to remedy it. Users can be asked to rate the incident according to how problematic it was seen to be. This might take the form of a scalar rating with '5' representing an irksome problem and '1' being a problem that was easily overcome.

Incident diaries are useful for gathering information about where problems occur and they do enable the team to look at how users have attempted to deal with the problems. They show how frequently problems have occurred and record the relative, subjective, rating of difficulty experienced by the user. However, this method is not advisable where problems are frequent because it will interfere too much with the way in which users work with the system. Secondly, it is invasive even where the diary doesn't have to be filled in often because users do not typically keep incident diaries! Finally, users may be reluctant to fill-in incident diaries because they may not wish to own-up to difficulties. They may not wish to discuss their problems and their solutions – after all, the final rating of the problem is *subjective*. Having said all that it is a cheap method for gaining information about problems and can be used for long-term data collection. It does require a level of trust and a level of cooperation from the user. It is not something that should be undertaken lightly since it does place a considerable burden on the user.

6.15 Logging use

Logging user usage of the how the system behaves is probably the least invasive method of gathering data about user response to the system, or at least on the surface it would seem to be non-invasive. It must not be done in secret – the user must be aware that logging will take place and user agreement must be obtained. This is not just a matter of morality and ethics but it is also a matter of law (see Chapter 2 for a more detailed discussion of this point). It could be argued that this will, therefore, affect end-user behaviour since the user's attention will have been drawn to the act of logging. However, it is likely that eventually the users will respond as if logging is not taking place since it is likely to be invisible. Logging by the system is not like recording using video equipment which can be very obvious. Perhaps a reasonably typical profile of user interaction with the system will be obtained eventually. At first, it is likely that users will be self-conscious of logging and may well act in an atypical fashion.

The real problem with logging is that it produces huge quantities of data that has to be analysed. This is not always easy and can be very time-consuming. It can also be difficult to decide what data is important and what ought to be ignored. The best forms of logging will involve analysis by machine and thus cut down on the work that has to be done on the data. The temptation with logging is to log everything and to fail to discriminate sufficiently. If the analysis can be done by machine then perhaps this is not a major problem but where analysis has to be done manually it is very important to concentrate only on factors that are deemed to be relevant.

6.16 The purpose of evaluation

The goal of the first stages of assessment of the system is to ensure that as many of the usability faults as possible are gathered at an early stage when change is comparatively easy and cheap. The later the problems are captured the more expensive it will be to solve them (Shneiderman, 1998).

Evaluation should be ongoing with designing and building. If problems are caught in the early stages then it easier and cheaper to fix them. The later changes ought to be minor and less costly, if a proper and carefully applied usability engineering process has been followed.

It is the task of the usability engineer to work out what types of evaluation should occur at the various stages of the development of the system. There is little point in evaluating if there is no intention to act upon the results of the evaluation but it is important that evaluation occurs when changes can still be made. It is not sufficient to rely upon the expertise of the usability engineer to dictate design. The usability engineer can guide design but evaluation must still be carried out.

Landauer suggests that the way in which systems can be improved is by making small, piecemeal advances. He says that:

> In IT development we find ourselves in an area where intuition and experience have proved poor guides... The way out is to improve our ability to know what works. The surest way to such discovery is the controlled experiment, and the time has come to use it. We want not deep truths about physical nature but merely little practical truths about what helps people and organizations do better work faster... We're after engineering experiments... to see if new designs help us fly farther, but also, and more important, to garner observations of where they wobble or need better controls, so that the next attempts will be better.
>
> Landauer; 1993, p343

There may still be problems even if we follow a usability engineering approach because the technology is still advancing. But we have to ensure that each effort is as good as we can make it.

CHAPTER SUMMARY

▶ Evaluation requires the collection of quantitative and qualitative data. Different types of evaluation are valid and useful at different points during the development.

▶ Formative evaluation helps the design process and refines and formulates the design. It should start at a very early stage since changes are cheaper the sooner they happen and users need to be involved in the design process from the start.

▶ Formative evaluation concentrates on qualitative information about the system. Summative evaluation is much more likely to require quantitative data and is useful when the design is complete.

▶ The experiment is the most rigorous method of testing a hypothesis. It involves the researcher testing out ideas in a controlled environment and setting the conditions to cause particular effects to happen.

▶ The object of experimental methods is to show that only one factor can account for an observed effect. This means that all other factors have to be discounted by careful control of the experiment and all extraneous factors. This is not easy because, in HCI, it is possible that extraneous factors will creep in.

▶ No matter how carefully experimenters set up the environment and the task, they cannot capture the real world and this does create problems.

▶ Some researchers attempt to carry out experiments in the subject's real environment. But, obviously, it is not always possible to carry out evaluations in this way. Perhaps ethnography provides a more suitable way of approaching the problems of how to gain information about people using systems.

▶ Talk aloud requires little expenditure and forms the basis for evaluation methods like cooperative evaluation. It does require the users to talk while they are working. Some users find this difficult and it may well affect the way in which they operate the system.

▶ The aim of cooperative evaluation is to identify and rectify problems with the prototype. It involves users by encouraging them to explain their behaviour at the level of the interface, whilst performing a task using the prototype. The method requires very little training and is cheap to carry out.

▶ Cooperative evaluation can be used to refine the specification.

▶ The Wizard of Oz can be used as a method of evaluation since the wizard is able to watch exactly what the user is doing.

▶ Usability laboratories lack the context of a working environment and in order to overcome this some organisations set out to replicate not just the immediate computerised system but also its environment.

▶ A laboratory trial is not the same thing as seeing a system in a real working environment and such trials are limited in their usefulness.

▶ A field study is one that is conducted in the user's environment. It gives the usability engineer a better idea about the context in which the system will operate. But it is full of distractions and cannot give a true picture of how the system will perform in reality because end-users may be influenced by the presence of the observer.

SELF TEST LIST

- analytical methods
- confounding variables
- control group
- cooperative evaluation
- counter balancing
- empirical methods
- experimental group
- fatigue effect
- field trials
- formative evaluation
- hypothesis
- independent measures design
- laboratory trials
- matching
- null hypothesis
- order effect
- practice effect
- related measures design
- qualitative evaluation
- quantitative evaluation
- summative evaluation
- talk aloud
- Wizard of Oz

EXERCISES

1   Choose a small system, or part of a system, that you know well and design a suitable task to be performed using it. Try the task list out on a subject. How easy was the task to understand? How would you improve the task list? What did you find out about the system?

2   Choose a well-known and popular software package. Make a list of about ten shortcut keys for frequent tasks using the package. Now design an experiment to discover whether subjects find it easy to remember the shortcut keys at the keyboard or away from a computer system and perhaps shown to them as a list on paper. You first need to formulate a hypothesis.

3   How could you find out if using shortcut keys is faster than using menus? Formulate a suitable hypothesis and design a suitable way of testing it.

4   What sort of systems might be tested using Wizard of Oz and why?

5   Try the Wizard of Oz on the voice-controlled drawing package. Ask a friend to be the computer and ask another to be the operator. Start with simple shapes. What are the problems? What are the solutions?

6   Examine the evaluation exercise carried out by the two students. Look for examples where the evaluator makes assumptions about the client's knowledge. What differences would you expect to find if the client was a novice user? How would the evaluator have to adopt his behaviour and language?

REFERENCES

Card S, Moran T and Newell A (1983) *The Psychology of Human Computer Interaction*. LEA, Hillsdale, New Jersey.

Draper S W (1993) 'The notion of Task in HCI' in Ashland S, Henderson A, Holland E and White T (eds) *Adjunct Proceedings of INTERCHI '93*.

Diaper D (1989) 'Bridging the Gulf Between Requirements and Design' in the proceedings of the *Ergonomics Society Conference on Simulation in the Development of User Interfaces*, pp. 129–145. Brighton, 18–19 May, 1989.

Faulkner C E (1991) 'Doing what comes naturally.' Unpublished internal paper, South Bank University.

Feynman, Richard (1988) *What Do You Care What Other People Think?* Norton, New York.

Feynman, Richard (1998) *The Meaning of it All*. Penguin Books, London.

Harris, Ed (1999) 'Mutterings as the BBC ends sounds of silence', *Evening Standard*, 14th october 1999, p17.

Hewitt, Thomas (1986) 'Iterative evaluation' in Harrison M D and Monk A F (eds) *People and Computers: Designing for Usability*, Proceedings of the Second Conference of the BCS HCI Specialist Group, September 1986.

Hughes J A, Sommerville I, Bentley R and Randall D (1993) 'Designing with ethnography: making work visible.' *Interacting with Computers*, vol. 5, no. 2, pp 239–53.

Jones, Steve (1996) *In the Blood*. HarperCollins, London.

Landauer T (1993) *The Trouble with Computers*. MIT Press, Cambridge, Massachusetts.

Lindley, David (1997) *Where does the Weirdness Go?* Vintage, London.

Monk A, Wright P, Haber J and Davenport L (1993) *Improving your Human-Computer Interface*. Prentice Hall, Hemel Hempstead.

Norman D (1988) *The Psychology of Everyday Things*. Basic Books, New York.

Norman D (1993) *Things That Make Us Smart*. Addison Wesley, Reading, Massachusetts.

Pirsig R M (1974) *Zen and the Art of Motorcycle Maintenance*. Vintage, London.

Redmond-Pyle D and Moore A (1995) *Graphical User Interface Design and Evaluation*. Prentice Hall, Hemel Hempstead.

Ren Xiangshi and Moriya Shinji (1998) 'The Influence of Target Size, Distance and Direction on the Design of selection Strategies' in Johnson H, Nigay L and Roast C (eds) *People and Computers XIII*. Proceedings of HCI '98, Springer-Verlag, London.

Rose, Steven (1997) *Lifelines*. Penguin Books, London.

Sanders M and McCormick E (1992) *Human Factors in Engineering and Design*. McGraw Hill, New York.

Shermer M (1997) *Why People Believe Weird Things*: Pseudoscience, Superstition, and Other Confusions of Our Time. W.H. Freeman and Company, New York.

Shneiderman B (1998) *Designing the User Interface*, 3rd edition. Addison Wesley, Reading, Massachusetts.

Tognazzini, Bruce (1992) *Tog on Interface*. Addison Wesley, Reading, Massachusetts.

Villazon, Luis (1998) "Old DOS for new", "Windows 95 Polish". *PC Format*. October 1998 (issue 87), p166.

Wolpert, Lewis (1993) *The Unnatural Nature of Science*. Faber and Faber, London.

FURTHER READING

Dawkins, Richard (1998) *Unweaving the Rainbow*. Allen Lane, Penguin Books, London.

Dawkins has one of the most readable explanations of experimental method. If that is all you are interested in then look at pages 166 to 173. However, this is an impressive book and a rewarding read.

Monk A, Wright P, Haber J and Davenport L (1993) *Improving your Human-Computer Interface.* Prentice Hall, Hemel Hempstead.

This is easy to read and very short so its worth looking at. Although it is ostensibly about cooperative evaluation it has some interesting material besides and some wonderful asides along the way.

Pratchett T, Stewart I, Cohen J (1999) *The Science of Discworld.* Ebury Press, London.

This is a delightful explanation of science and scientific method with a good story thrown in.

Wolpert, Lewis (1993) *The Unnatural Nature of Science.* Faber and Faber.

The sections on technology and science are interesting as are his ideas about scientific method and its relationship to the real world. This isn't a book to try to read if you are pressed for time but it is very readable– just not mainstream so far as HCI is concerned.

Design heuristics and expert evaluations

CHAPTER OVERVIEW

This chapter:

▶ considers the argument that usability engineering is expensive because it involves end-users;

▶ looks at methods of evaluating systems without the aid of end-users;

▶ examines various heuristics offered by experts in the field and looks at some of the other methods available for examining and evaluating systems during the early stages of design, during prototyping and after the product is complete.

7.1 Expert evaluations

In Chapter 5 a disadvantage of involving users in the development of a system was raised. Ben Shneiderman referred to the possible higher costs produced by user-centred system design and also how the process could be unnecessarily lengthened because of user involvement (Shneiderman 1998). As a response to these problems of possible protracted development time and perceived additional costs some HCI practitioners have been keen to evolve methods of evaluating a system without the need for extensive user involvement. They fear that the protracted development time and additional costs will cause developers to ignore the importance of usability and consequently hope that, by avoiding these pitfalls, products can be designed with usability in mind but without the need for extensive user evaluations. This chapter looks at some of the methods they propose and how those methods might be implemented.

Probably the best known proponent for this type of development method is Jakob Nielsen. Mack and Nielsen have catalogued a series of eight inspection methods which they believe enable usability inspection to be carried out (Nielsen and Mack, 1994).

Usability inspection is the name given to a set of methods available to evaluators who then inspect the interface in terms of its usability.

Mack and Nielsen take as their starting point that usability inspection occurs once the software product has been produced and the usability inspection will be carried out with a view to 'fixing the problems and improving the usability of the design' (Nielsen and Mack, 1994). Nielsen uses these evaluation methods as the basis for what he calls 'discount usability engineering' (Nielsen, 1993) – meaning usability engineering that is not too expensive. This is a process by which between three and five testers evaluate the system using one or more of the methods as a checklist against which they test the system in question. Nielsen says that HCI experts make the best testers especially if they have knowledge of the domain of the interface. However, in the absence of such experts he says that the method is easy to teach to developers, and is cheap and intuitive.

The eight usability inspection methods they list are as follows:

- ▶ heuristic evaluation;
- ▶ guideline review;
- ▶ pluralistic walkthrough;
- ▶ consistency inspections;
- ▶ standards inspections;
- ▶ cognitive walkthrough;
- ▶ formal usability inspections;
- ▶ feature inspections.

To these I wish to add:

- ▶ expert appraisals;
- ▶ property checklists.

The following sections will examine the various methods which can be used by an expert evaluator in order to assess the usability of a system. Some of these methods are those mentioned by Nielsen and Mack as effective in discount usability (Nielsen and Mack, 1994). In each case an explanation of how the process is carried out will be given; where possible, examples will be provided and comments on the advantages and disadvantages of the method will be offered.

7.1.1 Heuristic evaluation

Heuristic evaluation is based on the idea of testing the conformance of the interface to a set of predefined guidelines or heuristics similar to the ones met later in this chapter. Nielsen obviously advocates his own for use with the discount usability method but Shneiderman's eight golden rules (Shneiderman, 1998) or Norman's Seven Principles (Norman, 1988) could just as easily be used in this way.

The idea is that a good interface will adhere to the set of rules so by testing the rule against the interface it is possible to test for usability. Nielsen and Mack describe this as 'the most informal method' (Nielsen and Mack, 1994). There is some overlap in the heuristics with some authorities citing the same heuristic and using the same terminology. Sometimes different authorities will combine heuristics in different ways but they still cover the same ground. This is probably reassuring!

The heuristics will be examined in more detail in Section 7.2, later in this chapter.

7.1.2 Guideline review

Every software developer who has established a place in the market and every in-house developer armed with a word processor will be waving a set of style guidelines. These are quite a sensible reaction to the problem of inconsistency and based on sound principles. Guidelines can quite often point to the theory and practice of cognitive psychology to account for their presence in the set of guidelines. But sometimes these guidelines have got there by 'accident' or history because a system once acted in a particular way and now it would be difficult to persuade users to act in a different way.

If systems are developed for a particular platform then they will be expected to conform to the guidelines set by that platform. A guideline review checks for that conformance. It does not, unfortunately, ponder the wisdom of the guideline in the first place! It is very important that the usability engineer is able to distinguish between guidelines which are in place good reasons and guidelines that are present only through historical accident. Even the best interface-developers have sometimes compromised their positions because of an unfortunate misguided decision.

An aside...

Bruce Tognazzini explains how the idea of ejecting a disk on the Apple Mac by dragging it to the trashcan was thought up by an engineer who wanted to create a quick and easy gesture for ejecting disks. Although from an HCI point of view this is unsound, the method continues to be perpetrated because of two reasons:

'First, people have developed the habit of dragging disks to the trash, and it would be most unnatural to just suddenly have nothing happen... A second reason... is that this method of ejection works really well ergonomically.'

Tognazzini; 1992, p199

7.1.3 Pluralistic usability walkthrough

The pluralistic usability walkthrough technique is one which utilises users, developers and usability specialists. These various evaluators uses heuristic evaluation methods. The users are chosen to be representative of the area in which the system is to operate. They bring to the evaluation a thorough knowledge of the subject matter and the domain. Nielsen believes that this makes pluralistic evaluation especially useful where the usability specialists do not have knowledge of the specific domain. The idea is that the various evaluators perform their evaluations separately and then meet together in a full group discussion. Randolph Bias suggests that the evaluation is carried out a screen at a time and goes on to say that it is better if users present their ideas and opinions first so that they are not affected by the experts (cited by Nielsen, 1993).

The advantage of pluralistic walkthrough is that it brings together users, developers and usability specialists. In some ways it is rather like cooperative evaluation but rather more formal.

7.1.4   Consistency inspections

A consistency inspection is carried out by experts without the help of users. It is carried out to ensure that the system is consistent throughout. Lack of consistency can be a major source of difficulty for end-users. Gradually, consistency is spreading across packages so that activities performed in one package will do the same in another. For example, [control] + [x][1] on the Apple Macintosh will cut a section of text and [control] + [v] will paste it. In the past, a lack of consistency within the same package was quite often a major source of difficulty. The user might use [control] + [x] to exit one part of a package and [control] + [q] to quit another. Frequently, activities on one package might have catastrophic effects if carried out on another. For example [control] + [x] might cut text in one package and in another it might exit from the package.

An aside...

During the late stages of writing this book I moved platforms from the Apple Mac I had used for years to the PC running under Windows '95 at home and Windows NT at the office. On the Mac, clicking on the small box in the upper left-hand side of the window caused the window to close. On the PC the boxes on the right accomplish that and variations of it. I expect my problem will be all too obvious. I concentrated hard and easily learned to choose the right-hand side of the PC window. This was made easier because there wasn't a box on the left-hand side. However, if I now need to use the Mac I constantly enlarge and reduce the window by clicking on the right-hand side. I never notice this is happening and wonder why my clicking is having no effect and then am terribly puzzled because I assume the machine is 'hanging' – an event which is rare on a Mac!

However, the idea of consistency, which, on the face of it, is beneficial to the user (it reduces their memory burden) can in fact be a problem.

1. [control] + [x] means press the 'control' key, *hold it down* and press the letter 'x'. Same principle applies for other letters combined with the 'control' key.

Sometimes, when faced with all that sameness it can be difficult to remember one thing from another – making things *different* may be necessary. Occasionally, adhering to consistency will actually violate the user's sense of what is right and just. Bruce Tognazzini has a good example of the problems caused by consistency.

A spanner in the works...

Bruce Tognazzini says that:

'The Macintosh promises consistency, and it is a promise that is dreadfully hard to keep.'

Tognazzini, 1992

He goes on to describe several occasions when Apple broke its own consistency rules – most notably with HyperCard.

In fact, Tognazzini answers his own 'spanner' in that he suggests the most important consistency is the consistency of the user's expectations. Sometimes, maintaining consistency is a bad move because it would not fit in with how the user views the activities being carried out with a package. For example, Apple say that the menu bar should never be hidden but when slideshows are being run in HyperCard, for example, the menu bar is quite often hidden.

A final rather charming example of applying consistency is to be found in Pizza Tycoon which is a game by Microprose. The manual reads thus:

Pizza Tycoon has the same user interface throughout the whole game, which you should get used to fairly quickly.

Microprose, 1994

There are no attempts here by Microprose to make unreasonable claims about the game and its interface! I wish all software houses were like that! And, in fact, they were quite right; I did get used to it fairly quickly.

7.1.5 Standards inspections

Standards are not the same thing as guidelines. A standard is a formula that a software house or computer systems developer has adopted. Again, the standards are quite often sensible reactions to perceived difficulties and are frequently arrived at after stringent research. However, sometimes they get there because there is no obvious solution to a perceived problem and a standard simply has to be adopted. For example, there is no good reason for driving on the left or the right and various stories abound as to why particular societies have adopted different solutions. In this case, however, standardisation – at least on a country-by-country basis – is a sensible way forward, no pun intended! The alternative would be somewhat scary although probably very invigorating.

Standards inspections simply involve going through the system and ensuring that it does adhere to the particular standards that have been set for it by the specification. The standards can emerge from several different sources namely:

- ▶ **Internal developer standards** These will be standards that the organisation developing the system has evolved for itself and automatically applies. If the development is in-house then the standards will ensure that systems are consistent and standardised across the organisation. This can be a good thing.

- ▶ **Internal client standards** The developer may have little impact on standards that have been evolved by the client. They may simply have to be adhered to. Again, the comments made about developer standards will apply here. The client may have a holistic view of the organisation which is not available to the developer.

- ▶ **External industrial standards** These are standards that are adopted by industry in order to describe the particular product. Sometimes these standards emerge from the industries themselves and at other times they are imposed, or suggested by, external bodies. If they are imposed then the industrial standard must be adhered to. If they are suggestions then the industry concerned can choose whether or not to comply with them.

  For example, there are several British Standards (BS) TOG ratings for duvets with which industries can assign ratings to their products. For example, these might fall into bands from 15 TOG which is described as winter weight down to 4.5 TOG which is described as summer weight. Each band is described as a TOG and in order to be classified within a band a duvet must conform to that minimum weighting.

- ▶ **External national standards** Unlike the standards mentioned above these may well be imposed although sometimes there is no compulsion to adopt the standard. However, sales of a product can be adversely affected by failure to adopt the standard.

- ▶ **External international standards** This book has talked, at some length, about the International Organization for Standardization (ISO) regarding usability – so these standards will come as no surprise! International standards again do not, necessarily, carry any compulsion for them to be adopted. However, in reality, industries often help shape them and not conforming to the ISO can adversely affect the saleability of a product.

Standardisation is problematic in that before standards are adopted there tends to be a free market – externally between competitive developers and internally between teams. It does mean that a variety of solutions are available and can be pursued and developed until an obvious 'best' solution emerges. However, the problem is that the best solution may never arise or it may arise very late or even too late. If it never arises then it would have been better to have chosen a standard and adhered to it. If it arrives too late then it may simply never be adopted because changing over to it would be too costly. The QWERTY keyboard is a prime example. It was originally designed for mechanical typewriters in order to prevent typists from typing so fast they would jam the keys. Modern word processors have no keys to jam but we are stuck with a layout bequeathed us by a redundant and outmoded technology. The QWERTY keyboard does not distribute effort evenly over all fingers on both hands; unfortunately, negative transfer dictates that it is more economic to stick with what we have (Norman, 1988).

If standardisation arrives late then it can create pockets of eventually obsolete systems. This can be damaging economically for the organisations that have chosen the 'wrong' solution. Plenty of examples of late standardisation abound. For example, the video cassette recorder (VCR) standardised on VHS format rather than Betamax format. Those of us who are old enough to remember decimalization – that first step in bringing Britain closer to European standards – will recall the traumas of trying to figure out how much a chocolate bar would cost after the changeover.

Incidentally, VHS won the standards battle even though it is not as good as Betamax with regard to both image and sound quality. In the case of VHS the battle was won because at a crucial point in the fight for supremacy there were more current movies available in VHS format than Betamax. This minor advantage obtained by VHS became crucial. However, it is interesting to note that professional equipment still uses the Betamax format because of its technical superiority.

I suppose that there has been some standardisation on operating systems with MS-DOS replacing CP/M and with Windows '95 and Windows NT giving a severe hammering to the Mac operating system. CP/M, NextStep, GEM and suchlike have died out like dinosaurs after a particularly nasty shower of meteorites.

7.1.6　Cognitive walkthrough

The cognitive walkthrough is another evaluation method carried out by an expert. However, unlike other methods that involve expert appraisals of a system, the cognitive walkthrough requires the expert to go through a task, or tasks, with the view of imitating user performance and endeavouring to discover what problems the user might encounter at each stage. The expert pretends to be the user but at the same time has an expert appreciation of what the difficulties are likely to be.

Carrying out a cognitive walkthrough requires a close and considered appreciation of potential user behaviour. This means that the expert must know what sort of knowledge the potential user is likely to bring to the system otherwise the expert cannot predict where there are likely to be difficulties.

This method is relatively quick and cheap to carry out since it does not require a group of users. However, it does require considerable skill on the part of the expert who must understand the task that is to be done; must be able to break these down to the discrete stages; must be able to accurately predict likely user performance and must have an understanding of the user's likely cognitive abilities. None of this is easy. A cognitive walkthrough is only as good as the expert performing it. The cognitive walkthrough requires the following:

- ► A description of the users – including their level of experience and any assumptions made about them.
- ► A full description of the prototype or system. This method does not require the system or prototype to be fully operational but it does require a detailed description of operations and how they will be performed.
- ► A description of the task to be carried out during the cognitive walkthrough.
- ► A list of all the actions needed to complete the task using the given system.

For example, let's take the Pretty Slik Nail Painter and look at how a cognitive walkthrough might be designed and carried out for it. Box 7.1 shows what this might look like.

Box 7.1 A cognitive walkthrough for the Pretty Slik Nail Painter

Description of the users
The users are assumed to have no prior knowledge of how to operate the Pretty Slik Nail Painter. There are assumed to have experience of putting on nail varnish manually.

Description of the prototype
The prototype consists of a system that allows one finger to be placed into the machine at a time. The user programmes the machine for use by choosing:

- ► the number of fingers to be varnished;
- ► the colour of the nail varnish to be used;
- ► the number of coats to be applied.

Description of the task
The user must have all ten fingers varnished with one coat of purple varnish. The system is already switched on.

The action list

System Response: The system displays: 'How many fingers do you wish to varnish?'

User Action:	The user must select the number of fingers to be varnished – that is ten. This is selected by pressing the + or – buttons until the appropriate number is shown.
System Response:	The system responds by displaying the current number of fingers selected.
User Action:	The user must press OK when the correct number has been reached.
System Response:	The system responds by displaying: 'Choose the colour of the varnish you wish to apply.'
User Action:	The colour must be selected, in this case purple. This is chosen from the colour menu and selected by scrolling up or down until the appropriate colour is found. The user must press the OK button when the appropriate point has been scrolled to. This will indicate that a selection has been made.
System Response:	The system displays the number of fingers to be varnished and the colour. It asks for confirmation of both.
User Action:	The user presses OK to confirm.
System Response:	The system displays: 'Press start to begin varnishing.'
User Action:	The user then presses the start button.
System Response:	The machine requests that the first finger is placed into the slot.
User Action:	The user places the appropriate finger into the slot. When this is properly engaged varnishing of the first finger takes place.
System Response:	When the varnishing is complete the system requests removal of the finger.
User Action:	The user removes the finger.
System Response:	A request for the insertion of the next finger is then issued and so on until all fingers have been varnished.

For each of the stages shown in Box 7.1 it is necessary to ask a series of questions. These form the basis for the cognitive walkthrough. The questions are:

▶ Is the goal clear at this stage?

- ▶ Is the appropriate action obvious?
- ▶ Is it clear that the appropriate action leads to the goal?
- ▶ What problems are there in performing the action?

Box 7.2 shows an examination of the prototype using these questions on the first action performed by the user.

Box 7.2 The action list

> | **System Response:** | The system displays: 'How many fingers do you wish to varnish?' |
> | --- | --- |
> | *User Action:* | The user must select the number of fingers to be varnished – that is ten. This is selected by pressing the + or – buttons until the appropriate number is shown. |
>
> ***Is the goal clear at this stage?***
> The user is being asked to state the number of fingers to be varnished. The user may believe this is eight plus two thumbs. Or may assume that the system is dealing with one hand at a time. The + and – buttons assume knowledge of similar systems.
>
> ***Is the appropriate action obvious?***
> The system does not explain that the + and – buttons have to be pressed.
>
> ***Is it clear that the appropriate action leads to the goal?***
> If the + and – buttons are pressed then the numbers are clearly displayed.
>
> ***What problems are there in performing the action?***
> The action is simple to perform once the user has discovered that it is necessary.

7.1.7 Formal usability inspections

Some organisations carry out usability inspections using a team. This is done on the same sort of scale and under the same sort of conditions as the inspection of software might be carried out as part of the testing process. A team of three is probably sufficient. The team might go through the system using any of the methods discussed elsewhere but each part of the process will involve discussion and a formal description of what was discovered. It may lead to changes being proposed to the system.

7.1.8 Feature inspections

These are inspections concerned with features and functionality. The likelihood is that such inspections would be more concerned with discovering what features and functionality exists, how these are related and whether the specification is served by them.

7.1.9 Expert appraisals

Experts can work through the system, again using any of the methods discussed. The most obvious use of experts is through cognitive walkthrough but expert interface designers and evaluators are able to use systems and discover, through experience, some of the problems that are likely to emerge. Using experts is cheaper than using end-users. However, the evaluation will only be as good as the experts and the methods they use.

7.1.10 Property checklists

Property checklists are much like heuristics but take the form of high-level goals for usability which are then broken down into attributes that account for the high-level goal. The person applying the checklist goes through the interface and ticks off where the system adheres to the requirements set. For example, a high-level goal for the system might be consistency. The property checklists can then be used in order to ensure that consistency throughout the system can be accounted for and attested.

Several authors have produced suitable and sometimes very lengthy and exhaustive (perhaps even exhausting) checklists. Shneiderman has a very thorough and complete checklist in each of the editions of his book, (most recently, Shneiderman, 1998).

The advantage is that anyone can work through the interface and apply the checklist. If the system adheres to all of the rules laid down for the high-level goals then a fair degree of optimism can be adopted as regards the system's usability – at least on the basis of the property list attributes. Property lists are time-consuming to develop, but once prepared they are very cheap to apply because they can be used by non-experts. The problem with them is that there is an assumption that the property list is a sensible one in the first place and, of course, simply noting that a product does not adhere to a high-level goal or fails on certain attributes does not really suggest a solution to the problem. It merely helps identify areas that might be problematic and a solution to them still needs to be found. This may well require an expert.

7.2   Usability heuristics

Heuristics are broad-based rules. Usability heuristics refer to broad-based principles which ought to ensure a usable interface. It is argued that using them systematically on an interface will allow the usability engineer to find usability problems.

This chapter examines heuristics offered by three well-known HCI practitioners. I have chosen these three out of many possibilities and for reasons of personal preference. I readily admit bias.

Nielsen's heuristics are paraphrased from his book on *Usability Engineering* (Nielsen, 1993). Ben Shneiderman's heuristics are taken from those provided in his book *Designing the User Interface* (Shneiderman, 1998). Norman doesn't use the word 'heuristic'. However, his 'Seven Principles for Transforming a Difficult Task into a Simple One' (Norman, 1988) *amount* to heuristics.

An aside...

As a child in the UK, I (along with many other children) was given a copy of the Bible in my second year at Secondary School – perhaps the same principle should be applied with copies of Norman's Seven Principles given to new HCI entrants!

I have followed the Seven Principles with the design rules he offers (Norman, 1988) simply because they are so clear and useful that I couldn't in all honesty leave them out.

The following sections will examine these heuristics in more detail.

7.2.1   Nielsen's heuristics

Nielsen suggests the use of the following ten heuristics which can be applied by expert and non-expert evaluators to a given interface in order to help improve usability.

1   **Simple and natural dialogue** Nielsen suggests that a dialog should consist of the minimum. It should be natural and logical for the user to use.

2   **Speak the user's language** Dialogs should be expressed clearly in words, phrases and concepts that are familiar to the user. They should not be written in the language of information technology. They may well use the user's own jargon if that is appropriate.

3   **Minimise the user's memory load** The user should not have to remember information from one part of the dialog to another. Instructions for use of the system should be visible or if not shown on screen at that point, they should be easily retrieved.

4   **Consistency** Systems should use language and structures in a consistent fashion.

5 **Feedback** The user should be informed about what is happening. There should be ample indication about what the system's response has been to user action. Users should never be left in any doubt about the state of the system.

6 **Clearly marked exits** Users should be able to exit quickly from parts of the system, especially when they have got there by accident.

7 **Shortcuts** There should be accelerators to speed up the action of experts. These can be hidden from the novice if need be.

8 **Good error messages** Messages should be in plain, straightforward language. They should indicate the problem and explain how to recover from it. There should be no system jargon.

9 **Prevent errors** Systems should endeavour to prevent errors in the first place.

10 **Help and documentation** This should be concise, easy to search, related to the task and help should be concrete.

7.2.2 Shneiderman's heuristics (8 Golden Rules)

Shneiderman offers eight heuristics which again can be applied during the design stages or afterwards as an evaluation tool and as a means of checking for usability.

1 **Strive for consistency** Consistent sequences of actions should be required in similar circumstances. Identical terminology should be used for prompts, menus, help screens. Exceptions such as confirmation of the action of deleting, or not echoing passwords should be limited.

2 **Enable frequent users to use shortcuts** Shorter response times are attractive for frequent users and should be made available. Response times can never be too fast for frequent users – although novices like to spend more time examining the screen. In any case, however fast the system goes novices can still determine just how quickly they wish to respond to the system. It is probably best to have systems run as fast as possible.

3 **Offer informative feedback** For every operator action there should be feedback. This can be modest for a frequent or minor action. For infrequent or major actions the response should be more substantial.

4 **Design dialogs to yield closure** Actions should be organised to have a beginning, a middle and an end – just like a good short story. The informative feedback at the end enables closure to take place so that the users know they are free to move on to the next stage.

5 **Offer simple error handling** The possibilities for error should be designed out of the system wherever possible. The user should be offered simple, comprehensible mechanisms for handling errors. Erroneous commands, that is commands that do not mean anything to the system, should leave the system unchanged.

6 **Permit easy reversal of actions** Actions should be reversible. This relieves anxiety since the user knows that errors can be undone. It also encourages exploration because users know that any action can be easily reversed. Just think how much easier life would be if there was an 'undo' button and you could undo an action in life that you found had given an unfavourable outcome. You will then realise what 'undo' means to new users.

7 **Support internal locus of control** Experienced operators like to know they are in charge of the system. Users should initiate actions rather than being on the receiving end of them.

8 **Reduce short-term memory load** Displays should be simple; sufficient training time should be allowed and multiple-page displays should be consolidated. It must be remembered that the user has a limit to the amount of information they can hold in their area of conscious thought. It might be useful to remember George Miller's 'magical number seven plus or minus two'.

7.2.3 Norman – 'Seven Principles for Transforming Difficult Tasks into Simple Ones'

Norman's seven principles are quite clearly meant to operate during the design stage and although I've read all of his books all over again I can find no mention of 'heuristics' although the 'Principles' could be classified as such. I'm sure they could be applied in retrospect but that is quite clearly not Norman's intention so I leave it to the reader's conscience. Frankly, I'd rather apply the principles first and avoid gross error! I am certain if you followed all this advice you would have a better interface than you would if you didn't heed it! However, the principles can certainly be used as an evaluation tool.

1 **Use both knowledge in the world and knowledge in the head** The knowledge necessary for a task should be available in the world. It should not need to be remembered. Users should be able to derive system behaviour from interacting with the system.

2 **Simplify the structure of the task** Tasks should be simple and should minimise the amount of planning that has to take place.

3 **Make things visible. Bridge the Gulfs of Execution and Evaluation.** Designers should make it obvious what can be done and what the effects of actions actually are. Actions should match intentions. System states should be obvious. If the user does something 'big' to the system, the system should respond with something 'big' too. For example, Figure 7.1 shows a slider to make adjustments to the way in which a system is operating. A small change to the slider's position should produce a small change in the state of the system; a large change in position should make a large change to the state of the system

Figure 7.1 A slider

An aside...

At a recent conference I was pleased to find my *en suite* facilities included a power shower which produced really hot water at a considerable force. I was less amused to find that the area designated 'hot' on the temperature control was tiny so that small adjustments rapidly created a very cold shower. Unfortunately, I am not a 'morning' person and it did little to improve my already volatile temper!

4 **Get the mappings right** It is important to exploit natural mappings. Designers should make sure that the user can work out relationships between intentions and actions; between actions and their effects on the system and between the actual system state and what the system state appears to be either by sight, feel or sound. All too often users develop superstitious beliefs about systems. We have all heard them and probably said them 'It works sometimes if I wiggle it like this!' Yes, even the best of us are sometimes reduced to substituting 'easy' physical effort because it's harder to put brains into gear.

5 **Exploit the power of constraints both natural and artificial** It is sensible to use constraints that feel natural to the user – so that there is only one possible course of action. Think of putting a disk into a computer: it will go in one way only. What about trying a key in a lock – pick the wrong key and the door won't open! The nice thing about natural constraints is that quite often operators won't think of a failure as such. If you choose the wrong key, you simply select another one; most of the time this doesn't unduly worry you – in other words you don't think of it as error or failure.

An aside...

These ideas proved to be interesting to myself and a group of my students. I was interested in how people perceived swipe-card access to buildings so I asked a group of ergonomics students to carry out a study on a swipe-card entrance. They discovered that the perceived failure rate was much higher than the actual failure rate. For some reason, if swipe-cards failed to work this registered very emphatically with users that a failure had occurred.

6 **Design for error** It is necessary to assume that error will take place and plan for it. Designers should make it easy to reverse operations. Design explorable systems which allow users to wander around the system without fear of reprisal. If a user is scared of making mistakes that are irreversible they won't explore. It is better to design 'forcing functions' which make the user do the right thing.

An aside...

I was told this story by an engineer of a computerised system that was used in testing and licensed-out to external repair shops. One such shop complained that they had a problem with their system – it wasn't giving the correct diagnosis to problems. The test engineers duly went along and asked the user to take them through entering a fault into the system. At some stages the user simply skipped to the next screen, saying he couldn't be bothered to fill in the information or he didn't know how to. The system allowed him to skip these sections and came up with a totally inappropriate diagnosis!

If something is vital make sure it has to be filled in; force the user to do it and make sure they know what to do.

7 **When all else fails, standardise** If there isn't an obvious way then designers should standardise layout, design, mappings, functions, displays and outcomes. Norman is really suggesting that where there isn't a solution you choose the best option and make it the same. This is really the philosophy behind the style guides and it is sound thinking.

Notice that Norman has a contingency plan in Principle 7.

7.3   The seven stages of action and design

Don Norman suggests that the seven stages of action (see Chapter 3) can be used as a means of discovering how successful a design is. The questions are exquisitely simple, easy to understand and easy to answer. Put together with the Seven Principles they make for a good way to judge and evaluate an interface prior to proper evaluating with users.

Norman's seven questions amount to something like this:

1   How easy is it to work out the function of the device?
2   How easy is it to tell what actions are possible with the device and at that moment?
3   How easy is it to determine the mappings from the intention to the physical movement required in order to achieve the goal?
4   How easy is it to perform the action?
5   How easy is it to tell if the system is now in the desired state?
6   How easy is it to determine the mapping from the system state to the interpretation?
7   How easy is it to tell what state the system is in?

In fact, if these questions were used as a means of driving the cognitive walkthrough they would probably reveal most of the difficulties users are liable to encounter with a system.

7.4   Heuristics – advantages and disadvantages

Heuristics are useful for evaluating the system without involving end-users. They enable some of the more obvious problems that are already well known and documented to be dealt with. In the absence of a usability engineer on the team they amount to a better solution than leaving the interface to chance.

Heuristics can be used to make solutions obvious or at least the end of the solution obvious. For example, in applying a heuristic that is used to check for consistency, any lapse in consistency will need to be accounted for. The solution is quite obviously to achieve consistency – though the heuristic will not explain how this might be done.

However, use of the heuristic depends on how sound the heuristic was in the first place – it also depends on how it is interpreted and applied by the evaluator wielding it; although the solution may be obvious it cannot always be applied. The field is so new and there are so many contradictions that it is quite possible that the solutions implied by the heuristic are myriad.

Also, the interface consists of a whole. There will be a concept and identity for the interface and breaking one of the rules might be necessary for a particular application. Heuristics are broad-based guidelines – although it might sometimes be necessary to ignore those guidelines. An interface might be better by breaking rules and the usability engineer has to be prepared to do that and to justify the position.

Finally, the heuristics cannot consider every possible system that has to be developed. They are broad-based and, ultimately, somewhat crude methods of tackling the problem – they cannot be said to be specialised. For example, Suziah Sulaiman (at South Bank University) applied the Nielsen heuristics to a Computer Mediated Communication system (CMC) called CuSeeMe – a video conferencing system. She found that although some of the heuristics did enable evaluators to identify some of the problems with the system, they still left a fair percentage of problems undiscovered. The evaluators found more problems when left to their own devices than would have been implied simply by applying the heuristics. However, these evaluators were experts! On the basis of her work she went on to develop heuristics that were specifically designed for CSCW (Computer Supported Cooperative Work) systems (Sulaiman, 1998).

7.4.1   Sulaiman's heuristics for CMC evaluation

In her study of the CMC system – CUSeeMe – Sulaiman derived the following heuristics from an original application of the Nielsen heuristics to the CMC system and a close analysis of experts' comments on the heuristics applied in this way. She suggested that there were three major categories:

1   User Control.
2   User Communication.

3   Technological Boundary.

With three heuristics to account for the system's performance in each category:

User Control

▸ **Match between the system and the real world** The system should use language which is familiar to the user rather than computer or system jargon. Communication should follow the conventions of the real world and should appear natural and logical.

▸ **User control and freedom** The system should adapt to the users and not the other way round. It should assist users so that they are in control of their own navigation. It should support undo and redo.

▸ **Help users recognise, diagnose and recover from errors** Error messages should be expressed in plain language and indicate the precise problem. A constructive solution should be offered.

User Communication

▸ **Support easy connection** The system should allow users to establish connections easily and with the minimum amount of effort.

▸ **Show current status of users and/or system** The system should always keep users informed of the status of other participants. It should promote user awareness and show the system status whenever commands are sent.

▸ **Facilitate turn-taking** The system should give cues so that users are able to respond as in a conventional conversation. Voice intonations should be clear and all non-verbal communications should be visible and supported by the system.

Technological Boundary

▸ **Support synchronous communication** Users should not be confused by time-lags. All channels in the environment should be synchronous. ·

▸ **Indicate the quality of channels** The system should indicate the relative quality of the various channels and should allow users to decide between various other channels to facilitate communication.

▸ **Support media coupling** The system should allow the various media to be mixed as required. Users should be free to choose any channel they wish in order to facilitate interaction.

It could be that if Discount Usability is indeed the order of the day then more specialised heuristics will have to be developed. My own belief is that they are fine for getting rid of gross problems and ought to be applied as a matter of course but they are not, and cannot as yet, be a substitute for working with end-users and evaluating the system with them.

7.5 Expert appraisals – advantages and disadvantages

Expert appraisals are useful for ensuring that the gross problems are eliminated from the system prior to user trials. User evaluation trails are expensive and it would be foolish to try out a system on users when there are errors which can be corrected without resorting to user trials. Expert appraisals can undoubtedly ensure that the system that goes to user trials is the best possible system. The problems that are thrown up by user evaluation should be ones that experts were unable to trap.

Expert appraisals undoubtedly have their place. However, they are no substitute for proper user evaluation trials. Their proper place is early in the evaluation process so that when the user trials do take place gross error has already been avoided.

CHAPTER SUMMARY

▶ Some HCI practitioners have been keen to evolve methods of evaluating a system without the need for extensive user involvement which is often perceived as being time-consuming and expensive.

▶ Usability inspection is the name given to a set of methods available to evaluators who inspect the interface in terms of its usability. It occurs once the product has been produced and is carried out in the hope of fixing problems.

▶ Heuristic evaluation is based on the idea of testing the conformance of the interface to a set of predefined guidelines. Several authorities have developed suitable heuristics. These are frequently easy to apply as a means of evaluating a system.

▶ Guidelines can ensure that systems are internally and externally consistent – meaning that practice adopted for one interface will be the same for another on the same platform.

▶ The pluralistic usability walkthrough technique is one which utilises users, developers and usability specialists. The evaluators perform their evaluations separately and then meet together in a full group discussion. The method brings together users, developers and usability specialists.

▶ A consistency inspection is carried out by experts without the help of users.

▶ Standards inspections simply involve going through the system and ensuring that it does adhere to the particular standards that have been set for it by the specification.

▶ The cognitive walkthrough is carried out by an expert who goes through the user's task with the view of imitating user performance and endeavouring to discover what problems the user might encounter.

▶ Some organisations carry out usability inspections using a team. This is done on the same sort of scale and under the same sort of conditions under which the inspection of software might be carried out as part of the testing process.

▶ Using experts is cheaper than using end-users. However, the evaluation will only be as good as the experts and the methods they use.

▶ Property checklists are much like heuristics but take the form of high-level goals for usability which are then broken down into facets that need to be examined. The person applying the checklist goes through the interface and ticks off where the system adheres to the requirements set down in the checklist.

▶ Heuristics are broad-based rules. It is argued that using them systematically on an interface will allow the usability engineer to find usability problems.

▶ Heuristics are useful for evaluating the system without the use of users. They enable some of the more obvious problems to be dealt with. In the absence of a usability engineer they are a better solution than leaving the interface to chance.

▶ Heuristics can be used to make solutions obvious or at least the end of the solution obvious. However, their success or otherwise depends on how sound the heuristic was in the first place – it also depends on how it is interpreted and applied by the evaluator wielding it; although the solution may be obvious it cannot always be applied.

▶ Heuristics cannot consider every possible system that has to be developed. They are broad- based and, ultimately, somewhat crude methods of tackling the problem – they cannot be said to be specialised.

▶ Expert appraisals are useful for ensuring that the gross problems are eliminated from the system prior to user trials. User testing is expensive and it would be foolish to try out a system on users when there are errors that can be corrected without resorting to user trials.

SELF TEST LIST

- cognitive walkthrough
- consistency inspections
- expert appraisals
- feature inspections
- formal usability inspections
- guideline review
- heuristic evaluation
- heuristics
- pluralistic usability walkthrough
- property checklists
- standards inspections

EXERCISES

1   Using Box 7.1 carry out the rest of the cognitive walkthrough using the questions provided in the text (see pages 184–5).

2   Using Norman's seven questions, which have been formulated from the seven stages of action, go through the cognitive walkthrough again. There is no need to go through every stage, simply choose some of the more problematic areas you have identified from Question 1.

3   Compare the walkthroughs. Which provides a better understanding and why?

4   Choose a small system and carry out a heuristic evaluation using any or all of the heuristics in this chapter. How successful are they at finding problems?

5   Carry out an evaluation on the same system you used in Question 4 but this time use real users. What differences are there in the type of information you derive about the system?

REFERENCES

Microprose (1994) *Pizza Tycoon – User Guide*. Bristol.

Nielsen, J (1993) *Usability Engineering*. London: Academic Press.

Nielsen J and Mack R (1994) *Usability Inspection Methods*. John Wiley, New York.

Norman D (1988) *The Psychology of Everyday Things*. Basic Books, New York.

Shneiderman B (1998) *Designing the User Interface*. Addison Wesley, Reading Massachusetts.

Sulaiman S (1998) *Heuristics for Evaluating the Usability of CMC Systems*. MPhil thesis, South Bank University.

Tognazzini B (1992) *Tog on the Interface*. Addison Wesley, Reading Massachusetts.

FURTHER READING

Mayhew, Deborah J (1999) *The Usability Engineering Lifecycle*. Morgan Kaufmann, San Francisco, California.

This is an impressive book with lots of practical advice and sample documentation. It is also very thorough.

Nielsen, J (1993) *Usability Engineering*. Academic Press, London.

Nielsen's book is easy to read and very thorough. The historical perspective is interesting.

The spanners and what next…

This chapter:

▶ looks at some of the criticisms of usability engineering and suggests some tentative answers to the problems thus raised;

▶ looks at the direction that perhaps we need to take and suggests some suitable follow-up texts.

A complete alphabetical listing of books cited in the text or recommended as further reading can be found at the back of the book.

8.1 On spanners, science and engineering

This chapter is unusual in that I intend to look at the spanners hurled in the usability engineering works. In the past I have not always responded to these spanners, some of which I disagree with and some I believe to be more than likely right! Sometimes my decision not to respond to a spanner has been because I agree with it, or I don't want to impose my opinion at that point, or perhaps the spanner-wielder really deserved the last word! However, sometimes I haven't really known what the answer is and the spanner-wielder has left me with something of a problem. I expect those moments in the text will be all too obvious but in case they aren't I have tried to point them out. But, as I commented in the Preface, I am not pretending to be without bias. But I do wish to leave some of the questions open in the hope that the reader will return to the original argument instead of reading my potted and biased version. Furthermore, as Rose points out in *Lifelines* (Rose, 1998) there is no guarantee that any interpretation of anyone is correct. All authors can do is to explain what their interpretations are. However, we have to act on our interpretations and to make those interpretations clear and obvious. I shall still insist that so far as the spanners are concerned you should suck it yourself and see…

However, I am guided by my belief that HCI is somewhat promiscuous in its acceptance of beliefs. And it has to be. As we learn more about human behaviour at the interface so we will have to amend our ideas and dispense with those theories and practices which we find to be untrue or redundant. We can afford no loyalty to ideas in HCI. I don't believe in telepathy but if someone proves it tomorrow to my satisfaction I'll convert in an instant and take it on board.

Many of the theories of HCI are influenced by cognitive psychology which is itself comparatively young and still developing. As cognitive psychology and computer science deliver more of the goods so our ideas about HCI will develop and change. Lewis Wolpert says this rather well when he describes the way in which scientific ideas advance:

> The whole history of science is filled with new discoveries and the overthrow or modification of ideas which were held to be true.
>
> Wolpert, 1993

Anyone working in the field of HCI has to be ready to give up passionately held beliefs when something better comes along. This isn't easy but it is necessary. Thus, some of the contradictions that are problematic now may well disappear when we have a theory for HCI that will provide a framework from which we can work. Max Planck,[1] writing about science, suggested that scientific paradigms are replaced not by revolution but by the dying-off of most of the people holding those beliefs. I hope he isn't right and that in our field we would be able to abandon ideas as they cease to provide the right answer. For me, Steven Rose, a biologist, puts the idea of scientific advance rather nicely. He says that as each new discovery is made so biologists act as if that discovery didn't actually exist before it was found. He says:

> [we speak] not as if yesterday we *thought* one thing and today we *know* better, but rather as if the change were in the 'real' world outside us; yesterday this world took a particular form, while today it takes another. Not 'we now know that there are eight different forms of the metabolic glutamate receptor, whereas last year we knew of only seven', but 'there *are* now eight metabolic glutamate receptors'. We speak as if the world inside our heads had primacy over the natural world outside...
>
> Rose; 1998, p64–5

In some ways this strikes me as a healthy abandonment of erroneous thinking without the messiness and self-indulgence of allocating blame or

---

1. Max Planck (1858–1947). German physicist, a pioneer of quantum mechanics theory.

censure for not getting it right first time. One project student, with whom I spent some time interviewing for some research I was carrying out during the last stages of writing this book, has brought home to me just how perfect a science hindsight is. Speaking of the program he had been developing he said that now he knew what needed to be done writing the code would take just a few weeks and he was embarrassed by the amount of rewriting he had gone through. But, of course, it was all necessary. The final product could not be there without the programs he had written and disposed of along the way. It was only obvious now because of the hard work and the rewriting and rethinking he had done.

Archaeology can provide another good example of this. It is frustrating to look back at how much has been destroyed by the primitive archaeological methods of the past when today's practices can deliver so much more information and can offer much better methods of preservation and restoration. However, we have to remember that the methods of today will seem primitive by the standards of tomorrow and also that the methods of today were delivered by the primitive methods of the past and will deliver the ever more sophisticated methods of the future.

Sometimes when I look at science and engineering I feel somewhat envious but I can remind myself that even with all of the experience of science or engineering mistakes are still made. Computer science may have the millennium bug to face up to but, as recently as this century, civil engineering can blush at the thought of bridges that have collapsed during building or shortly after completion.

Lewis Wolpert points out that despite the existence of science, engineering hasn't always, and presumably still doesn't, look to science for confirmation and reassurance. Instead, bridges have been built on what he calls the Five Minute Rule – if they stay up five minutes then they will last forever (Wolpert, 1993). The Channel Tunnel fire is also an example of the failure of engineering to predict some of the problems – though others were ignored for economic reasons. The first lightweight tower blocks swayed and bent in the wind, all because civil engineering failed to predict it would happen. At first, they even misunderstood the cause and then had to rectify the problem after the building had been constructed (Petroski, 1996).

It is all very well and all too easy to declare that computer science should have 'anticipated this' or that software engineering 'should not have made that mistake' but the field is still very young. The millennium bug, poorly designed interfaces, and so on, are simply problems 'along the way' that any new field is bound to fail to anticipate. It does not reduce the disciplines to less than science or engineering. That is not how they obtain their definitions. If computer science isn't a science it is not because of its failures but rather because of its content and structure. The same goes for software engineering and usability engineering. Engineering does not, and cannot, always predict: it is always 'wise after the event' until it has sufficient experience with which to anticipate problems; even then it will make mistakes somewhere else because it will have moved on. It should always be able to explain, eventually. I shouldn't like to say – as physicists do from time-to-time – that one day all usability engineering problems will be understood and solvable. What I do know is that the fact that we make mistakes does not mean we should not only throw the baby out with the bath water but give up washing as well! When I first came into the field I was lucky enough to be given a paper by Thomas Green. I still have the copy today, clipped together with an enormous paperclip that the lecturer concerned put on it as he gave me this 'gift'. That paper explained how we couldn't afford to wait for cognitive psychology. We had to go ahead and make our own mistakes (Green, 1990). The trick is not to indulge in the luxury of regret or self-castigation. We don't blame children for mistakes and HCI is still but a child with teenage parents – computer science and cognitive psychology – errors and howlers are bound to be very much in evidence. David Lindley suggests that there is a fine line between acting on very little evidence and perhaps being wrong and ignoring it because it does not seem to be strong enough to warrant the risks (Lindley, 1997).

Computer science, software engineering and HCI are still very new and we are bound to have plenty of mistakes in our theories and practices. I might argue passionately for a set of ideas today that tomorrow I throw away because something better has turned up. I urge anyone entering the discipline to do likewise. An open mind is probably the most valuable of assets and the ability to move on without self-indulgent backward glances at old theories and mistakes.

8.2   When should evaluation take place?

However, we still have the matter of several spanners that need to be answered, so let's look at them.

A spanner in the works...

Paul Booth argues persuasively that the problem with Eason's

'…ideal approach, when taken to its extreme, is that is suggests that we must build and implement a system, and then wait to see what happens if we wish to evaluate its usability.'

Booth; 1989, p110

Obviously, if usability engineers were to wait to the last minute to evaluate a system – with no idea how that system might perform – they would lay themselves open to severe criticism. However, the whole point of usability metrics is that they are part of the process of usability engineering. They are not the whole of usability engineering. Usability engineering is a process that starts with understanding the user's environment, captures requirements, sets planned levels of performance for the system and then tests those levels against the original specification. This does not mean that other forms of evaluation are ruled out. Some of the metrics – satisfaction, for example – (Shackel's 'attitude') would best be measured by traditional methods of working directly with the user – through collaborative evaluation, for example, (Monk *et al*, 1993). Usability engineering is not just about metrics in just the same way that it is not simply about user centred-design or evaluating with end-users.

8.3 On definitions

> **A spanner in the works...**
> Paul Booth writing in 1989 said that:
>
> 'Unfortunately, despite the gradual refinement of the term *usability,* it appears unlikely that a general agreed definition of usability will emerge within the next few years. The main reason for this is that the term *usability* is used by many researchers to mean many different things. Indeed, some researchers have argued that the term is so vague and ambiguous that it ought to be abandoned.'

This feels a bit like a severe attack of *déjà vu*. I am reminded of 'user friendly' and Norman and Draper's comments about 'user friendly' systems (Norman and Draper, 1986). In order to reinforce the sense of *déjà vu* I would like to examine a comment made by John Karat.

> **A spanner in the works...**
> Writing in 1996 (in the ACM's own journal *Interactions*), John Karat was discussing User Centred Design (UCD) – which is really a concept that is at the heart of usability engineering – and said:
>
> 'Rather than becoming more clearly defined as the CHI [Computer Human Interaction] community matured, is the term "user-centered design" (UCD) becoming akin to "family values" in nature – a concept which everyone subscribed to, but for which there seemed to be no agreed definition?'
>
> Karat, 1996

Karat goes on to say that UCD is undefined and can describe 'anything that usability specialists do'. My problem with this is a profound one in that I don't believe anyone agrees what a usability specialist is. For me, usability engineering is a process which produces systems fit for their purpose; systems that conform to the relevant ISO standard and are truly usable. Notice, I say 'systems' not software. Usability engineers could be involved in producing products too. But they will be engineers. They will engineer something – be it a video recorder, the Pretty Slik Nail Painter, the Breakfast Buddy Toaster, a word processing package or whatever. A usability engineer sees the process all the way through from start to finish: from requirements capture to user-acceptance testing. Other people may be involved but they won't be called usability engineers unless they do exactly that! Usability evaluators might be involved in the testing as specialists who know about getting information from users and gathering user attitudes. If we had a clear picture of what we meant by usability specialists then maybe we would know whether or not a UCD process was being followed.

Unlike the case of 'user friendly' there have been attempts to be more careful about how the label should be applied. Terminology in HCI, as I have remarked earlier, is still finding its feet and terms do quite often take some time to firm-up and stabilise. Sometimes they go out of vogue because the need for them disappears. Sometimes they are replaced by something a little more apt and concrete. In a newly-emerging field this playing with words is probably inevitable as we try to find out just what the problems are and just what the framework of our discipline should be. In this respect the work of people like John Long is very useful. In fact, I say in a newly-emerging field, but judging from remarks made by scientists in other fields, naming is not always done wisely and quite often appears to be the results of what I think could be described as fashion (Rose, 1998).

8.4 Who sets the goals?

Let's have another look at a spanner.

> **A spanner in the works...**
> Paul Booth says that:
>
> 'The usability approach has been characterized as one that begins by analyzing the user's needs and setting usability goals for the intended system (or product). The idea of setting usability goals for products has been well accepted within both academia and industry. Unfortunately, the question of who sets usability goals and how they are set, has received less attention.'

I would prefer to talk about usability *targets* because the term 'goals' tends to be used when talking about a user's actions and tasks. However, the question of who should decide 'what is the target' is a sensible one. If you view usability engineering as a process that involves usability engineers from start to finish then the answer is painfully obvious – it has to be the usability engineer in conjunction with the user. The usability engineer understands the user's problems, knows what level of performance is required from the system and can produce these as targets.

8.5 A rose by any other name...

Shakespeare's Juliet was not yet 14 when she met and fell in love with Romeo. When I think of her speech: 'a rose by any other name would smell as sweet' I remind myself that she was awfully young! What's in a name? In fact, lots. In Chapter 1 I briefly mentioned that usability had replaced the older term of 'user friendliness' and that in some way it was a pity because people seemed to know what user friendliness meant. As I finish this book I am also finishing reading *The Politics of Usability* by Trenner and Bawa. I have greatly enjoyed their book and now intend to share one of its nuggets. Trenner, writing on the importance of 'spreading the word' and getting usability into the forefront, mentions that when faced with usability trials readers of PC magazine were puzzled by the terminology. She comments that:

> …almost no one in the focus groups had a clear understanding of what usability meant and when discussing usability issues were more likely to talk in terms of understanding, user friendliness, ease of learning, or liking, making no connection between these terms and the term usability.
>
> Trenner and Bawa, 1998

The concepts the focus group mentioned are close to our definitions of usability but the term itself was alien to the people who actually wanted to know about how usable products are. Interestingly, at the launch of its usability programme in August 1998, the video clip from PC Magazine's CD shows Maggie Williams – the Usability Editor – who says that:

> Usability is about how easy it [a product] is to use rather than how many functions it has.
>
> Williams, 1998

Those of us in the field of HCI are close to concepts of the ideal. It is easy to feel passionately about how systems ought to be available for people to use effectively. I use a computer virtually every day of my life. If I don't it probably means I'm too ill to get out of bed! I log on to the VAX/VMS remotely and stay in touch with my students even when I am at home, or at weekends. I now turn to the computer to do all kinds of tasks for which I would previously have used pencil and paper, the telephone, or visited a library. My reliance on the computer is so total that one weekend when it failed I told my mother that I seemed to be able to manage a weekend without seeing any people but a weekend without a computer drove me to despair because I couldn't do anything!

The way in which, in my circle at least, e-mail has taken over the role once fulfilled by the postal system, and to a certain extent the phone, was brought home to me quite forceably by two comments made by colleague. I mentioned to one that a friend had written to me. The colleague replied: 'Do you mean a real letter with pen and ink? How quaint.' The colleague I share an office with and who is a constant source of my insights into how people operate systems once told a student he was speaking to on the phone that there were many ways in which the student could make contact. He went on to list them – phone, e-mail, fax, voice mail. And then he added, 'And what's that other thing called? Yes, ordinary post.' All this underlines the fact that tasks using computer systems have to be made so that people can operate them easily and without fear of something going wrong.

For me, the computer is a tool and a source of entertainment that I should not want to be without. I find it hard when I see people who could benefit from the tool being locked out of the technology because it is overly complex. Technology should not create a section of society who are enabled and a section that is excluded. It should be available for everyone so that the basis on which they make the decision to employ a computer or not is not down to computers being too difficult. I meet more people outside of the academic circle I live in who are afraid of computers than those who have been empowered by them. Most of those who are afraid say they aren't good with computers because, 'They always go wrong for me.' This is not an indictment of human behaviour or humans adversely affecting computers. The computers don't always go wrong for them – computers seem to go wrong because they are difficult and awkward to use. They go wrong for everyone. They are difficult and awkward to use by those of us who are familiar with them.

When I told my students about the *The Sunday Times* survey cited in Chapter 1 and the number of people who hit their computers out of frustration, a large number of the class raised their hands. I was puzzled until they explained that they were admitting to the same 'crime'. If computer systems reduce experts to anger and frustration what must they do to people who don't have the expert's familiarity with how systems operate?

I am appalled by parts of systems that easily allow users to make changes that may cause the operating system to cease to function. A relative told me a little while back that his printer no longer worked so I made suggestions about possible cures and eventually went to have a look for myself. After a little while I got the printer to work again by reinstalling parts of the system software. My relative had been experimenting and had caused a problem with the system software. But the system had happily let him do that. I told him that actually you weren't *supposed* to play about with those parts of the system. He asked, 'Why not?' He liked playing about with things and he wanted to know what was in there. I know the feeling I do it myself. How am I or anyone else supposed to know what I'm not allowed to play about with? I have a hard boney skull round my brain. I guess that's to stop me from fiddling about with it. If the makers of this system wish to prevent me from fiddling around with their operating system then a hard, boney structure that I can't so easily get past would be a good idea too! Some system software now carries these warnings or prevents users from carrying out activities that would be harmful to the system itself. But systems have to stop expecting so much from users. It is time they grew up and took some responsibility instead of expecting far too much of their users. It is all too often far from clear how serious a modification to a system might actually be.

How can systems be made easier to use? The answer must be by concentrating on what people want to do with computer systems. The things that can be done should be dictated by the needs of the user and not the other way round. The way in which the computer communicates should be according to the ideas of the user and not the other way round. Users should not be subjected to ideas that are used in an alien way.

8.6 Whither usability engineering?

In writing this I have returned to some of the material I started off with when I first came into the field of HCI. Rereading Norman and Draper's *User Centred System Design* reminded me how forward-thinking that book was and it made me just a little sad to realise that in some ways not enough progress has been made. Like this book's preface, this conclusion is going to be self-indulgent!

The idea of a usability engineer who does all of the things I have suggested is not one that is widespread. It is not one that many people think is possible. But for me it seems like the only possible way forward for the time being.

I started this book talking about how the term user friendly had become something of a pariah amongst the HCI community. When it was first coined it seemed to be what we were aiming for but over time it came to mean things we hated and despised. But time and the *Oxford Dictionary* seem to have been kinder and given it a new image even if we haven't. The idea of user friendliness, however misguided, is firmly entrenched in the minds of many ordinary users and it seems to be prevalent as a concept in the mind of the general public. Language defines itself in use. I might be irritated by the computer world's misuse of 'metaphor', 'desktop', 'icon' and so on but at the same time I can accept that language has to change. It is not a constant. I suppose at the end of the day as long as the concepts and attitudes of usability engineering remain, what they get called shouldn't bother me. But I find myself concerned because the hopping from name to name might be symptomatic of something more profound. Juliet might suggest that the rose might be as beautiful called something else, or that Romeo will still be Romeo if he is called Sid but I have my doubts. Language is more than the concept. The sound of a word is important and the words it is associated with are equally relevant. The tragedy of Romeo and Juliet would not be so poignant if their names were replaced by Sid and Daisy. If we are searching for an appropriate label to identify characteristics that we hold dear then perhaps we did not make good choices in the past and need to find one that really defines what we mean. But perhaps it is the characteristics that are really the problem.

After user friendly the HCI community turned its attention to user-centred design. This was the thing we should aim for and how systems should be built.

In the article by Karat (cited above) he goes on to say that if he was forced to define a UCD process he would point to Gould (1988) and Whiteside *et al* (1988). In other words Karat defines UCD in terms of usability engineering. I can't agree with him more. I wish there was a terrible penalty for using the term 'usability engineering' when what is meant is software development without a user in sight or, even worse, evaluation – with or without users. But underlying Karat's assurance that there is a UCD process is the nagging feeling that perhaps UCD is about to go the way of 'user friendly' and then will 'usability', 'usability engineering' and 'usability engineers' go the same way because our definition is so woolly? Certainly Andy Smith has the view that 'usability is indeed a fuzzy concept, (Smith, 1997). He believes this fuzziness is caused by the proliferation of definitions of usability.

Sometimes, when I think of Norman's *User Centred System Design*; the papers by Gould; the papers by Whiteside, Bennett and Holtzblatt and the work done by Shackel in the 1970s and early 1980s, I feel exasperated and angry at the lack of progress. Why is it we can all sit about saying it should be like this and it still isn't? For someone as impatient as I am it isn't easy to watch over a decade pass with very little apparent change. But is that true? Has there been so little change? Very late one night, when I was revising the first chapter, I re-read the Norman, Draper and Bannon glossary. Reading what they had to say about 'user friendly' reminded me of the systems I first used and how awful some of them were by the standards of their day. Comparing them to now is hardly fair. But then I can also remember some very slick – dare I say 'user friendly' – systems which, given the technology, I doubt anyone could have done much better – even today. At that time, the best systems I came across were a word processor called *LocoScript* and some amazing games which were totally enthralling; however, I never got to the end of those games because they were unstable – due to lack of proper software engineering and unreliable hardware! Oh, for a time-machine and a bunch of usability engineers to fix those software problems of the past.

We are getting there. One day systems will be truly usable. They will seem to be natural and perhaps even intuitive though the way in which that word is banded about reminds me of 'user friendly'. They will be properly engineered and stable. I think that the way to speed that moment is via usability engineering. Time and time again in my reading I come across authors lamenting problems that could have been solved by involving users in the process and by engineering the product. I am not sure finally what involvement users will have in the production of systems. For me, with my affection for ergonomics, I hope the answer is through a closer understanding of user environment and culture. I think the ethnographers probably have some of the answers to our ability to grasp that particular nettle. For me, a real usability engineering approach would be a mixture of the ethnographical approach in the early stages and hard usability metrics in the later ones. I see no contradiction in mixing what Andrew Monk has so aptly described as 'oil and water' – although he was thinking more in terms of bringing together experimentation and ethnography (Monk *et al*, 1993). Spoons are good for eating soup. Forks are useless for that purpose and chopsticks even worse. However, I'm not about to chuck out every chopstick and fork I own because sooner or later I may want a vegetable chow mein or a nut cutlet.

At the start of this book I suggested that usability engineering and user-centred design might be a problematic in their implementation, but that the process of ignoring both was too high and that really there was no alternative but to endeavour to adopt both attitudes.

Originally, the interface became important because of the need to ensure that computers could be used as tools to get other tasks done. Computers are no longer simply items of interest in their own right; they are used by people doing all sorts of tasks so they must be easy to operate. If you are a doctor using a computer to keep records, consult those records and dispense prescriptions, then the *patient* is your real interest: the computer is simply a *tool* to facilitate the task of curing your patient. You don't want to concentrate on the interface or the operating system, you want to concentrate on the patient. My own doctor once told me he hated the computer on his desk because it got in the way of caring for sick people. It was meant to help him but he saw it as a barrier between him and the people he was trying to care for. Systems should not take over; they should support and facilitate.

Computer systems, computerised systems or any product at all ought to be as easy to use as possible and should not involve the users in needing to think about the functioning of whatever tool it is that they are using. The use of the tool ought to appear to be natural and unproblematic. The problem is that in the race to develop the system it is all too tempting to forget that systems need to be operated by people. And people are so adaptable. Machines aren't that adaptable so when it is difficult to design it is easier to do the best you can with the product, the machine, the system and expect the human user, wearer, doer to adapt around the less versatile manufactured item.

Richard Seymour gave me real pause for thought when he was talking about the bra in *Designs on your Bra*, the Channel 4 television programme shown in the UK in 1998 and mentioned by me in Chapter 4. He said that the bra consisted of a solution to a perceived problem. This solution consisted of providing structure and support through the use of wires. There were then many other bits added to the bra to solve the problems produced by the solution. And the final product was frequently uncomfortable and inconvenient because it could not be thrown into the washing machine because of the design solution. He made me think because, of course, products and systems are designed like that all of the time. In computing I am used to seeing solutions that are problematic because part of the solution caused another problem. I am used to seeing problems created by structures that have nothing to do with what needs to be done. This reminds me of an episode of the Simpsons in which Homer goes on a space mission. The mission inevitably experiences disaster. At one point we are shown the control centre with all of its equipment. We are shown this equipment in action. It is truly impressive and the inevitable question is asked: 'And how is the spacecraft doing?' To which the reply is: 'All this equipment is just there to monitor the TV ratings. I don't know.' All too often our systems are just like that – containing structures which have nothing to do with the task in hand. It is time for systems to be more simple, to be more approachable, to do what we need them to do, to be truly usable by us without anxiety and mishap.

Usability engineering is awfully young. I hope it doesn't get stifled at birth because I believe it has problems to solve, people to influence, places to go.

But any reader who has got this far, or has skipped to the end to find out where to go next may well want some pointers.

8.7   What next?

Jakob Nielsen's book *Usability Engineering* is excellent on usability evaluation methods.

Gould's 1988 paper should be required usability engineering reading material but there's a very nice version in Baecker (*et al*) *Readings in HCI, Toward the Year 2000*. This has the advantage that it also has Jonathan Grudin's excellent paper and Norman and Lewis on error. My only gripe is they cut Gerald Murch to a breathless two pages and there is less of an ergonomics flavour to this collection than the earlier one. Read Norman. Start with *The Design of Every day Things* and work through the series. *User Centred System Design* is still worth dipping into but I fear it's akin to people like me listening to Bob Dylan and Free – it's a nostalgia trip! Some of the ideas have become so fundamental that anyone new to HCI will wonder what all the fuss is about because it is now so obvious that these things are true! Whiteside, Bennett and Holtzblatt's 'Usability Engineering our Experience' needs to be read and re-read. All these years on it is still difficult to find a more sensible description of usability engineering. Shackel is good for an excellent historical analysis (Shackel, 1990). I still hanker after his definition of usability and wish the ISO had adopted 'attitude' instead of 'satisfaction'. The 1990 paper is probably the most accessible although I enjoyed, and still enjoy, the 1986 paper.

Sommerville's *Requirements Engineering* is a good start. Requirements Engineering is an emerging part of software development and this is a readable text. For an HCI perspective on usability engineering then the Hix and Harman text *Developing User Interfaces* is a good bet. If, like me, you can't resist what product engineers are doing then Pat Jordan's two books would be a sensible place to go – *Usability Engineering in Industry* is a delightful collection of essays and Jordan's own book *An Introduction to Usability* is a gem. Both are excellent and well worth reading. I think this is because of the ergonomics influence but anyone who knows me will say I am biased! The collection of essays is highly interesting and Jordan's own book is a delight – a nice, unpretentious and succinct book that is fun to read and has some interesting pictures.

Redmond-Pyle and Moore have a software development approach to usability. I like their book called, very appropriately, *Graphical User Interface Design and Evaluation*. It is truly impressive in its scope and its attention to detail. Note that it is an engineer's book and takes for granted that you can build.

When you've done with all that get hold of Andrew Monk *et al* on cooperative evaluation, the book is called *Improving Your Human Computer Interface*. It costs an arm and a leg so I'm going to be mean about their royalties and suggest that if you're a student you should borrow it from the library; however, it is excellent and has evaluation sheets which can be photocopied and used. I should add that Monk *et al* actually *urge* the reader to photocopy those pages so I am *not* suggesting an action that would infringe copyright! Of all the evaluation methods I've come across which purport to be useful and easily carried out, cooperative evaluation is the one my students and I have most enjoyed and found to be the most effective. The book itself is a treat, full of sound common-sense and lots of tips. It's also very short and can easily be read in an evening. The style is clear and concise and has a no nonsense feel about it. My students always enjoy this text and, like me, lament the price.

As I neared the completion of this book I came across *The Politics of Usability* by Trenner and Bawa. Like Thomas Landauer's book this is an eye-opener and well worth looking at. It's a collection of essays so you can just look at the ones that catch your fancy.

I like Andy Smith's nice, unpretentious book *Human Computer Factors*, which has interesting sections on usability and user-centred design and is highly readable. Deborah Mayhew's *The Usability Engineering Lifecycle* is a must. It is impossible not to be impressed by the scope and practicality of that book.

During the draft revisions of this book Don Norman's *The Invisible Computer* was published. I deliberately held off reading that book but curiosity eventually got the better of me. I have to recommend it. On the basis of my reading I have added a few references to it but I don't do it justice. It is yet another treat.

The Web is also a good source of material on usability. Jakob Nielsen has a site devoted to usability and has methods for evaluating the usability of Web pages. They are well worth looking at and, at the time of writing, are constantly being updated and reviewed. See:

```
http://www.useit.com/
```

Nielsen's alert boxes are amounting to a series of heuristics and are well worth looking at. I am very curious as to what sort of lifespan the alert boxes can have and whether he will turn them into the heuristics they seem to be evolving into. In any case they are a good source of the latest usability news and thinking and as usability is a moving target the Web is perhaps the best place to start studying it.

And now, you should stop skulking amongst my conclusions and go off to become a usability engineer. There are systems that need building and interfaces to be fixed. Go do it! Someone has to.

CHAPTER SUMMARY

▶ Usability engineering is relatively new and is still evolving. There are problems with it but as our understanding increases perhaps some solutions can be found.

▶ HCI has been heavily influenced by, and has leaned on, the products of psychology and cognitive psychology. Developments in those areas might help to shape still further directions for HCI.

▶ To some people 'usability' seems to be relatively undefined and this could lead to its abandonment. User friendly had a similar problem.

EXERCISES

1 Look at definitions of user friendly, usability, usability evaluation and usability engineering. What do writers think they mean by the terms? How do these interpretations differ? Are there any elements in common?

2 Draw up a list of points you would look for in an interface. Could these be turned into heuristics? Compare them to the heuristics we examined in the previous chapter.

3 Ask non-computer-literate friends and relatives – all those who use computers as tools but have no contact with computing as a discipline – what they think the term 'user friendly' means. Find out how many have heard of 'usability'. What do they think it might mean?

4 Choose a system you have in the house and try to computerise it. For example, what would a computerised toaster or central heating system look like?

REFERENCES

Booth, Paul (1989) *An Introduction to HCI*. LEA, Hove.
Gould J (1988) 'How to design usable systems' in Helander M (ed.) *Handbook of Human-Computer Interaction*. Elsevier, Amsterdam, North Holland.

Green, Thomas (1990) 'Limited Theories As A Framework For Human–Computer Interaction' in Ackermann and Tauber (eds) *Mental Models and Human Computer Interaction I*. Elsevier, North Holland pp. 3–39.

Jordan P (1998) *An Introduction to Usability*. Taylor and Francis, London.

Jordan P, Thomas B, Weerdmeester A and McClelland I (1996) *Usability Evaluation in Industry*. Taylor and Francis, London.

Karat John (1996) 'User centred Design: Quality or Quackery?' *Interactions*, vol. 11.4, ACM.

Lindley, David (1997) *Where does the Weirdness Go?* Vintage, London.

Mayhew, Deborah J (1999) *The Usability Engineering Lifecycle*. Morgan Kaufmann, San Francisco, California.

Monk A (*et al*) *Improving Your Human Computer Interface*. Prentice Hall.

Norman D and Draper S (1988) *User Centred System Design*. LEA, Hillsdale, New Jersey.

Norman D (1998) *The Invisible Computer*. MIT Press, Cambridge, Massachusetts.

Petroski H (1996) *Invention by Design*. Harvard University Press, Cambridge, Massachusetts.

Redmond-Pyle D and Moore A (1995) *Graphical User Interface Design and Evaluation*. Prentice Hall, Hemel Hempstead.

Rose S (1998) *Lifelines*. Penguin Books, London.

Shackel B (1981) 'The concept of usability' in Bennett J L *et al* (eds) (1984) *Visual Display Terminals: Usability Issues and Health Concerns*. Prentice Hall, Englewood Cliffs New Jersey.

Shackel B (1986) 'Ergonomics in Design for Usability' in Harrison M D and Monk A F (eds) *People and Computers: Designing for Usability*, Proceedings of the Second Conference of the BCS HCI Specialist Group, September 1986.

Shackel B (1990) 'Human Factors and Usability' in Preece and Keller (eds) *Human Computer Interaction*. Prentice Hall, Hemel Hempstead.

Smith, Andy (1997) *Human Computer Factors: A Study of Users and Information Systems*. McGraw Hill, London.

Sommerville, Ian and Sawyer, Pete (1997) *Requirements Engineering*. John Wiley, Chichester.

Trenner, Lesley and Bawa, Joanna (1998) *The Politics of Usability*. Springer-Verlag, London.

Whiteside J, Bennett J and Holtzblatt K (1988) 'Usability Engineering; our Experience and Evolution' in Helander M (ed.) *Handbook of Human-Computer Interaction*. Elsevier, North Holland.

Williams M (1998) 'Introducing Usability'. PC Magazine CD, August 1998.

Wolpert L (1993) *The Unnatural Nature of Science*. Penguin Books, London.

A case study– the Tuttles

This chapter is a case study based on work carried out at the School of Computing, South Bank University.

9.1 Background to the Tuttles

The following case study is based on work carried out with final-year students on the BSc (Hons) Computing Studies degree at the School of Computing, South Bank University. The students are from the Usability Engineering and Evaluative Methods unit taught by Fintan Culwin and myself. The Tuttles Project has now come to an end and has been replaced by the Brewsers Project which is referred to elsewhere in the text.

The Tuttles project was started a few years ago when Fintan Culwin had an idea for something different to make the second semester more interesting and productive both for the students and ourselves. We were concerned that although we told the students that HCI and software engineering should be integrated, we didn't actually practice that in our classes. We decided to work together in the same room, on the same project and integrate the two halves of our course around a project. It has undergone major fundamental and cosmetic surgery since that first year although the aims remain the same – to integrate HCI and software engineering through usability engineering.

The project derives its name from Fintan's original typing error. I was so taken by Tuttle instead of Turtle that I asked him to keep the name.

Originally the exercise was designed to be carried out in X/Motif. The first students who acted as our 'guinea pigs' for our ideas about integrating the practical and theoretical build side of engineering the interface with the practical and theoretical side of HCI provided a lot of feedback about what we were doing wrong. They also reassured us that most of what we had done to them was probably right! A more detailed description of this work can be found in Faulkner and Culwin, 1997 and 1999.

Although the first year of the Tuttles was a success – largely due to the devotion of that first year of very able and robust students – we recognised that X-Motif was a hard environment for groups to work with in a short space of time. We therefore moved to Tck/Tcl – which was too easy, and caused our students to break out in a nasty rash of what Fintan described as 'featuritis'. We moved over to Java which, like baby-bear's porridge, has proved to be just right.

I divide the students into teams on the basis of their skills so that we have a good cocktail of talents and abilities. Each team draws an envelope from the hat and the envelope contains the requirements for the system that team has to build. Each team is allocated a team leader but may choose one other person to act as HCI coordinator. The team leader works with Fintan Culwin, the entire cohort and myself but the HCI coordinator works with me and the cohort.

The aim of the exercise is to produce working programs to be used as prototypes for evaluation. Fintan and I act as clients and expert consultants although we try not to interfere if the mistakes that are about to be made are interesting and won't cause too much distress to our students!

The following pages show:

- ▶ a description of the project as received by the students;
- ▶ a description of the requirements they receive;
- ▶ details of the evaluation phase which they produce for their evaluation work.

Typically, the evaluation is in the form of a field trial or survey with a task list, evaluation questionnaire and observer's checklist. We also carry out some usability metrics. The metrics carried out in 1997–8 are available as part of this case study.

The systems are evaluated with students from South Bank University. In the first year we used visitors to the university and rewarded them with chocolates afterwards. But the last two years have consisted of trials taking place with students and staff from South Bank. In 1997 we used our Learning Resource Centre and set up a room full of the systems to be evaluated. Students could drop-in as they wished to help with the evaluation. In 1998 we carried out two trials. One was carried out in the psychology observation laboratory which was then newly built. The laboratory technician was keen to have some feedback on the laboratory and we were keen to do a test with the systems under laboratory conditions. We set up the trial, sent in an observer, openly videoed our subjects and observed them behind a two-way mirror. On the basis of this trial we were able to correct faults in our evaluation tool as well as producing a wishlist for improvements to be made to the systems. This was followed by a drop-in session – this time carried out in one of the School's own laboratories.

The students work in small teams of four or five. But the whole cohort has to work together for the evaluation process and for some aspects of the build. We believe that this need for cooperation makes the task as realistic as possible.

The following pages show the output from the student's evaluation study. I have reproduced their work – warts and all! I start off with two of the four specifications to give the reader a feel for what we did and to see our starting point. It has to be remembered that the students have ten weeks to complete all of this work – from build to evaluate – so it is somewhat rushed!

9.2 The specifications

The following are samples from the specifications given to the students.

9.2.1 Specification B

The *LoggingTuttle* (Java) class is to be used for this specification and facilities to undo and log the user's actions should be provided.

This specification is to extend the existing semi-direct manipulation interface so that it affords the user the opportunity to move the Tuttle any number of steps in its current direction. (This part of the specification is common to Specification A and a common approach may be used).

Additionally, a *RadioTuttleButton* class is to be produced and instances of it used to indicate the currently available foreground and background colours.

A single application including the facilities of Specifications A and B is to be produced.

9.2.2 Specification D

The *LoggingTuttle* class is to be used for this specification and facilities to undo and log the user's actions should be provided.

This specification is to extend the existing Main Menu Bar interface so that it affords the user the opportunity to move the Tuttle any number of steps in its current direction. This is to be accomplished by the provision of additional dialogs.

9.3 The usability specification

The usability specification is shown below. This specification was drawn up with planned levels based on the average performances over all interfaces during a trial run in the psychology observation laboratory at South Bank University. We worked with five users for this exercise. We intended to dry-run the protocol and the evaluation material to produce a set of times and performance levels. By taking an average across these figures we obtained the planned levels.

Tuttles Usability Specification

Version no 3. Dated 12 May 1998.

1. Measuarable Attributes

In order to evaluate the usability of the different systems, the usability will be broken down into measurable attributes; each measurable attribute will have an objective indicator. Information about each will be obtained by:

- logging the user's activity with the system;
- analysing the results from the questionnaire.

Metric	Attribute measured	Objective indicator	Source	Planned level
Ease of use	System transparency level	Number of users with a perceivable view of the system functionality	Questionnaire Logging	75%
	Conformance level	Number of tasks which can be carried out with the system	User logging	All 3 tasks
	System responsiveness	User rating of system responsiveness	Questionnaire	75% rate Adequate or fast
	System helpfulness	Number of help facilities used successfully	User logging Questionnaire	1
Flexibility	System function utilisation level	Number of functions used to not used	User logging	More functions used than not used
Learnability	Training level	Time it takes to learn how to operate the system	User logging Questionnaire	5 minutes
	Level of task achievement	Number of completed tasks	User logging	3
	Level of task failure	Number of uncompleted tasks	User logging	0
	Help request level	Number of times help is requested	User logging Questionnaire	3
	Task time execution level	Time it takes to carry out the task	User logging	25 minutes
Attitude	Satisfaction level	Number of users who would use the system again	Questionnaire	50%
	User tiredness level	Number of users fatigued by the system	User logging Questionnaire	25%

2. Classification of Users

Users will be classified according to their level of computing expertise. The knowledge and experience level with the system will be assumed to be the same with all users since no one will have used this system before. Users are to be classified from their own assignment and the level of experience they indicate.

Type of user	Knowledge of the system	Experience with similar systems	Computer experience
Novice	None	None	None/Low
Casual	None	Low	Medium
Expert	None	All levels	High

9.4 Evaluation material

The next sections show material used for the conducting the survey:

▶ Section 9.5 shows the instructions for observers.
▶ Section 9.6 shows the summary of the running order.
▶ Section 9.7 shows the logging mechanism for subject allocation to the specific interfaces.

This constitutes all of the material for evaluators to use and follow for the survey.

▶ Section 9.8 shows the observervation forms filled in by observers.
▶ Section 9.9 shows the usability observation forms.
▶ Secrtion 9.10 shows the task list given to the subjects. The same task list was used for each interface.
▶ Section 9.11 consists of the questionnaire given to the subjects after they had finished the task.

9.5 Instructions for observers

• The observation form can be used to provide consistent evaluation of usability of the system.
• Tell the subject that they have 5 minutes to explore the system after which they will be given a list of tasks to test its usability.
• Enter the time they start on the observation form.
• When they are ready, or after the 5 minutes are up, give them the task list and explain that we would like them to see how usable the interface is without outside help. However, if they reach a standstill and cannot progress, they are free to ask.
• Enter time on the observation form.

- Make notes as the subject uses the interface. The observation form asks for the observer's opinion regarding the understanding of each subtask within the main tasks. (So for Task 1, there are four subtasks a, b, c and d). There is also a space on each page of the observation form for other comments to be made regarding difficulties encountered etc.
- As the subject finishes a task or moves on to the next, make a note of the time and whether they finished the task or not. If an accurate estimation of the amount of task completed could be made then enter this. Otherwise leave it blank.
- Once the user has finished the tasks, make a note of the time and ask them if they mind filling in a questionnaire. Place a sequential number preceded by the interface letter in the top left corner of both the observation form and the questionnaire so that they may be matched up later i.e., for group A – A1, A2 etc.
- Save the log file under the same name as the number placed on the paperwork.
- Show the subject to a desk that they can use to fill in the questionnaire (this should preferably be facing away from the interfaces so that their answers are not skewed by other interfaces or subjects).

9.6 Summary of evaluation running order

This should be used in conjunction with, and not as a replacement for, the investigators instructions produced earlier.

1. Set up interfaces (1 for each group).
2. We will need one person responsible for greeting and allocating subjects to different interfaces. They will need to spread levels of user evenly across the four interfaces.
   A form has been created that will allow such a spread to be more easily achieved.
3. Each team should supply 2 people to look after their interface.
4. A person will be needed to look after the questionnaires and to provide subjects with explanatory help if required.
   Once the questionnaire is complete, the subject should be thanked for their help.

People needed:

- One person responsible for greeting and allocating subjects to different interfaces.
- Two people from each group to look after their interface.
- One person to look after the questionnaires and to provide subjects with explanatory help if required.

9.7 Subject allocation sheet

Please ask each subject for their opinion of their level of expertise choosing from novice user, casual user and expert user.

With this information assign the subject to an interface placing priority to those interfaces with the least number of subjects within the given user category.

Enter a tally mark into the box associated with the type of subject and the Interface assigned to them.

	Interface A	Interface B	Interface C	Interface D
Novice users				
Casual users				
Expert Users				

Thank the subject and direct them to the selected interface.

9.8 Observation forms

Task 1 Observation Form

Start Time   :
Finish Time   :
Complete   :   yes/no

Personal Assistance

Help Requested	Help Given	Resulting Action

Usage of Interface Help Facility

Help Facility Accessed	Resulting Action

Observed Understanding of Tasks and of Interface

This section requires the observer to assess the subject's understanding of both the task to be performed and of the means by which that task can be achieved.

Task Understanding   **Understanding of Interface**

a) Understood completely ☐   Understood completely ☐

    Vague understanding ☐   Vague understanding ☐

    Not understood ☐   Not understood ☐

b) Understood completely ☐   Understood completely ☐

    Vague understanding ☐   Vague understanding ☐

    Not understood ☐   Not understood ☐

c) Understood completely ☐   Understood completely ☐

    Vague understanding ☐   Vague understanding ☐

    Not understood ☐   Not understood ☐

d) Understood completely ☐   Understood completely ☐

    Vague understanding ☐   Vague understanding ☐

    Not understood ☐   Not understood ☐

Further Observational Notes:

Task 2 Observation Form

Start Time   :
Finish Time   :
Complete   :   yes/no

Personal Assistance

Help Requested	Help Given	Resulting Action

Usage of Interface Help Facility

Help Facility Accessed	Resulting Action

Observed Understanding of Tasks and of Interface

This section requires the observer to assess the subject's understanding of both the task to be performed and of the means by which that task can be achieved.

Task Understanding   **Understanding of Interface**

a) Understood completely ☐   Understood completely ☐
    Vague understanding   ☐   Vague understanding   ☐
    Not understood   ☐   Not understood   ☐

b) Understood completely ☐   Understood completely ☐
    Vague understanding   ☐   Vague understanding   ☐
    Not understood   ☐   Not understood   ☐

Further Observational Notes:

```



```

Task 3 Observation Form

Start Time :
Finish Time :
Complete : yes/no

Personal Assistance

Help Requested	Help Given	Resulting Action

Observed Understanding of Tasks and of Interface

This section requires the observer to assess the subject's understanding of both the task to be performed and of the means by which that task can be achieved.

Usage of Interface Help Facility

Help Facility Accessed	Resulting Action

Task Understanding

a) Understood completely ☐
    Vague understanding ☐
    Not understood ☐

Understanding of Interface

Understood completely ☐
Vague understanding ☐
Not understood ☐

Letters selected to complete task:

This section requires the observer to sketch the letters drawn by the subject. The way in which a letter is drawn may provide clues as to the level of understanding gained.

Letter 1	Letter 2	Letter 3

Further Observational Notes:

9.9 Usability observation form

This was used by the observers to give some indication as to what they should be looking for when they carried out the observations. Normally, observers would be trained but our limited amount of time meant we could only have one short training session using volunteers from the group.

Tuttle Usability Observation Form

This form is intended for use by observers as an information collection tool. Its purpose is to act as a guide only and as such should not be considered to provide a definitive list of observation points.

User Familiarity Observation

Start Time   :
Observation Notes   :

Task List Observation

Start Time   :
Finish Time   :
Observation Notes   :

9.10   The task list

This was given to each user so that results from each interface could be compared.

Task List

This task list consists of a number of actions that can be performed using the Tuttle. The column to the right contains examples of the intended result from each action. It also shows the amount of steps required for each movement of the Tuttle.

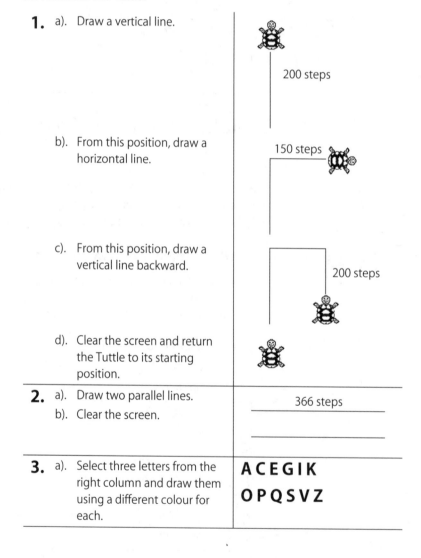

1. a). Draw a vertical line.

200 steps

   b). From this position, draw a horizontal line.

150 steps

   c). From this position, draw a vertical line backward.

200 steps

   d). Clear the screen and return the Tuttle to its starting position.

2. a). Draw two parallel lines.
   b). Clear the screen.

366 steps

3. a). Select three letters from the right column and draw them using a different colour for each.

A C E G I K

O P Q S V Z

9.11 Questionnaire on the Tuttle systems

Tuttles Questionnaire

Background

What is your age? 18–25 ☐

26–35 ☐

36–45 ☐

46+ ☐

What is your occupation (if not a student)?

Sex: M ☐ F ☐

What is your first language?

Experience

Do you use a computer at home?

Yes ☐ No ☐

Do you use a computer at work?

Yes ☐ No ☐

What software packages are you familiar with?

Word processing ☐ Spreadsheets ☐ Database builder ☐
Drawing packages ☐ Cad systems ☐ Other ☐

How would you rate your computer experience?

None ☐ some ☐ average ☐ above average ☐ loads ☐

How did you feel?

Did you feel comfortable during this user trial?

Yes ☐ No ☐

What would you alter to make you feel more at ease?

System functionality

Which system did you use?

MenuBar Tuttle ☐ SemiDirect Tuttle ☐ TextMenu Tuttle ☐

Was it obvious how the system worked from first glance?

Yes ☐ No ☐

Did you think the system was…

Slow ☐ Adequate ☐ Fast ☐

Would you use this system again?

Yes ☐ No ☐

What changes to the system would you like?

Tasks

Did you need help at any time?

Yes ☐ No ☐

If yes, did you use the help on the menu or did you ask someone?

Help system ☐ Asked someone ☐

How many mistakes did you feel you made?

0 ☐ 1 ☐ 2–5 ☐ more than 5 ☐

Which 3 letters did you choose to draw for task 3?

A☐ C☐ E☐ G☐ I☐ K☐ O☐ P☐ Q☐ S☐ V☐ Z☐

Why did you choose these letters?

Rating

Please rate on a difficulty level of 1–5 what you thought of each of these tasks (i.e., 1 would be very easy, 5 would be very difficult).

Drawing a line: 1 ☐ 2 ☐ 3 ☐ 4 ☐ 5 ☐

Turning left or right: 1 ☐ 2 ☐ 3 ☐ 4 ☐ 5 ☐

Pen up: (stops drawing a line behind the Tuttle)	1 ☐	2 ☐	3 ☐	4 ☐	5 ☐
Pen down: (draws the line behind the Tuttle)	1 ☐	2 ☐	3 ☐	4 ☐	5 ☐
Checking the state of the Tuttle:	1 ☐	2 ☐	3 ☐	4 ☐	5 ☐
Clearing the screen:	1 ☐	2 ☐	3 ☐	4 ☐	5 ☐
Undo:	1 ☐	2 ☐	3 ☐	4 ☐	5 ☐
Resetting the Tuttle to the starting point:	1 ☐	2 ☐	3 ☐	4 ☐	5 ☐
Changing the background colour:	1 ☐	2 ☐	3 ☐	4 ☐	5 ☐
Changing the colour of the Tuttle:	1 ☐	2 ☐	3 ☐	4 ☐	5 ☐

Thank you very much for your assistance. Without your help this evaluation could not be done.

REFERENCES

Faulkner C and Culwin F (1997) 'The Return of the Tuttles' in the Proceedings of the 5th CTI Dublin Conference, 1997. pp. 75–8.

Faulkner, Xristine and Culwin, Fintan (1999) 'From Tuttles to Brewsers: Integrating HCI and Software Engineering Using the Whole Class Project' in the proceedings of Project '99 Conference, 14–15 September, 1999. University of Exeter.

References

ACM SIGCHI (1992) *Curricula for Human-Computer Interaction*. ACM Press.

Allwood C (1984) Analysis of the field survey in Allwood C M and Lieff E (eds) *Better Terminal Use*, pp. 72–7, University of Goteberg: Syslab-G.

Ashworth G (1991) 'Evaluation case study II: a voice-operated database enquiry service' in Andy Downton (ed.) *Engineering the User Interface*. McGraw-Hill, London.

Bannon L (1995) 'From Human Factors to Human Actors: The Role of Psychology and Human Computer Interaction Studies in System Design' in Baecker, Grudin, Buxton and Greenberg (eds) *Readings in HCI: Towards the Year 2000*. Morgan Kaufmann, San Francisco.

BCS HIC Group (1995) BCS Model Syllabus 'Challenging Computing Curricula'. *Interfaces,* no. 28.

Bennett J (1984) 'Managing to meet usability requirements' in Bennett J L *et al* (eds) *Visual Display Terminals: Usability Issues and Health Concerns*. Prentice Hall, Englewood Cliffs, New Jersey.

BIUSEM (1995) *Benefits of Integrating Usability and Software Engineering Methods*. ESSI project 10290. See also:

`http://www.esi.es/ESSI/Reports/All/10290/Objectives.html`

Booth, Paul (1989) *An Introduction to HCI*. LEA, Hove.

Card S, Moran T and Newell A (1983) *The Psychology of Human Computer Interaction*. LEA, Hillsdale, New Jersey.

Carroll J M and Mazur S A (1986) 'Lisa Learning'. *IEEE Computer,* 19(10), November 1986, pp. 35–49.

Carroll J M and Rosson M B (1989) 'Paradox of the Active User' in Carroll J M (ed.) *Interfacing Thought*. MIT Press, Cambridge, Massachusetts.

The Concise Oxford Dictionary (1986) 9th edition. BCA, London.

Culwin F and Faulkner C (1997) 'Integration of Usability Considerations within the CS/SE Curriculum'. Proceedings of 3rd CTI Dublin Conference.

Diaper D 1986 'Identifying the Knowledge Requirements of an Expert System's Natural Language Processing Interface.' Proceedings of the Second Conference of the BCS HCI Specialist Group, September 1986.

Diaper D (1989) Simulation in the Development of User Interfaces, May 1989.

Dix A *et al* (1998) *Human Computer Interaction*. Prentice Hall, Hemel Hempstead.

Downton A (1991) *Engineering the Human Computer Interface*. McGraw Hill, Maidenhead.

Draper S (1985) 'The Nature of Expertise in UNIX' in Shackel B (ed.) *Human-Computer Interaction*. INTERACT '84 , pp. 465–71. North-Holland, Amsterdam.

Draper S W (1993) 'The notion of Task in HCI' in Ashland S, Henderson A, Holland E and White T (eds) *Adjunct Proceedings of INTERCHI '93*.

DTI (1990) *A Guide to Usability, Usability Now!* Open University.

Faulkner C (1998) *Essence of Human Computer Interaction*. Prentice Hall, Hemel Hempstead.

Faulkner C and Culwin F (1999) 'Integration of Usability Issues within Initial Software Development Education' in *Proceedings of the Thirtieth SIGCSE Technical Symposium on Computer Science Education*, March 1999.

Faulkner C E (1991) 'Doing what comes naturally.' Unpublished internal paper, South Bank University.

Faulkner, Xristine and Culwin, Fintan (1999) 'From Tuttles to Brewsers: Integrating HCI and Software Engineering Using the Whole Class Project' in the proceedings of Project '99 Conference, 14–15 September, 1999. University of Exeter.

Feynman, Richard (1988) *What Do You Care What Other People Think?* Norton, New York.

Feynman, Richard (1998) *The Meaning of it All*. Penguin Books, London.

Gould J (1988) 'How to design usable systems' in Helander M (ed.) *Handbook of Human–Computer Interaction*. Elsevier, North Holland.

Gould J (1995) 'How to Design Usable Systems' in Baecker, Grudin, Buxton and Greenberg (eds)*Readings in HCI: Towards the Year 2000*. Morgan Kaufmann, San Francisco.

Gould, Stephen Jay (1997) *Life's Grandeur*. Vintage, London.

Grudin J (1990) 'The computer reaches out: the historical continuities in interface design' ACM.

Grudin J (1991) 'Interactive Systems: Bridging the Gaps Between Developers and Users' in Baecker, Grudin, Buxton and Greenberg (eds) *Readings in HCI: Towards the Year 2000*. Morgan Kaufmann, San Francisco.

Grudin J (1990) 'The computer reaches out: the historical continuities in interface design' in Chew and Whiteside (eds) Empowering People, conference proceedings of CHI '90, pp. 261–8. ACM, New York.

Harris, Ed (1999) 'Mutterings as the BBC ends sounds of silence', *Evening Standard*, 14th october 1999, p17.

Hewitt, Thomas (1986) 'Iterative evaluation' in Harrison M D and Monk A F (eds) *People and Computers: Designing for Usability*, Proceedings of the Second Conference of the BCS HCI Specialist Group, September 1986.

Hix D and Hartson R (1993) *Developing User Interfaces*. John Wiley, New York.

Holtzblatt K and Jones S (1995) 'Conducting and Analyzing a Contextual Interview' in Baecker, Grudin, Buxton and Greenberg (eds) *Readings in HCI: Towards the Year 2000*. Morgan Kaufmann, San Francisco.

Hughes J A, Sommerville I, Bentley R and Randall D (1993) 'Designing with ethnography: making work visible.' *Interacting with Computers*, vol. 5, no. 2, pp. 239–53.

Jones, Steve (1996) *In the Blood*. HarperCollins, London.

Jordan P (1998) *An Introduction to Usability*. Taylor and Francis, London.

Jordan P, Thomas B, Weerdmeester A, and McClelland I (1996) *Usability Evaluation in Industry*. Taylor and Francis, London.

Karat J (1996) 'User Centred Design: Quality or Quakery?' in *Interactions*, vol. 11.4, ACM.

Killin J (1989) 'Interview Techniques'. The Knowledge Based Systems Centre, South Bank Polytechnic. Internal paper.

Kim, Scott (1995) 'Interdisciplinary Cooperation' in Baecker, Grudin, Buxton and Greenberg (eds) *Readings in HCI: Towards the Year 2000*. Morgan Kaufmann, San Francisco.

Landauer, Thomas (1993) *The Trouble with Computers*. MIT Press, Cambridge, Massachusetts.

LAS (1993) *Report of the Inquiry into the London Ambulance Service*. London: LAS.

Lewis C and Norman D (1986) 'Designing for Error' in Norman D and Draper S (1986) *User Centred System Design*. LEA, Hillsdale, New Jersey.

Lindley, David (1997) *Where does the Weirdness Go?* Vintage, London.

Maguire M (1997) *RESPECT User Requirements Framework Handbook*, Deliverable D5.1. RESPECT Consortium.

Mayes *et al* (1990) 'Information Flow in a User Interface: The Effect of Experience and Context on the Recall of MacWrite Screens' in Preece J and Keller L (eds) *Human Computer Interaction*. Prentice Hall, Hemel Hempstead.

Mayhew, Deborah J (1999) *The Usability Engineering Lifecycle*. Morgan Kaufmann, San Francisco, California.

Maynard, Mary (1989) *Sociological Theory*. Longman, London.

Microprose (1994) *Pizza Tycoon – User Guide*. Bristol.

Monk A, Wright P, Haber J and Davenport L (1993) *Improving your Human Computer Interface*. Prentice Hall, Hemel Hempstead.

Monk A *et al* (1993) 'Mixing Oil and Water' in Ashland S, Henderson A, Holland E and White T (eds) INTERCHI '93 Adjunct Proceedings.

Mumford E and Sutton D (1991) 'Designing Organisational Harmony' in *The Computer Bulletin*. August 12–14.

Nielsen J (1993) *Usability Engineering*. AP Professional, Cambridge, Massachusetts.

Nielsen J and Mack R (1994) *Usability Inspection Methods*. John Wiley, New York.

Nielsen J, Mack R, Bergendorff K and Grishchkowsky N (1986) 'Integrated Software Usage in Professional Work Environment: Evidence from Questionnaires and Interviews', conference proceedings of CHI '86, pp. 162–7.

Norman D and Draper S (1986) *User Centred System Design*. LEA, Hillsdale, New Jersey.

Norman D (1988) *The Psychology of Everyday Things*. Basic Books, New York.

Norman D (1992) *Turn Signals are the Facial Expressions of Automobiles*. Addison Wesley, Reading, Massachusetts.

Norman D (1993) *Things That Make Us Smart*. Addison Wesley, Reading, Massachusetts.

Petroski H (1996) *Invention by Design*. Harvard University Press, Cambridge, Massachusetts.

Pirsig R M (1974) *Zen and the Art of Motorcycle Maintenance*. Vintage, London.

Plous S (1993) *The Psychology of Judgement and Decision Making*. McGraw Hill, New York.

Pratchett T, Stewart I, Cohen J (1999) *The Science of Discworld*. Ebury Press, London.

Preece J *et al* (1994) *Human-Computer Interaction*. Addison Wesley, Wokingham, England.

Pressman R (1987) *Software Engineering: A Practitioner's Approach*, 2nd edition. McGraw Hill.

Reason J (1991) *Human Error*. Cambridge University Press, Cambridge.

Redmond-Pyle D and Moore A (1995) *Graphical User Interface Design and Evaluation*. Prentice Hall, Hemel Hempstead.

Ren Xiangshi and Moriya Shinji (1998) 'The Influence of Target Size, Distance and Direction on the Design of selection Strategies' in Johnson H, Nigay L and Roast C (eds) *People and Computers XIII*. Proceedings of HCI '98, Springer-Verlag, London.

Root R W and Draper S (1983) 'Questionnaires as a software evaluation tool' in Janda A (ed.) *Human Factors in Computing Systems*, conference proceedings of CHI '83, pp. 78–82. ACM Press, New York.

Rose, Steven (1997) *Lifelines*. Penguin Books, London.

Sanders M and McCormick E (1992) *Human Factors in Engineering and Design*. McGraw Hill, New York.

Sayers D (1970) *Gaudy Night*. Hodder and Stoughton, London.

Shackel B (1981) 'The concept of usability' in Bennett J L *et al* (eds) (1984) *Visual Display Terminals: Usability Issues and Health Concerns*. Prentice Hall, Englewood Cliffs, New Jersey.

Shackel B (1986) 'Ergonomics in Design for Usability' n Harrison M D and Monk A F (eds) *People and Computers: Designing for Usability*. Proceedings of the Second Conference of the BCS HCI Specialist Group, September 1986.

Shackel B (1990) 'Human Factors and Usability' in Preece and Keller (eds) *Human Computer Interaction*. Prentice Hall, Hemel Hempstead.

Sherman, Barry (1985) *The New Revolution*. John Wiley, London.

Shermer M (1997) *Why People Believe Weird Things: Pseudoscience, Superstition, and Other Confusions of Our Time*. W.H. Freeman and Company, New York.

Shneiderman B (1998) *Designing the User Interface*, 3rd edition. Addison Wesley, Reading, Massachusetts.

Smith, Andy (1997) *Human Computer Factors: A Study of Users and Information Systems*. McGraw Hill, London.

Sommerville, Ian and Sawyer, Pete (1997) *Requirements Engineering*. John Wiley, Chichester.

Sulaiman S (1998) *Heuristics for Evaluating the Usability of CMC Systems*. MPhil thesis, South Bank University.

Tognazzini, Bruce (1992) *Tog on Interface*. Addison Wesley, Reading, Massachusetts.

Trenner, Lesley and Bawa, Joanna (1998) *The Politics of Usability*. Springer-Verlag, London.

Tyldesley D (1990) 'Employing usability engineering in the development of office products' in Preece and Keller (eds) *Human Computer Interaction*. Prentice Hall, Hemel Hempstead.

Villazon, Luis (1998) "Old DOS for new" "Windows 95 Polish". *PC Format*. October 1998 (issue 87), p166.

Whiteside J, Bennett J and Holtzblatt K (1988) 'Usability Engineering: our Experience and Evolution' in Helander M (ed.) *Handbook of Human–Computer Interaction*. Elsevier, North Holland.

Williams M (1998) *Introducing Usability*. PC Magazine CD, August 1998.

Wolpert, Lewis (1993) *The Unnatural Nature of Science*. Faber and Faber, London.

Glossary

accelerators – term used to describe methods provided to speed-up activity through a system; quite often in the form of shortcut keys.

action – the physical interaction with a system in order to carry out the user's goal.

Action Cycle – Norman's explanation for the cycle that accounts for actions.

analytical methods – methods of analysis using pen and paper as opposed to field trials.

answer garden – system that keeps a record of questions and answers and adds new questions and answers according to requirements of the users.

attitude – one of the attributes described by Shackel as making up usability.

catastrophic errors – errors which prevent the task from being done and from which it is not possible to recover without a knock-on effect.

checklists – lists of things to do, or lists of items to be chosen from, used in questionnaires.

cognitive walkthrough – a method by which an expert can walk through the task working out what the cognitive processes and performance are likely to be.

confounding variables – variables that interfere with an experiment.

consistency inspections – checks on a system to ensure that they are the same throughout.

control group – group that is used to measure the effect on the experimental group as a comparison.

cooperative evaluation – evaluation method developed by Andrew Monk *et al* by which the evaluator and the subject cooperate to examine the system. It is a development of talk aloud.

counter balancing – method in experimentation by which groups perform the tasks in different order.

design–build–evaluate cycle – method by which software should be developed using evaluation at each cycle.

direct users – people who use the computer systems themselves and for their own activities.

discretionary users – people who can chose whether or not they will use a computer system.

effectiveness – a measurement in usability to express how appropriate the system is in terms of getting the task done.

efficiency – one of the attributes used in usability engineering.

empirical methods – methods that use experimentation and field studies.

error rate – rate at which errors occur; can be expressed in a variety of ways such as success to failure ratio or as an expression of error in time.

end-user class – the class of users who will actually be using the computer system.

ethnography – a way of studying groups of people derived from anthropology and based on observation.

experimental group – the group that receives the independent variable.

expert appraisals – examinations of systems carried out by HCI experts.

expert users – groups of users who are proficient in the use of a system.

fatal errors – errors that cannot easily be rectified without major effort and time loss and will prevent the completion of the task.

fatigue effect – the effect of tiredness on experiments.

feasibility study – a study to make sure that a system can actually be developed given the time and resources available.

feature inspections – examination of a system to ensure that what is available is what is appropriate and required.

field trials – trials of systems that take place in workplaces or outside the laboratory.

flexibility – a measure of how far the system can be adapted to user and task.

formal usability inspections – inspections carried out by a team in order to assess the usability of a product.

formative evaluation – evaluation that is used to drive the design.

goal – the aim of an action.

guideline review – review of a system that checks it against the guidelines issued by the company.

Gulf of Evaluation – gap between what the user wants to achieve and what is implied can be achieved by the system.

Gulf of Execution – gap between what the user wants to do and what actions the system can support.

Hawthorne effect – effect on groups of users being observed.

heuristic evaluation – evaluation of a system using rules.

heuristics – rules or general guidelines.

Hierarchical Task Analysis – form of task analysis which structures the task into a hierarchy of task and subtask.

hypothesis – the research question.

indirect users – users who employ a system on someone else's behalf.

intermediate users – users who are between novice and expert.

intermittent users – users who use a system sporadically.

Jackson Structured Programming – method of representing programs.

knowledge in the head – knowledge that has to be learned.

knowledge in the world – knowledge that can be derived from examining the system.

laboratory trials – trials that take place in a laboratory.

LEAF – Learnability, Effectiveness, Attitude, Flexibility – from Shackel's definition of usability.

learnability – a usability measure of how easy a system is to learn.

Likert scale – a scalar questionnaire.

major errors – errors that will take some time and effort to rectify.

mandatory users – users who have no choice but to use a system.

matching – method by which subjects are matched to ensure that both groups contain the same type of subject – for example, by age, experience or gender.

minor errors – small errors that are easily recovered from.

multi-choice questions – questions that are given several alternative answers for the user to choose from.

novice – beginner.

null hypothesis – at a simple level, the null hypothesis states that the different conditions used in an experiment will not cause a difference to the dependent variable.

order effect – biasing of an experiment because of the order in which tasks are done.

pluralistic usability walkthrough – this is a technique for evaluating a system which utilises users, developers and usability specialists.

practice effect – the subject of an experiment improves because of repetition of a task.

property checklists – lists that can be used to ensure that a system contains all the aspects it is supposed to contain.

prototyping – method of producing an example for the user to examine. It may be incomplete or it may not cover the whole system.

qualitative evaluation – evaluation that looks at how the user feels about the system. It can be categorised but will not reduce to numerical measurements.

quantitative evaluation – evaluation that takes measurements.

rapid prototyping – method of producing prototypes quickly and cheaply so that they can be evaluated by the user. As with a prototype, the system may be lacking functionality or may be only part of the projected product.

related measures design – this is a technique used in experimental method. The performance of each individual is compared with that individual's own performance. It could be assumed then that individual differences have been controlled. It is also known as *within subjects design* or *related subjects design*.

remote users – users who connect to a distant system.

requirements specification – list of what a system is required to do.

scalar questionnaires – questionnaires that scale responses.

scenarios – descriptions of possible interactions that may take place with a system. They can be used for checking that a system is able to cope with all of the likely circumstances – and some unlikely ones!

simulations – mock-up of systems that may not have much, or indeed any, functionality.

socio-technical design – method of design that looks at the way a system will operate inside the organisation.

standards inspections – inspections carried out to ensure that systems comply to standards set for them.

state transition diagrams – method of representing a system to show possible states of the interface and how they will interact with each other.

storyboards – method of representing screen designs in the form of screenshots with indications as to how the user will proceed through the system. Storyboards can be made of card or paper.

structured interviews – interviews that follow a set pattern, perhaps in the form of a questionnaire or questions. They tend to be more formal.

summative evaluation – evaluation that comes at the end of a cycle and checks acceptability.

support users – users who provide help and support to other users.

talk aloud – method of evaluation that gets the user to talk about what they are doing.

Taylorism – method by which work was divided up into small tasks.

transformation – the change that takes place to an input.

unstructured interviews – interviews that do not follow a questionnaire or a given set of questions but allow the interviewee freer scope.

usability – how easy it is to learn and use a system.

usability attributes – aspects of usability that can be measured.

usability engineer – software engineer who has a profound understanding of user needs or an HCI expert who has a profound understanding of, and is able to develop, software.

usability engineering – a method of software engineering that incorporates HCI principles and adopts user centred-design and development.

usability evaluation – methods for evaluating the usability of a product.

usability metrics – measurements taken to find out whether a system is usable.

usability specification – list of performances for the system.

User Centred Design – design method that puts the user at the centre and incorporates feedback from users at regular stages during design and build.

user friendliness – now a much-maligned term, it was used to denote that a system was 'kind' to its users.

user satisfaction – a usability measure to account for user acceptance of a system.

Wizard of Oz – this is a method of evaluation which mocks-up the system using a member of the design team to provide the system responses.

Index

A

accelerators 29, 189
acceptability 8
ACM 11, 113
action 57, 192
　cycle 58
activity
　logging 41
　sampling 41
air traffic control 76
aircraft 61
Allwood, C 2
analytical evaluation 139
answer garden 26
Apple 4, 103
　iMac 4
　Macintosh 28, 180
archaeology 201
Archimedes 73
ashtray 88
Ashworth, G 107
assumptions 30
attitude 7, 122
attributes 125–27
autoskip 192

B

Bannon, L 24
Bawa, J 2
BCS 11, 113
Bennett, J 6
Betamax 183
Beynon, H 56
bias 36, 41
BIUSEM 91, 99, 112
Booth, P; 113, 117, 122, 131–32,
　202–204
bras 87
Breakfast Buddy Toaster 96, 203
Brewsers 41, 143
budget 95

C

Card, S 139
Carroll, J M; 27, 124
Carroll, Lewis 57
categorisation 25
Channel Tunnel 201
checklist 37, 47, 168
Chinese Whispers 88–89, 91
Clarrie 85
closed questions 35
closure 189
cockpit 61
code of conduct 145
cognitive walkthrough 178,
　183–86, 192
comfort 116
command line 4, 29
Computer Science 201
Computer Supported Co-
　operative Work 46, 76–77
confirmation 28
confounding variables 149
consistency 189
　inspections 178, 180–81
contract 98
control group 148
co-operative evaluation
　157–166
counter balancing 150
Culwin, F; 13, 106, 215
customers 92, 94

D

Dawkins, R 175
deduction 145
dependent variable 148
design 64, 78–79, 85, 88
　representation 99–109
　team 35–36
design–build–evaluate cycle 12,
　80, 107
designers 62, 87
Designs on your… 87, 109, 209
Desktop 207
Diaper, D; 107–108, 167

D (cont.)

Dickens, C 146
discount usability 178, 194
Dix, A; 77, 91
dog 85–86, 116, 124–25
Downton, A 12
Draper, S W; 8, 25, 28, 84, 116,
　152–53
DTI 11
Dylan, Bob 210

E

ease of use 6
effectiveness 6, 7, 114, 116–118
efficiency 7, 114, 116–119
electric cars 87
Eliot, T S 58
e-mail 205–206
empirical evaluation 139
end-user 13, 31
　class 23
　group 32
enjoyment 124
error 73, 97, 124–27, 189, 191,
　194
　catastrophic 127
　fatal 127
　major 127
　minor 126
　rate 125–26
ethics 42–43
ethnography 46, 75, 92–93, 208
ethnomethodology 159
eureka 73
evaluation 171
　carrying out 140–45
　methods, subjective 35
　preparing for 141–43
　qualitative 136, 138, 167
　quantitative 10, 136, 138, 169
exits 189
experimental
　group 149
　method 146–48
experiments 40, 145
　problems with 148–56
expert
　appraisals 178, 187
　evaluations 177, 195
　users 28–30

expertise 25
experts 23, 28, 35, 73

F

failure rate 118
falsification 150
fatigue effect 150
Faulkner, C; 1, 6, 13, 191, 215
feasibility 93, 95
feature inspections 178, 187
features 168
feedback 26, 28, 133, 189
Feynman, R; 152, 155–56
fidget rate 116
field
    studies 154, 168
    trials 168
findings 144, 158
Five Minute Rule 201
flexibility 6, 120, 122
formative evaluation 138
Free 210
fun 124
functionality 46, 93, 168, 170

G

games 88, 181, 208
gates 85
GEM 183
goals 57, 59, 61–62
GOMS 139
Gould, J; 12, 22, 26, 31, 40, 55,
    107–108, 210
Gradgrind 146
Green, T 202
Grudin, J 76
GUI 22, 29, 106
guideline review 178–79
Gulf of Evaluation 58, 60–61,
    190
Gulf of Execution 58, 60–61, 190

H

Hartson, H; 11, 117
Hawthorne effect 40
help 26, 28, 189
    manuals 4, 28
heuristics 177–79,
    188–193, 211
Hewitt, T; 137–38, 139
hierarchical task analysis 63–66
Hix, D; 11, 117, 136

Holtzblatt, K; 46, 55, 75
Homer Simpson 210
Hughes, J; 77–78, 92, 159
HyperCard 103
hypertext 102
hypothesis 147–48

I

icon 32, 207
incident diaries 170
independent
    measures 149
    variable 148
induction 145
inspiration 63
intention 59–60
interview 42
interviewer 35, 42
ISO 7, 8, 61, 115–117, 119, 120

J

Jones, S 156
Jordan, P; 2–4, 113, 126, 136,
    210
JSP 63

K

Karat, J; 12, 109, 112, 203, 208
Killin, J 45
Kim, S 77
knowledge
    ellicitation 45
    in the head 121, 190
    in the world 120–21, 190

L

laboratory studies 167
Landauer, T; 3, 19, 155, 172
LEAF 117
learnability 7, 119–121,
    123–24
learning 124
Lewis, C 126
Likert scale 38
Lindley, D; 155, 202
LocoScript 208
logging on 73
logging 171
London Ambulance Service 14,
    19, 31, 98

M

Macbeth 150
Maguire, M 3
mappings 191
Martial 98
matching 149
Mayhew, D 197
Maynard, M 77
metaphor 207
metrics 119, 130, 202
millenium bug 201
mistakes 126
modem 73
Monk, A; 76, 140, 158–59, 176,
    203, 209, 210
multi-choice questions 37
Mumford, E 79

N

nail polishing 66
negative transfer 183
Newton, Isaac 73
NextStep 183
Nielsen, J; 2, 8, 22, 45, 177–78,
    180, 197, 210–211
noise 32
Norman, D; 8, 19, 41, 58–60, 93,
    120, 153–54, 178, 188,
    190–92, 208, 211
Norman's action cycle model
    58–60
novices 14, 22, 26–28, 30, 32, 120
null hypothesis 148

O

observation 39–41, 145
OHP 100
open-ended questions 35–36, 42
order effect 149
organisational needs 93

P

Petroski, H; 61, 78, 84, 201
Pirsig, R M 147
Pizza Tycoon 181
Planck, M 200
planning 60
Plous, S 38
pluralistic walkthrough 178–80

Popper, Karl 150
Powell, D; 87, 109
practice effect 150
Pratchett, T 176
Preece, J 57
Pressman, R; 90, 95
Pretty Slik Nail Painter 105, 110, 184, 203
productivity 3
promises 98
property checklists 178, 187
prototype 101, 103, 139, 184
    paper 101
public 39

Q

questionnaires 5, 35–39
questions
    closed 35
    open 35
quiet environments 32, 167
QWERTY keyboard 183

R

ranked order questionnaire 38
rapid prototyping 99, 106–107, 129
Reason, J 125
recording 40, 43–44, 143, 158
Redmond-Pyle, D; 84, 140, 211
reductionism 152
remote users 24
Ren, X 155
requirements 23, 46, 88, 90–93, 95, 104
    document 99
    engineering 210
robustness 26–27
Romeo and Juliet 204, 207
Root, R W; 5, 46
Rose, S; 147, 150, 152, 156, 199, 200

S

Sale of Goods 5
Sayers, D; 39
scalar questionnaires 37
scenarios 99, 104–105, 169
self-administered
    questionnaires 36
semantic differential scale 38
Seymour, R; 87, 109, 209

Shackel, B; 6, 19, 21, 117, 210
Shakespeare, W; 150, 204
Sherman, B 9
Shermer, M; 145–46, 156
Shneiderman, B; 31, 40, 78, 88, 177–78, 189
shortcut keys 29, 189
Simpsons 210
simulations 99, 103
slips 126
Smith, A; 3, 208, 211
social context 75–76
socio-technical design 78–79, 92
Sommerville, I; 112, 210
South Bank University 41, 51, 74–75, 215–216
spreadsheet 94
standardisation 192
standards 183
standards inspections 178, 181–83
Star Trek 60, 94
    Mr Spock 60
state transition diagrams 99, 105–106
storyboards 99–102
structured interviews 43
student projects 95, 100, 116, 201
Sulaiman, S 193–94
summative evaluation 138–39
surveys 4–5
Sutton, D 79
swipe cards 191
synonyms 29

T

talk aloud 156
tape recording 43–44
target group identification 140
task 6, 7, 25, 30, 114–115, 140, 158
    analysis 64, 73
    control 66
    dependency 66
    frequency 66
    initiation 65
    interruptions 66
    model 63
    subtask 63–64, 115
Taylorism 80
telepathy 200
time 127
Tognazinni, B; 140, 179, 181
training 23, 31
transformation 65
Trenner, L; 2, 113, 205

Tuttles 215–229
Tyldesley, D 10

U

undo 27, 189, 190
UNIX 25
unstructured interviews 43
usability 6, 7, 12, 208
    aims 127–28
    approach 113
    attributes 116–117
    engineering 1–12, 13, 128–133, 215
    engineers 26, 128
    evaluation 12, 137–172
    inspections 178, 186
    levels 10
    metrics 6, 130–33
    problems 2
    specification 129–130
user-centred
    design 12, 13, 108–109, 203, 208
    development 31
user friendliness 8–10, 208
user friendly 3, 8, 9, 203–204, 208
user group characteristics 47
user satisfaction 5, 7, 114–115, 119–121, 137
users 21–23, 30, 62
    categorising 25, 30
    direct 23
    discretionary 24
    discussions with 31–32, 34
    indirect 24
    intermittent 25, 27
    involving 31, 108–109, 208
    mandatory 24
    recruiting 140, 158
    support 24
    types of 23–24

V

valuation method 169–170
VAX 28, 73–75, 168, 205
verification 145
VHS 183
video recordings 40
vigilance 153
Villazon, L 154
Vinall, N 89

W–Z

walk up and use 23, 120

Web 132, 211
whiteboard 100
Whiteside, J; 10, 12, 113, 136,
    208, 210
Williams, M 205

Wizard of Oz 99, 107–108,
    166–67
Wolpert, L; 73, 145, 151, 154,
    156, 176, 200–201
working environment 32, 114,
    167

workload 66
workplace 23, 31–32, 92

X-Motif 216